I ALWAYS WANTED TO FLY

Memoirs of a World War II Flight Engineer/Gunner

JOHN J. SHIVER JR.

Copyright © 2012 John J. Shiver Jr.
All rights reserved.

ISBN: 0615667767
ISBN-13: 9780615667768

This book is dedicated to my wife, Myrtle;
our children, Martha and Jeff;
their spouses, David and Laura;
our grandchildren,
and our great-grandchildren.

Our faith comes in moments; our vice is habitual

–Ralph Waldo Emerson

*He has told you, O man, what is good,
and what does the Lord require of you, but to do justice,
to love kindness, and to walk humbly with your God*

–Micah 6:8 ESV (*English Standard Version*)

What time I am afraid, I will trust in thee

–Psalm 56:3 (*Douay-Rheims Bible*)

*Restore unto me the joy of thy salvation,
and uphold me with thy free spirit*

–Psalm 51:12 KJV (*King James Version*)

<u>Always Remember</u>
*Men of genius are admired
Men of wealth are envied
Men of power are feared
But only men of character are trusted.*
–Alfred Adler

ACKNOWLEDGEMENTS

Without the encouragement of my son, Jeff Shiver, and my niece, Gwen Myers, the handwritten memoirs I wrote of my experiences in World War II would have been known only to a few. Their belief that others might appreciate the dream of a young man who wanted to fly and ended up doing so in a way he never imagined was the motivation to put my notes in print. This allowed me to share the challenges and struggles I had in World War II as a flight engineer and gunner. I thank them for their dedication in putting these remembrances into print.

Three others involved with transforming my notes are my daughter, Martha Walker of Atmore, Alabama, Jane King of Medford, Massachusetts, and Sandra Fischer of Beaufort, South Carolina. I thank them for the many hours typing, proofreading and editing the material to put in a readable form.

–John J. Shiver, Jr.

PREFACE

This book is meant to present my view as an airman and my service as a flight engineer/gunner in World War II. It is not meant to give a technical nor critical view of the military experience in that war.

My descriptions of the events and people in this book are written from my personal perspective and have no other purpose than to describe them according to my recognition and understanding of them.

During my tour of duty in World War II, I served in the Army Air Corps in the following divisions:

8th Air Force. 389th Bomb Group (England)
9th Air Force. 98th Bomb Group, 344th Squadron (Libya)
12th Air Force. 98th Bomb Group, 344th Squadron (North Africa)
15th Air Force. 98th Bomb Group, 344th Squadron (Italy)

–John J. Shiver, Jr.

TABLE OF CONTENTS

Acknowledgements..v
Preface...vii
Chapter 1   A Young Man's Dream......................................1
Chapter 2   The Training of an Airman..............................9
Chapter 3   Transfers and Advanced Training 45
Chapter 4   An Eight Day Leave 83
Chapter 5   Final Training and Deployment to the
            War in Europe..93
Chapter 6   Benghazi, Libya 109
Chapter 7   Hergla, Tunisia 119
Chapter 8   Brindisi, Italy 133
Chapter 9   Manduria, Italy 147
Chapter 10 Lecce, Italy 161
Chapter 11 Combat Missions 201
Chapter 12 Finally Heading Home 241
Chapter 13 Stateside Duty 259
Chapter 14 An Airman's Reflections 301
Final Thoughts 311

Chapter 1

A YOUNG MAN'S DREAM

"The Boy Who Wanted to Fly"

As a young boy at three years old, I would look up into the sky and see the birds flying and I wanted to see the things on the ground from where they were. One day I was out in the yard playing when I heard a loud noise coming from the sky and I looked up and saw an old two wing, yellow painted thing flying over me. My mother came outside and saw it and told me it was an airplane.

When I was five years old, I saw a dirigible as it came over Atmore. We lived on 3rd Ave in 1925 and the Greenlawn Hospital addition had been completed. The streets had been made and the ditches on each side of the streets had been graded out. There was only one house at the south end of 4th Avenue. A bi-plane landed on 5th Avenue one day and started flying people on trips over Atmore for a fee. The pilot would sit in the back seat and his customer would sit in the front one. It was parked in front of Church Street and I always enjoyed watching the plane's take-offs and landings. It stayed there several days because on one of the landings, the pilot let the plane's propeller hit the ground and broke it. The propeller was a wooden one and it was in a number of pieces. I went over and saw it as the pilot was removing it, and I heard him tell someone he would be back with a new one in a couple of days. I talked my mother into taking me over to the plane while the pilot was away and lifting me up to see inside the plane. I was excited to see the instruments and the stick and foot controls that the pilot used to control the plane in the air.

"The George Stone Story and Living on 3rd Avenue"

My father had a house built on 3rd Avenue in 1925 and we moved there when it was completed. I have a lot of memories of living there and playing with my friend, George Stone. George's parents' home was down the street from our house, and, weather permitting, we would visit and play together almost every day. Our favorite place was in the street ditches in front of our homes. The times were bad when I was young and growing up in Atmore, but I didn't know we were poor. Most of the people were like we were – the old saying, "All were in the same boat." We always had something to eat. We would have a spring and a fall garden, and neighbors helped each other.

George and I would make our toys. We would take a piece of wood board, add jar lids for wheels, and using a handsaw, nails, and hammer, in a short time we had made a little truck. We had a number of different types and all sizes of them to play with. We also made airplanes – all types and sizes of them - one wing and two wing planes. I made a two-seated, one wing type of plane. Then, I found a piece of isinglass and made two windshields for the two cockpits. That plane was my prized possession for a long time. George and I liked to play our games of marbles, also. We enjoyed playing together and I don't recall any time we had any trouble with each other.

George had a grandmother who lived with them and she was confined to her bed all the time with an illness. I don't remember if she was Mr. or Mrs. Stone's mother. She enjoyed me coming in to visit with her, and she would talk to George and me and pat us on our heads when we left her bed. George would tell me what day and what time his grandmother was expecting us. We would wash our faces and hands before we went in to visit her. I don't remember the health problem she had. I'm thinking it was her heart.

After a few years, the Stones moved to Florida not far from the Alabama-Florida state line and I don't think George and I ever saw each other again. He was a state representative for Escambia County, Florida, for a long time until he was killed in a traffic accident a number of years ago. He must have been a good representative for that county because they built a large fishing lake, recreation and camping area off Highway 4 in Escambia County and named it for him.

I have a lot of memories of 3rd Avenue while I was a small boy and growing up on that street. On the north side, next to us, lived the Brown family. On the south of us lived the Blue family, and next to them was the Black family. Skip one house and the White family lived there. Across the street from the Whites lived the Green family. On one half block of 3rd Avenue lived the Brown, Blue, Black, White, and Green families.

On Christmas morning, in 1928 or 1929, I got an airplane. It was about ten or twelve inches long, metal, and was named "The Spirit of St. Louis". It was a model of Charles Lindberg's plane. I was proud of that plane and kept it in the box it came in for a long time. I have thought about that plane a number of times in my life, but I don't know where it went. "That's life – here today gone tomorrow". *But, we still have memories.*

"My First Plane Ride"

In the early thirties, I went with my father to the Ewing Air Field out from Atmore when he was going to work on the engine used to run the generator that charged a bank of batteries. The U.S. Navy used this field for cadets to practice take-offs and landings during the day and at night. There was a beacon light that rotated and marked the field and landing strip marker lights. I remember the large glass batteries with the acid and water in them. The Navy stopped using the field and in approximately 1941, a tri-motor Ford plane used the field. I went out there and took my first airplane ride. That was some kind of flight. Noise is not the word to describe the kind of racket and disturbing things going on all the time. I didn't feel safe with the metal skin that was in the plane, flopping and flapping around me. The ride around the Atmore area was about thirty minutes; then, we were back at the field landing. As we touched down on the grass, the pilot let the little tail wheel touch the ground first and bent the support. He stopped the plane as soon as he could, looked at the damage done and got back inside the plane. He told us the damaged wheel bracket would have to be fixed before the plane could be moved and we had to walk back to where our cars were parked. No one complained. We were happy to be on the ground.

That was my first plane ride and I still wanted to go into the Army Air Corps. I went to Mobile by bus to the recruiting office and tried to get into the Cadet program but was told I would have to have at least two years of college. I tried Maxwell Field and was told the same thing. Some months later, I was told the Cadet program had dropped the two years of college requirement, and I rode the bus to Mobile and tried again. The sergeant told me he had heard rumors about it, but he hadn't gotten any official notice of it. The requirement was still two years of college to get into the Cadet program. But, I still wanted to fly.

"The War, a Wedding, and Enlistment"

The Japanese attacked the United States at Pearl Harbor on Dec. 7, 1941 – the United States was at war. I registered for service at Local Board #2 on February 16, 1942. My number was 10587, signed by Mrs. Lucille Moore.

Myrtle Dean was my high school sweetheart. We had dated beyond high school and planned to be married, so we decided to get married now, since I had already registered for the service. And we did. Judge Harvey E.

Page married us in Pensacola, Florida, on May 27, 1942, and <u>that was the best thing I ever did in my life.</u> I received my classification card on June 2, 1942; I was 1-A, signed by Dr. H.H. Rogers.

On June 21, 1942, I received a card to report for a physical exam at Fort McClellan, Alabama, on July 20, 1942, signed by Mr. C.M. Mullins - Board Clerk. I reported to the Board at the post office in Atmore early on the morning of July 20, 1942, and was handed a large sealed envelope with records of approximately thirty men in it. An old bus arrived, and I was told when I turned the envelope in at Fort McClellan, to tell them we were one man short from the list of men on the records they had sent – that's what I did. There was a no-show and they didn't tell me his name. We stopped at a place for a noon meal. I had been given a paper by the Board in Atmore for our meal.

We arrived at Fort McClellan about two o'clock that evening and they were expecting us. We had to undress and before five o'clock, they had finished with the physical exam. Someone said they carried us through that medical exam like we were animals. Doctors were on each side of us most of the time and when one was looking in one of our ears, another doctor was looking in the other ear. Someone said, "If they don't see each other, you're okay".

There were a few who were turned down for the Army, but I was glad I was in good condition. We were served the evening meal and marched into a supply room, given a sheet and a blanket, then were led to a barracks and told to pick out a bunk. We were given a tag with our name on it and told to put it on the end of the bunk. Lights went out at 8:00 pm.

About 2:00 in the morning, a GI woke me up and told me to put on my clothes and go to the hospital with him. On the way to the hospital, I asked him, "What's up?"

He answered, "I don't know – I was told to find you and bring you to the hospital."

I thought I had something bad and as soon as I got to the hospital, I asked them. They told me, "We have lost your chest x-ray and we will have to take it again. Stay with us awhile and we will tell you about your x-ray."

I stayed, and after about thirty minutes, I got a good report and was led back to the barracks.

They got us up early the next morning and after breakfast we had a break for an hour and then they put us on the go – from one meeting to another and, then, to the swearing-in ceremony. Next, we went to the supply building and were issued all of our Army clothes and equipment. The shoes were the last things we received. There was just one line to get in for shoes and it was moving along at a good speed, but then it stopped. I could see and hear why it had stopped. There were two little ramps you walked up and you placed your feet into two shoe-size measuring gauges and a GI on each side called out your shoe size and another GI set it down with your name. A man was standing on the gauges and his toes were off the gauges. They didn't know what to do and were waiting for an officer to come and tell them what to do. About five minutes later, an officer came and settled the problem. I heard him say, "The only thing we can do is undo what we have done. We will have to give him an honorable discharge for the convenience of the government and give him a copy to show his draft board."

They had to take back all the clothes and other things that had been issued to him. I got up to the gauges in a short time and I had size 9C shoes as long as I was in service. I left the supply building with two barrack bags full and my name and service number (34335079) on each bag.

It was time to go to the mess hall. As soon as we finished the noon meal, we loaded our bags and headed south to Atmore. We didn't stop for a meal on the way home and we arrived back in Atmore at around 8:00 on the evening of July 21, 1942. My orders were to report to the post office in Atmore on the morning of August 3, 1942, by 8:00 a.m. I received a card from Mr. C.M. Mullins on July 28, 1942. The bus to the recreation center at Fort McPherson, Georgia, left Atmore at 9:32 a.m. on Monday and I was on active service in the U.S. Army on August 3, 1942. I was on inactive service from July 21, 1942, to August 3, 1942.

Orders read:

Army of U.S. Selective Service and Training to serve for duration of war plus six months.

Age at induction: 21 years and 11 months

Height – 5'8"
Weight – 171 ½ pounds
Eyes – Grey
Hair – Brown
Complexion – Fair
Waist – 38"

Chapter 2

THE TRAINING OF AN AIRMAN

"Training at Fort McPherson"

FORT MCPHERSON
ATLANTA, GEORGIA
Orders - McClellan to McPherson
HQ – RCTQ and Ind. Sta. McClellan, Ala 7/12/42 to
C.O. Rec. Center – Ft. McPherson, GA –
Par.7-S.O. #98 – HQ. RCTQ. and Induction Station

I was with a group of men who left Atmore on Monday, August 3, 1942, by bus at 9:32 a.m. going to Ft. McPherson, Atlanta, Georgia, for active service in the Army. We arrived about mid-evening and it wasn't long until we realized "we were in the Army now". A corporal was put in charge over us, and he was in charge over us because he told us so. He really felt his position at that time with us. Someone remarked later, when he couldn't hear what we were talking about, "If I could buy him for what he's worth and sell him for what he thinks he's worth, I would be a rich man."

He marched us everywhere we went. He led us to a mess hall and we got an evening meal. That was extra good, because we had no noon meal that day. Then he marched us to our barracks and we received his orders for the next day. We would be awakened fifteen minutes before reveille (5:00 a.m.). In fifteen minutes, we put on our fatigue clothes, made our bunks, put on our shoes, and assembled in front of the barracks by the time the bugler blew his horn for reveille. After that, we would return to our barracks, shave, and use the bathroom. But, if we had any time left and we wanted to sit down, we had to sit on the floor – it was a no-no to sit on our bunks. The corporal marched us to breakfast, then back to the barracks for a short break. Still, no sitting on our bunks. The corporal walked up and down the barracks, telling us what we would be doing during the short time at Fort McPherson. We would be going to a building and getting our five shots, and then he would be leading us to another building for us to be classified as to what part of the Army we would be assigned. We would be expected to pull KP in one of the mess halls or guard duty. We would be going to lectures and marching and we could be expecting some close order drill lessons by a drill sergeant.

The corporal said, "Now, if you think I have been tough on you, just wait until that drill sergeant gets you out on the drill field - your tongue will be hanging out and you will want water so bad, but he will still be drilling you and drilling you some more."

We marched to the building for our shots and I got two in one arm and three in the other one. The corporal then marched us to the building for our interview. I sat down at a desk and a captain started talking to me. He told me I would do well as a mechanic in a motor pool or a mechanic for a tank unit in the Army.

"Which one do you want?" the captain asked.

"I don't want either one. I want to fly a plane in the Air Corps."

He remarked, "But you haven't got two years of college."

"I know that, but please send me someplace in the Air Corps. I want to fly. I have always wanted to fly – ever since I was a little boy. I don't want to work on trucks or tanks."

The captain said, "You are surely a determined young man, but I still think you would make a good mechanic. I am going to send you to Atlantic City and you can go from there. Does that make you happy?"

"Yes sir, and thank you, sir. I'm happy." I left his office on cloud nine and thinking - you don't always get what you want, but you can always try.

That afternoon, we were introduced to our drill sergeant. He marched us to the drill field and gave us some lessons on what we would be doing and what he was expecting from us. He said he would be at our barracks in the morning to start our drill lessons. The next day, when we had been marching about thirty minutes, he gave us a little rest break. Close to us, there was another squad that had been marching and had stopped. One of the soldiers was talking and said he had enough of this crap and he wasn't marching another step. That soldier was a big bully type of guy, and he was really causing trouble. The drill sergeant had been talking to him but wasn't getting anywhere with him. The drill sergeant told one of the GIs to go to a certain building and tell a lieutenant there he was needed on the drill field now.

In a few minutes the GI arrived with the lieutenant at the squadron. The drill sergeant explained to the lieutenant the trouble he was having with this particular soldier. Our drill sergeant told us we needed to hear and see this, so we stayed. The lieutenant tried to get the bully to do what the drill sergeant wanted him to do and to be quiet. The bully told the lieutenant if he didn't have those lieutenant bars he would take care of him.

The lieutenant said, "Do you really mean that's what you want?"

The bully replied, "I sure do!"

The lieutenant was a really small man, but the lieutenant took the bars off his shirt and handed them to the sergeant and told him to hold them for him. The bully was all for a quick job on the lieutenant and told his squad to look at him as he took a swing at the lieutenant. The lieutenant must have been a boxer. He ducked under the bully's swing and at the same time, gave the bully a one-two punch and the bully fell to the ground. The lieutenant helped him up and asked him if he had enough and the bully said yes. The lieutenant told him he was sorry that he had to do what he did, but he had asked for it and must learn to take orders.

He said, "You are in the Army now and I hope you realize it."

Our marching got back to where we were before the bully learned his lesson. We did a lot of marching that week before we left Fort McPherson.

One day as I was entering the mess hall, I saw Red Lumpkin from Atmore. He was on a detail job of counting the number of men who were coming in to eat. I just said" hello" to him. On Thursday, I saw my name on the board for KP duty the next day. There were seven of us from my barracks who had a shift from 3:00 a.m. to 3:00 p.m. We had to be at the mess hall at 3:00 a.m., so we were awakened about 2:30 and were marched over to the mess hall in a group and delivered to the mess sergeant as a group. He was cooking some things for the breakfast then, but he put about three others to washing big pots and pans. The other three and I were given the job of cleaning the tables, filling all the salt and pepper shakers, and sweeping the floor. The tables were to be our job for breakfast and the noon meal. We were to be replaced by a new group at 3:00 p.m. The mess sergeant told us to do a good job for him and after the noon meal was over, he would cook us anything we wanted. We did a very good job, even washing all the windows and, when we had finished our job, he inspected it and said it was good.

The mess sergeant was a man of his word and he asked us what we wanted to eat. I think all of us wanted steaks. We sat down and enjoyed a meal with the mess sergeant. I think we earned it but we didn't know what was coming up. The mess sergeant was told there was not a group coming to relieve us. Someone had dropped the ball. The mess sergeant asked us to help him with the evening meal and as we were cleaning the mess hall, the sergeant showed us six bushels of field peas that needed to be shelled for the officers' meal the next day. We gave a fast job on the cleaning detail and got busy shelling peas. The sergeant was very happy and said we needed an early breakfast. He baked us biscuits and fried bacon and eggs. That was very good and he thanked us for helping him out of the bad situation he was in and told us if we were ever on KP again, he would never forget what we had done for him. A new group relieved us at 3:00 a.m. Since we had been on KP for twenty-four straight hours, the sergeant wrote a note for us to sleep the next day. The orders came out Saturday, August 8, 1942. I left Fort McPherson on a train on Sunday, August 9, 1942, going to Atlantic City, New Jersey.

"Training at Atlantic City, New Jersey"

<u>Fort McPherson to Atlantic City, NJ</u>
To C.O. Air Force RTC – Atlantic City, NJ
Par. #4-S.O. #202 – HQ –R.C. - Aug. 8, 1942

The Training of an Airman

We left Fort McPherson on Sunday, August 9, 1942, by train and arrived in Atlantic City, New Jersey the next day – August 10, 1942. We were taken to a large hotel (The Strand Hotel) that was a half block from the famous Atlantic City Boardwalk. We were told that we couldn't use the elevators at any time, that was a "no-no" now, but we would be told at a time when we could. We were told to go to the fifth floor and we would be assigned a room. There were two stairs to every floor so that was a total of ten flights of stairs we had to climb each time we went to our room. I know that was part of our training to get us into physical condition fast.

We didn't get to choose our roommates. They tried to mix everyone up as much as they could, and they did a good job of doing that. I knew only one GI at Atlantic City, and that was Ralph Wise from McCullough, Alabama. He and I met up one or two times and talked about Atmore. Ralph told me his brother, Ulay, was an officer and was at one of the other hotels in the city. They had a temporary partition put up in every hotel room to make it into two rooms with two cots in each room. That was okay, except it made it bad for us in the mornings when four were using one bathroom. We made do with what we had. We had a consolidated mess hall where they were feeding 10,000 GIs, three meals a day. We had to use our mess kit every meal. I was assigned to KP duty and to guard duty one time each.

While I was at Atlantic City, we had a staff sergeant for our drill sergeant and he was with us all the time. He was at least 6' tall – slim and neat – had a sharp, loud voice and he was all Army. I'm sure he was a regular Army man, but he did know how to teach us how to march and how to do close order drills.

We had to start out early each morning, except Sunday. Sunday was a day of rest, except for those who had KP or guard duty. I had guard duty one time about 5:00 a.m. on a Saturday morning for four hours, walking back and forth at the front of the hotel. The sergeant would blow his whistle – the signal to get up, dress in our fatigues, put on our fatigue hats, and run down those ten flights of stairs to assemble on the street in front of the hotel. The sergeant would look at his watch and say, "I'm sorry fellows; I've got you up too early. Go back up to your room, but no sitting on your cot."

About the time our seats hit the floor, he would blow that whistle again, and then he would send us back up to the room again. That was repeated over and over each morning until it was our time to go to the mess hall for breakfast. We had to march down the boardwalk and arrive at the hotel at the designated time. The drill sergeant would always keep us busy; if we had any spare time when he wasn't marching or talking to us, then we had to study and commit to memory the Army manual which contained a large number of "do's and don'ts".

Atlantic City was known as a coastal resort city on the Atlantic Ocean. There was a large auditorium and convention hall that had a number of rooms all around the auditorium and, I was told, had football games played inside it. In some of these rooms, we were given tests on different days to help the officers decide where they were going to send us. That was the first time I had someone teaching the Morse Signal Code to us – both sound and lights. That was the only test I took that I deliberately tried to fail. I didn't want to be a radioman. I wanted to fly an airplane.

One of those officers told me, "I don't understand how you made good grades on all your tests except radio, and you failed that one. I think you set out to fail it."

I didn't say anything except, "I want to get in the Cadet Training Program."

He said," When you meet the lieutenant who will be classifying you for what school to send you to, tell him you want to take the Cadet Training Test."

Later that day my name was called to go to a certain room for assignment. I was told I was being sent to an Air Corps mechanic school in North Carolina in a few days. I told the lieutenant I wanted to take the test for the cadet-flying program.

"You can't pass that test," he said.

"You may be right or you may be wrong. We won't know until I take it, will we?" I replied.

The lieutenant told me to be back in the morning at 8:00 to take the test and it would take one and a half hours. He said, "I will have to have time to grade it, so you tell your sergeant you will be back at 10:30 or 11:00." He told me I was a stubborn GI.

I returned to his office the next morning and he was ready to give me the test. He told me some things that would help me to get a good grade on it. The first thing he told me was to go through and answer the questions I knew and then work on the hard ones. It was a speed test and a long one. I made a good grade, 127 out of a perfect score of 150. If a person made a 100 on it, he could apply for cadet training and his name would be put on a list of names to be called at a later time. If someone made a grade of 110 or more, he could go at once to cadet training. The lieutenant was surprised at my score. I told him I was ready to go but he said he didn't know where to send me. I asked him to call someone and find out. He told me to go on to the mechanic's school and my orders to go into cadet training would catch up with me later. I was a happy person.

We had one GI we called "Kentucky" who was a comical character all the time. We would laugh at him when we looked at him because of the way he had his fatigue hat on his head. He would get us looking at him, and then he would do and say things to make us laugh. He would make the drill sergeant get so mad at him and he would come down hard on Kentucky, but that didn't change Kentucky. Kentucky would do the same thing over and over again.

We would be doing close-order drills and Kentucky would get 50 to 75 feet away from the squad and the sergeant would stop us and call Kentucky to come back to the squad and dress him down again, but Kentucky would just smile at him. When we were marching on the boardwalk to the mess hall, Kentucky would use his spoon and his mess kit to give us a beat to march with. Kentucky enjoyed getting the sergeant mad at him and there was nothing the sergeant could do about it.

We were told on the last Saturday we were in Atlantic City we would have an inspection at 10:00 in front of the hotel. It was for the base commander and we had to wear our khakis and tie, and have our shoes shining. We were in our proper place when the inspection group arrived at the hotel. I'm sure our drill sergeant was very proud of his squad as we came to attention when the general and his team came to look us over. I was in the last row of our squad and Kentucky was in the row in front of me.

When the general stopped to look over Kentucky, he asked the general, "Sir, will you please give me change for a quarter?"

The general said, "Son, why do you need change for a quarter now?"

Everyone was surprised because we were not supposed to blink an eye when an officer was looking us over. Everyone who heard Kentucky was excited and we didn't know what his answer was going to be.

Kentucky replied, "Sir, when we are turned loose and this inspection is over, there will be a long line at the drink machine at the hotel, and if I have to hunt change, then it will be empty." The general turned to the officer behind him and told him to be sure this man got his change before anyone was dismissed. I said to the one standing next to me after we were through with that inspection, "Kentucky is the only one in the Army who would do that and get away with it."

The GI said, "You're right and it's a good thing; the Army doesn't need another Kentucky."

As far as I know, no one said anything to Kentucky about this episode and I never heard if the drill sergeant said anything to him or not. There is nothing that can be done to undo something that has happened, but I'm sure glad the general had some laughs about it.

I was put on the KP list to be at the mess hall at 6:00 p.m. to work the night duty until 6:00 a.m. the next morning. The mess sergeant talked to us and explained to us the different things he wanted done. The first job he put me on was breaking eggs for the Sunday morning breakfast. I don't know how many crates of eggs were brought out for us to crack, but we had crates stacked everywhere. Two large pots were placed on the floor with four stools for each pot and the mess sergeant showed us how to take two eggs in each hand and at the same time break them on the rim of the pot and get them inside the pot. He told us not to worry if an eggshell fell into the pot.

"Let it be. They will be cooked and eaten with the eggs and you haven't the time to get them out", he said.

There were eight of us at that job and we wondered how many eggs we had put into the pots that night, but we didn't ask. Some of the cooks would keep watch and would keep us supplied with empty pots when the ones we were working with had a certain amount of eggs. They were putting the pots in a cooler room until they started cooking breakfast.

About 9:00 or 9:30 p.m., the mess sergeant came to me (after we had finished the eggs) and told me to go with him. We went into another large room with tables and a double row of ovens. He said I was going to be cooking hams for the rest of the night. The hams were for Sunday's noon meal. I told him I didn't know anything about cooking hams and he needed to get someone else for the job.

"I'm going to show you how," he told me.

He said to watch him as he prepared a few of them and then I could take over. There was a stack of metal pans on one of the tables and he took one of the pans and put two hams in it and made a number of cuts on the hams. He went to the cooler and got a large container of pineapple slices and a gallon jug of a juice mixture. He told me to get all of the ovens ready and put two hams in each one. The hams were to be scored on the tops and the oven doors left open. He would be checking on me and would be back when I finished. I did all he told me to do and sat down for a few minutes' rest. He returned and asked me if I was ready to start cooking hams. I told him I was and he said, "Let's get busy."

He put one pineapple slice on each ham. Then he put some of the juice mixture in a small pan and applied it to each ham with a brush, shut the oven door, set the oven thermostat and told me to do the next one. After he saw me do that one, and as I set the thermostat, he said, "Don't stop. When you finish putting the last ham in the oven, it will be time to go back to the first oven and brush some of the juice mixture on all the hams. Repeat the brushing again, and remember - the ovens are hot, so don't get burned. I will be checking on you."

I went to work and time went by fast because I was busy. I don't remember how many hams I cooked that night with the mess sergeant's help, but it was a large number. When 10,000 men are to be fed, it takes a lot of food. I stopped working with hams about 5:30 that morning and the sergeant let us have breakfast in the kitchen area before they started serving breakfast. The mess sergeant thanked us and we returned to the hotel and went to sleep.

The boardwalk was parallel to the ocean and close to the surf. It was seven or eight miles long with piers about 2500 feet long extending out over the Atlantic Ocean. We never marched the entire length of the boardwalk from one end to the other, but we marched a long way on it. On a number of days, we would march a long way on it, get off and go out of the city, passing by the city garbage dump. We went to an open area where we had an hour of calisthenics led by a Notre Dame football player. Our time to take calisthenics was from 10:00 a.m. to 11:00 a.m. That was at a hot time of the day, but he was one who took his job seriously and he believed in keeping us at it for the full hour. He had a platform about six feet high in the middle of the area where all could see him and he could see everyone. We were getting in better condition because we were not complaining as much as we had been. No one, at any time, asked if we wanted to do something – they didn't give us a choice. They told us what to do and when. That's the military way, and that's the way it should be. We were always glad to get the calisthenics done for the day.

Here are a few facts about Atlantic City when I was there: The city was the largest seaside resort in the world. It is located on a narrow sandbar approximately ten miles long and ¾ mile wide, four miles away from New Jersey. There are bays and meadows in between it and the mainland. People visit there summers and winters. The boardwalk is seven or eight miles long, made of steel and concrete with flooring made of wooden pine planks. It is sixty feet wide. There are hotels, big and small, everywhere. There are amusement places, parks, shops, eating places, theaters, and five long piers that start at the boardwalk and go out over the Atlantic Ocean for a long way – almost a half mile. It had its famous "Atlantic City Auditorium and Convention Hall". I went one time to "The Steel Pier" and walked and looked at some of the shops. I saw and heard one of the "Big Bands" of 1942.

One afternoon, about 5:30 p.m. the sergeant came up and started some trouble in the room next to my room. He should not have been on the floor at that late time in the afternoon. We were told that after five o'clock we could sit on the cots. Sometime after five he had come up and checked some of the cots by dropping a nickel on the blankets to see how tight they were. That time the sergeant picked the wrong GI and the wrong cot and the wrong time to do his cot check. The sergeant had the GI standing at attention and was really dressing him down when the noise drew a large number of us to the doorway to see what the trouble was. The GI was a tall, red-headed, slim man. He was acting like a "mad" man. In a moment's time, he had a long-bladed knife at the sergeant's throat. He was at the sergeant's back and had his left arm around the sergeant's chest and arms, and he held the knife in his right hand. The red-headed GI was a crazy man, and we didn't know what was going to happen. He held the knife to the sergeant's throat as he told him what he wanted to tell him. This is what he said plainly, using a lot of cuss words in the telling.

He told the sergeant what a bad man he had been to us and he needed to ease up on us. He told the sergeant he was not to report what had happened and when he removed the knife and let him go, the sergeant was to make up the cot like it was when he walked in (the sergeant had pulled the blanket off the GI's cot). We were ready for this situation to end. There weren't any words spoken after that. The redhead removed the knife and let go of the sergeant. The sergeant made up the cot and left the room. The crowd of GIs went back to their rooms and no one ever talked about this episode again. We were happy it was over – it could have been bad. I didn't have but a short time left in Atlantic City after this event took place.

When we were in Atlantic City, one of the men called a few of us together and told us about his roommate. He said for us not to get close to this roommate in a crowded area because he had a nervous problem and we might get hurt. This was his problem. If he heard someone make a clicking noise with his mouth, he would immediately close his eyes, cross his arms, bring his arms and hands with his fists close to his chest and then let the arms and fists leave his chest and swing out fast and hard. If anyone was close to him, they would be hit and I mean hit hard. The roommate said he had tried to stop him but could not stop him. Even the doctors tried to come up with some cure for it but failed.

This man should not have been in the service, but I don't know if he had told them about his problem or not. I saw him have one of those spells one time when I was in the elevator at the Strand Hotel. This was during the last week of my stay in Atlantic City, and it happened when one of the GIs deliberately pointed his finger at him and made a clicking sound with his mouth. That was something to see and hear. One fist hit the elevator operator and the other fist hit the wall of the elevator. That should not have happened, and I told the one who caused this he should be ashamed for doing it.

I was happy to hear I was leaving Atlantic City and as always, I was with a new group of GIs. They sure knew how to mix us up. Here is the order to leave:

Atlantic City to Goldsboro, NC

Orders BTC (7) AAFTTC – Atlantic City, NJ

Aug. 30, 1942 to Goldsboro, NC –S.O. #61

Hg. BTC AAFTTC – Left Aug 31, 1942

"A Fast Train Ride"

I left by train with a group in a regular coach rail car on the rear of a fast train from New York City to Miami, Florida. That was a fast train ride. The black porter came into our coach car about 9:30 that night and asked us if he could ride in the car with us for an hour or two. We told him he was welcome to stay as long as he wanted to. He told us a lot of stories about things that had happened on the train trips he had been on, especially the New York to Miami runs, when certain engineers were at the controls. He explained the last car on a long train gets a lot of whiplash on some of the tracks, and there was a bad spot in the tracks not far from where we were. He added, "I hope old so-and-so who is on this run tonight will slow down a little for that spot. But I wouldn't bet on that."

The porter told us about an engineer on this same spot and on a coach car with GIs like us going to Miami. The car wheels hopped off the rails and then got back on the tracks after a couple of miles. He said he knew it was the truth, because the engineer stopped and backed up, and he took a look to check for any damage to the car. There was no damage to the car and wheels, but the cross ties showed the wheel marks. He was sure some of the ties had to be replaced. Then, the porter said the engineer was not going to slow down for that spot and there was a speedometer on the dining car wall.

"I'm going to go and see how fast we are going", he said, leaving us to manage as best we could the whiplash headed our way. He came back about thirty minutes later. He told us the speedometer showed us at 78 miles per hour and that was too fast for the curve.

"How bad was it back here?" he asked. We replied it was bad. We told him he had picked the right time to leave us and go to the dining car, hadn't he? We made it okay and arrived at Goldsboro the next day, September 1, 1942.

"Training at Goldsboro, North Carolina"

We arrived in Goldsboro on September 1, 1942, to start classes at a new school for training to be airplane mechanics at Seymour Johnson Field. The Army Air Force's Technical Training Command near Goldsboro was building this school. The area was a wet and muddy place and we called it a swamp. They were not completely through building it when we arrived. I think we were the second class to start there. The first class arrived one week before we did. We had temporary barracks to stay in and they were always moving us from one barracks to another depending on what time we had classes. They had a very good school setup and had good and well-equipped classrooms.

There was mud everywhere and they had some board walkways in some areas but not everywhere we had to go. They were building constantly on the base at that time, but there was only one mess hall and that was bad when we had classes night and day. I think we changed shifts every month. It was bad to go to the mess hall when we wanted to get breakfast and had to eat turnips and beans instead. Or, when we would finish night school we would get to go to the mess hall and eat breakfast instead of an evening meal because we had to sleep during the day. We were moved to barracks at the back of the base and they gave us blankets to put over the windows.

They still wanted us to get our Army training with our schooling, so we had some hiking and marching to do. We had an obstacle course to run every week and it was some obstacle course! It was made in a big U-shape with a GI trainer at each station. We had to do every obstacle - there was no such thing as going around one of them. We had to do all of them or stay at each one until we did. After a few times around, we began to master all of them. It was every Friday, rain or shine. With calisthenics, running, marching, and the obstacle course, we got into good physical shape.

The instructors at the school were very good. They had mock-ups, books, films, diagrams, charts and blackboards to use along with their teaching. There were a number of subjects taught by different instructors. There was a class on airplanes for all kinds of military jobs. This was a study of all the metals used in airplanes, all parts of the main body, wings, and controls. Included were wiring diagrams, magnetism, electromotive forces, physics of static electricity, and electrolysis. Also covered were all electrical units, engineering for all types from the small plane to the large airplane engine, both air and water cooled types, hydraulics, and instruments. There was also a study of all types of bearings, fuels, oils and greases. When I say study, I mean from theory to practice. These classes were taught using cutaways of different parts and some of them were working units with moving parts visible through Plexiglas. They taught the theory of electricity by using a film made by Walt Disney with only three characters – Mr. Volt, Amp, and Ohm and a bridge as resistance. It was a simple way to teach, but the lessons stayed with us. I still remember them after sixty-six years. They only had a few months to make us into plane mechanics and they did a good job.

Goldsboro to Goldsboro
Orders 794th Tech Sch. Sqn. (SP) Goldsboro – Oct. 12, 1942
To 799th T.S.S. (SP) S.O. #124 P8-HQ Oct. 29, 1942

We had a building that had all types of engines mounted on stands in separate cells with controls. We were in a room with glass viewing windows and took turns at creating troubling situations while other class members determined what the problem was and fixed it. That was a noisy place when all the engines were running. There was one engine in the building that was an experimental engine built to be used in the Navy PT boat. It was a

32-cylinder engine. They had put two V-16 Allison water-cooled engines together with only one large output shaft on the rear. That was a large engine, and the instructor told us they had tried it in the experiment. He told us he wasn't told why it was used. We ran it on the test stand and it did make a lot of noise and had plenty of power.

There was a GI from Alabama who was always in the bunk next to me. He was a little older than me and was an insurance man at a place close to Birmingham. He was a heavy drinker and would get a pass to go into Goldsboro when our school schedule would let him. He wouldn't return until about 11:00 p.m. and he enjoyed waking everyone up, turning the two hanging light bulbs on and hollering, "Wake up everyone! - two naps are better than one!"

Almost all the time, he would go to one or two of the barracks next to us and get them mad at him. One of the men in our barracks said, the next time he went into town he was going to fix his bunk with a box of Grape Nuts. He had a box from the mess hall. The man went into Goldsboro that night and for two nights after that, the man with the Grape Nuts went to work. He took everything off the other man's bunk and covered the mattress with the cereal. Then he put the bunk back like it was supposed to be. At the usual time the man returned and went through his routine and all of us in our barracks were just waiting for his reaction to his bunk when he got in it. To our surprise, there was not a word from him and all of us went back to sleep.

The next morning, we thought he would find the cereal when he fixed his bunk, but he got up and just pulled his blanket tight and tucked it in place. We didn't know if he would go back to town that night or not, but he did. We were sure he would certainly discover the cereal the second night. But, the second night was the same as before. We were all really surprised he didn't feel the Grape Nuts as he lay on the cot.

The third night was a different story. As soon as he hit the sack, he got up and turned on both lights and said, "Get up everybody! Someone has been eating coconut cake in my bed." He made several trips up and down the barracks saying that and then he went to the other barracks and told them about it. I don't remember if anyone ever told him it had been done three days before. After that night a number of the men wouldn't let him forget about what happened. He tried to find out who fixed up his bunk, but no one told him who did it.

Myrtle came to Goldsboro and stayed about two months. We found a room she could rent at a home in town with a couple whose name was Crowe. Mr. and Mrs. Crowe were very good to Myrtle and me and we did appreciate their friendship. It snowed at times and we had some hard times, but we were happy to be together. During the war, people helped each other, and they especially helped the service men and their wives.

"Episodes at Goldsboro"

While I was at the school in Goldsboro, we were told there was a possibility we could be crew members on a bomber. A number of times, we were sent to a building and were given different kinds of eye and hearing tests. Some of the fellows who didn't want to be in combat would fake bad eyesight by asking someone who had glasses to let him use them while taking the tests. I saw and heard them doing that a number of times. I would ask them, "How do you live with yourself? That's not the right thing to do."

They would say, "It doesn't bother me."

"That doesn't make it right." I would answer. "Someone is going to do the fighting for you."

Most of the time, I was with fellows from the New England states. I had some good friends from there. I met some who didn't want to carry their part of the load. But, that's a part of life. I soon learned to accept it, but I didn't have to like it.

We were sent to a medical building one afternoon to take a test for tuberculosis. They gave us an injection in the inside of the left arm, about halfway between the wrist and the elbow.

They could tell the results in a short time. They told us to have a seat on the long bench by the side of the building, lean over and hold our head down as low as we could and stay in that position for a certain number of minutes to keep from passing out. We did as we were told to do and a big soldier came by and called us a big bunch of sissies. He said, "You boys need to act like a real man, like me. I'm leaving now."

We were told to leave by the back of the building and there were about eight feet of steps there. The back door was open and we heard a commotion out back. The big soldier who didn't sit on the bench as he was told to do, passed out as he started down the steps and fell head first out of the back door and cut his head. Since he was unconscious, someone called for an ambulance to come and take him to the hospital. I'm sure he was taught a lesson from this.

In our barracks was one odd GI who was an artist. He was always painting a landscape or a portrait from a picture. He was a tall, redhead about thirty years old, and he told us he was an orphan, raised by a rich aunt and uncle since his parents died. They had sent him to Paris to an art school for several years and he had studied there and at a school in Mexico City. The men in the barracks let him have an end bunk at the back and let him have a little extra space for his easels and painting supplies. Every week, he would receive a box of exotic foods, such as rattlesnake meat, foreign sardines packed in olive oil, all kinds of fish foods, including salmon, and, well, you name it, he would have it. If not, he hadn't heard of it. He would pass some of it around to all of us in the barracks, and some would sample it (especially the rattlesnake meat, so they could say they had eaten some of it). I ate one of the sardines and it was good. It should have been good, because he said it came from Norway, and a small tin cost a dollar. The regular price for a can of sardines was ten cents in the United States and it was a larger size than the Norway tin.

This redheaded GI would take some cans of these fish foods with him to the school classrooms and open and eat them during classes and he got away with it. The smell was bad. It was really bad - especially the salmon - right out of the can and not cooked. I think the instructors were told to let him have his way by our squadron lieutenant. The lieutenant had the

GI paint a portrait of his girlfriend from a picture of her. The painting was really beautiful and we saw it being painted a little at a time by a real artist.

In our barracks was an older man who was in his forties who was waiting and wanting to get out of the Army. He was told his discharge orders would be there in a few days. We had named him, "Papa Davis." His last name was Davis and everyone would add the "Papa" to his name. Almost all the GIs were called by their last name. We had been together in the barracks for several weeks when Red told Papa Davis he had met him somewhere a long time ago. They got into a conversation and Red recalled when and where it was. Red was driving in Arizona in 1937 and Papa Davis was hitchhiking. Red was on his way to Mexico City and stopped and gave him a ride. Both enjoyed meeting again.

It wasn't long before Papa Davis was discharged from the army. I remember when I saw a picture of the first service man being released from service because of age. That was Houston Wolfe of Atmore, Alabama, my hometown, and a friend of my father and me.

When we arrived at Goldsboro, we were assigned to our squadron and told we could pay for our laundry service when we were paid on the first day of each month. The squadron supply officer had made a deal with the laundry shop in town to do all our clothes for a certain amount each month. We could turn them into the supply room each week, and they would be returned during the week. There could not be any clothes washed in the latrine at any time, day or night. At first, we turned in two of everything and the only thing left were the clothes we had on. But, no laundry came back from town.

Now, you talk about troubles. We were told the laundry would arrive in a day or two, but days turned into weeks and weeks got to be months. We got desperate. They had collected two times for laundry services, and we had no clothes but the ones we had on. We asked for permission to wash our underwear, but they said no. We had gotten to the point we had to do something. We waited until 10:00 or 11:00 p.m. and then went to the latrine and washed the underwear and held them close to the boiler to dry them a little. We put them on our bunks at the foot ends to finish drying. We took turns in the night for our washing and we got by with it. The laundry in town got on the ball after two months or more and we had clean clothes for the rest of our time at Goldsboro. It was about time, but we didn't get any money back.

We had a man in our barracks at Goldsboro, older than us, who said he was a gambler from New York City. He operated a gambling business in New York and also had three racehorses. He told us he had turned everything over to a brother-in-law to operate while he was in the Army. He told us we should never gamble with a gambler, because we would always lose. "A gambler is in business to make money and he will win most of the time. Basketball games are my moneymakers because there are usually at least two games being played in or around the city each night. I never take bets on baseball games; they are so unpredictable. I have to know how the odds are at all times, how much money I have in bets on each team to win or lose, and to stop making bets at a certain amount. I try to predict the winner of a game, and if I have picked the right team, I will make more money than I would make if I had made the wrong pick. But, if I have played the odds right and stopped taking bets at the correct amounts, I will not lose; I will make a little money", he said.

After the World Series games in the fall of 1942, the gambler called us together the evening of the last game and told us about his troubles. His brother-in-law had bet on the series and had not played the odds right and didn't have the money to cover the bets. He said he had just got back from seeing the squadron commander and had asked for a three-day pass to go to New York City and sell his three racehorses, but he was turned down. He said he had to go there. He didn't have a choice. He told us he was going AWOL (absent without leave) for three days - one day to get there, one day to sell the three racehorses, and one day to get back to Goldsboro. He said to tell everyone he had no choice, but don't tell them tonight.

He left the base that night after the lights were turned out, and we told our instructors at the school about his leaving. They said they would help him on the lessons that he missed. We didn't know if he was going to get to New York City or not, but he returned to Goldsboro on the night of the third day. He told us he made the trip without being stopped by the MPs and we were glad. He went to the squadron office and reported in. He explained his being AWOL to the commander and told him it was something he had to do. He asked for mercy and got it. The commander restricted him to the base for a month. He got off with a light punishment, and he told us so.

I enjoyed the classes at the airplane mechanic school in Goldsboro. I tried to study extra hard for tests that were given to us. There was a classmate from New York City by the name of Kaplan, who was a smart student and made good grades without doing much studying. He was good at it, and he wanted everyone to know it. We were finishing our studies, and our main instructor gave us some instructions on what we would be doing to prepare for the final test. He had already told us I was the number one student at that time, but Kaplan was close, and the final exam would decide who would finish at the top of the class. I had not asked for this situation, but Kaplan had. He made it known he was going to beat me on the final exam and be at the top of the class.

A number of the men in the barracks came and talked to me about it and said they wanted to help me beat Kaplan by doing things for me and giving me more time to study. I told them to forget it, but they said they wanted to do my barracks' work for me. So, for two weeks they cleaned and mopped and made my bunk for me. I tried to get ready for the final test, but I could see Kaplan was also studying for it. I told the men they were expecting too much out of me and for them not to be surprised if Kaplan came out on top.

"He is a smart man, so we will wait and see." I said.

The instructor had heard about the challenge between Kaplan and me and said some changes needed to be made before he gave out our test papers. He put Kaplan at a desk on the right front corner of the room and put me at a desk on the left back corner and then passed out the exam papers. I don't recall how hard a test we had, but he told us he would give us the grade reports the next day. We returned the next day, our last day at the Goldsboro school. We entered the classroom and sat down. The instructor came into the room and said all had made a good grade on the test and he wished us well in our military service. Everyone was waiting to hear the test scores, and he said, "Kaplan and Shiver, you made the same grade. You both missed one question on soldiering, the same one, and that was one tricky one. I deliberately phrased that one to catch someone and I caught the top two in the class."

He then passed the graded test papers out to us and thanked us, and we were dismissed. We were through with school and on the 10th of January, 1943, I received my diploma from the United States Army Air Force Technical Training Command signed by Brigadier General Reid, the base commander at Seymour Johnson Field, Goldsboro, North Carolina. I was now a 747 airplane mechanic.

After we got back to the barracks I talked to Kaplan and the men. I told them they were wrong in their part by trying to get someone to a number one position at anytime and anywhere. I was still the #1 student in the class that just finished and I was just a little bit ahead of Kaplan, but that didn't make me a better person. I was only #1 by a fraction of a point in the grading system. I told Kaplan if he had studied as much as I had, then he would have passed me. That was the truth, and it helped all who heard me. Since we had to be together for a few more days, I thought we needed to part as friends. Kaplan and I shook hands and everyone was happy and enjoyed the time of doing nothing for a few days.

It was during the Christmas season of 1942 in the PX at Goldsboro when I first heard Bing Crosby sing "White Christmas" on the radio.

We left Goldsboro on January 14, 1943, by train for an advanced school at St. Louis, Missouri.

<u>Orders</u>
Goldsboro to St. Louis
799th Tech. Sch. Sqn. (SP) AAF to C.O.
AAF Det. Curtiss-Wright-S.O. #11 – Par. #11

"Advanced Training at St. Louis, Missouri"

A group of us arrived in St. Louis, Missouri, by train from Goldsboro, North Carolina, on January 15, 1943. We were carried out to the Curtiss-Wright factory at Lambert Field Airport. We were told we would be there approximately one month, going to school on a new A-25 plane the Army wanted. They had built one hangar and a barracks for us and had one instructor. We had a captain in charge over us and he explained the situation to us. The school hadn't been completely equipped, and there were no instruction manuals or books for us. The instructor at the school did have a number of lessons taught to us. One of them was on the electric propeller. He had a cut-away model along with some teaching setups.

The Air Corps wasn't sure the A-25 was the plane they needed. They had the A-20 two-engine attack plane, and they had planned on Curtiss-Wright modifying the Navy Hell Diver plane and calling it the A-25. The Hell Diver was used on carriers with folding wings and had an arresting hook on the rear for landing on carriers.

The school had no mess hall for us and the captain said we would have a few classroom sessions, but most of our days would be spent observing the planes being built in the factory. He explained we were to eat three meals a day in the factory cafeteria; we did and really enjoyed the food. We could go back and get any amount and they always had a variety of everything.

Here are some other things I remember that happened at St. Louis:

We would have about an hour of exercise and calisthenics each day, except Saturday and Sunday.

The Curtiss-Wright Factory was across the runway at the airport, Lambert Field, St. Louis.

I saw the Delta Queen, a Mississippi riverboat, tied up at St. Louis.

One of the men had met a young lady in St. Louis, and they were going to get married. They invited all of us to an engagement party at the Plantation Club one night. Six of us got a cab to carry us to the party. It was from 6:00 to 10:00 that evening. We had a good meal and the main entertainment was a show featuring Ted Louis. We had checked out to be back at the barracks by 10:00 p.m., so we left about 9:30.

I enjoyed the time at the factory in St. Louis. There were different sections, and we could visit any and stay as long as we wanted to at them. There were a number of drop presses where they were stamping parts out, and these presses did make noise! There were a large number of women operating the riveting guns and a number of midgets working in small places inside the planes. There was a section with a number of long tables where women were making all kinds of wiring harnesses. The planes were going to be carriers and all parts had to be painted and treated with non-corrosive coatings. I spent a long time in special paint booths where the parts were painted.

There was a waterfall at the rear of these paint booths with fans blowing toward the waterfalls. There were racks and racks of small and large parts that had to be painted. The operator would close the doors on the booth, start the waterfall, and turn on the fans. Then he would start the painting. I didn't ask how many coats of the material he put on, but he put a large number on. He told me they saved a lot of the material by using the waterfall to trap it, and they told me it was very expensive material.

One day, when I was in the cafeteria eating my noon meal, I was alone at a little two-seat table when a man asked me if he could join me. I told him I would enjoy having him join me. He introduced himself to me and said he had been with the company a long time. He was a designer and said that in 1934, he drew the plans for the Japanese Zero plane. The U.S. Army turned down his plans. It had two 30 caliber machine guns on it, one on each side, mounted on the wings. He said he had often wondered how they got those plans. He said it was a good fighter plane and he drew the plans.

When the planes were finished the test pilots would take them out to make a few runs up and down the runway. Sometimes, they would bring them back to a hangar at the rear of the factory, and sometimes they would fly them off and stay gone a long time before they would return. When the factory test pilots were through with the test flights, then the Navy test pilots would take them up and check them out. When the Navy test pilots were through with their flights and returned, the Army test pilots would take them up. All the pilots had a pad fastened to their legs to write notes on. We talked about the Army Air Corps testing the planes when they had not decided they were going to use them. I didn't see any fixed wing planes being made while I was in the factory and all the planes had the arresting hooks on them.

At the very back of the factory, there was a big transport plane made of wood. This plane's fuselage, wings, and stabilizers were made of laminated piano wood. It had two engines and the outside of the plane had been completely marked off with approximately two inch squares. In the middle of each block, there was a small string taped - about three inches long. I had to find out what that strange looking plane was doing there. I was told it was an experimental plane that had been flown close alongside a plane carrying a photographer taking pictures of every part of the outside of the plane from all angles. They were studying the strings and finding out the wind flow by how the strings were at all angles in the pictures. They also were checking the laminated piano wood used to make the fuselage, wings, horizontal, and vertical stabilizers. I don't know if it was ever flown again, but I do know it was a strange looking plane.

Some of the men were trying to get a group to go across the river and check out East St. Louis in Illinois. I didn't want to go, because I had heard it was a bad place to go to. One man, older than most of us, told the men that sometime in the 1930's he had lived in East St. Louis and had been known as a 'big time gambler from New York City'.

He said, "I am afraid someone will recognize me. I welshed on a big gambling debt and my life wouldn't be worth a wooden nickel. I would be dead before nightfall and thrown in the Mississippi. I haven't gone into St. Louis since we have been here and that's the reason."

I didn't go and the man from New York didn't go.

When we were ready to leave St. Louis, the captain had a session with us. He told us he had received reports from a number of men in the factory about what they observed while we were in the factory and cafeteria. He told us they told him we had not caused any problems with anyone, and we had acted like gentlemen with everyone. In fact, there had not been any complaint from anyone – that was the way it was and that was good news to us.

The captain told us some more good news. The Army had sent him three dollars a day per man; he had just returned from the factory office after paying our cafeteria bill and they had charged us only $2.25 a day. He asked us, "Have you fellows ever been paid to eat at a place before? Well, I have 75 cents per day for all of you!'

I graduated from Curtiss-Wright Factory A-25 Airplane School on Thursday, February18, 1943. I was schooled as an advanced A-25, 1st and 2nd echelon mechanic, qualified to do all maintenance services. I left St. Louis with a group on a train at 3:00 p.m. for Fort Myers, Florida, on Friday, February 19, 1943. We were going to an aerial gunnery (Flex) school to be trained as gunners on a bomber.

"Aerial Gunnery School - Fort Myers, Florida"

We arrived at Fort Myers, Florida, on Saturday, February 21, 1943, at 1:30 p.m. and went out to the base at 4:00 that afternoon. We were assigned to BK 213 Third Student Squadron School to become gunners on a plane. The school was known as the Aerial Gunnery (Flex) School at Buckingham Field, Fort Myers, Florida.

As soon as we got to the school, some of those who were at the school were telling us all about the bad things concerning training there. Especially tough was the physical training ahead of us at the obstacle course every Thursday evening and the "Burma Road" we would have to run every Friday evening. They were telling the truth. Both of those days were bad, really bad, and Monday, Tuesday, and Wednesday, we had at least a full hour of calisthenics. They said they had just about six weeks to get us in physical condition for flying and, later on, we would appreciate what they had done for us. That was true, but at the time, we thought they were trying to kill us.

The obstacle course was a particularly tough and hard one. The one we had in Goldsboro wasn't anything compared to this one. It was a tough one, and I mean tough, tough. When we got through with this course, we didn't go to the mess hall, we went to the barracks and flopped on our bunks and lay there for three hours. We didn't want to eat – we were too tired and always skipped the evening meal on Thursdays and Fridays. The man in front of us, leading us on our "Burma Road" run every Friday afternoon, had to be in great physical condition. He told us we were going to jog at a steady pace for two and a half miles. "If anyone drops out and falls, don't stop to help him, let him be. After the run, a truck will come and get those who couldn't make it."

When we would stop for a ten minute break, about the time our seat touched the sand, the man would say, "Get up! We need to take some calisthenics. We don't want our muscles to tighten up, do we?"

So, we would exercise and then he would say, "Let's hit the trail back."

We would follow him. All of this was done on a trail in Florida. There was sand about four to six inches deep on the trail and it was thick with palmetto trees and bushes. We had GI shoes on. It was hard to even walk on the trail, and we had to jog it five miles every Friday. We looked forward to Saturday and Sunday coming, so we could relax and get ready for the next week. The break was always welcomed. I never failed to complete the trail run, but some did.

We arrived on a Sunday afternoon and they called us as a group to a meeting at 8:00 Monday morning. They told us about what they would have us doing in our short time of approximately six weeks there. We were expected to learn about plane identification, plane wing lengths, turrets, guns, sights, and to become familiar with both .30 and .50 caliber Browning machine guns and ammunition. We had to practice skeet shooting and learn to make machine gun repairs with our eyes covered. We were taught how to shoot with BBs, .22 rifles, 12-gauge shotguns, and .30 and .50 caliber machine guns (Flex and in turrets). We practiced shooting at clay targets at the skeet stations and also standing on a flatbed truck with no one else on the back but an instructor. We shot the Browning machine gun at a moving target mounted on a jeep running on an oval track and from the rear seat of an AT-6 with three other planes and gunners in the rear seats.

We were each assigned a color. The ammunition was dipped in different colors so the hits could be counted on the target sleeve, which was white and was towed by a cable behind a plane. My color was always green. The other colors were black, red, and yellow. The white sleeve was marked and tagged (time of day, the number of the plane that towed the target and the gunner's name). At the end of the day, the hits were counted and recorded and our grade was determined. Near the end of our training there, we and three others at a time (four of different color ammo) were put on a two-engine plane with a Martin turret on it for a trip down the Gulf, past the Florida Keys and back. We shot at a target from the turret with two guns. We were told: "You will have a number of different instructors and they are good at what they do. Listen and do what they tell you, and you will be an aerial gunner when you leave here. It's going to be hard and fast, but you can do it."

"Episodes at Fort Myers"

They started us off with target practice in a shooting booth using a BB machine gun with a light that illuminated the silver colored BBs. Then they advanced us to a .22 caliber rifle in a booth with rows and rows of moving targets. This was like those they have in carnivals. I really enjoyed the shooting booth training, but when you have to do anything a long time, you get tired of it. They had us in a classroom part of the day, so that did give us time to relax and get away from shooting.

After training on the rifle, they moved us up to shooting 12-gauge shotguns. They started us out with clay targets being thrown from two huts about forty or fifty yards apart, and we moved to different stations. One of the huts from which the clay targets were shot into the air was high and the other one low. The angle the clay targets took when they were thrown into the air was changing all the time. I think we had eight stations at the skeet range, and we changed stations after every shot. There was a whole truckload of shell boxes brought out to the shooting range in the morning, and they would be gone that evening. I had a very good skeet instructor - his name was Duncan. He was good at skeet, and he rarely missed a target. He told us about duck hunting and alligator wrestling in his home-state, Louisiana. He said a friend and he loved to roll off their flat-bottom boat in the bayous of Louisiana with their knives in their mouths and wrestle an alligators. He told us the hardest part was getting the alligator in the boat. I was told Duncan went to Miami to shoot skeet in a shooting match on a Sunday and lost. I asked him about his losing out and he replied, "Me and the winner was tied at 198 straight hits and I missed the 199th disc, but he made his. His score was 200 and mine was 199. I just missed one, but he was perfect. I lost the match."

I wasn't too good at skeet. I usually scored about sixteen to twenty hits out of twenty-five shots. I knew what my problem was, but I could never correct it. As soon as I pulled the trigger, I stopped the gun's movement, and if I had completed my arm swing, I would have scattered the shell pellets over a larger area. I had to be quick on the trigger, especially when I was shooting doubles. Two discs would be shot out at the same time, and I would have to decide which one was going to be in the air the longest time and shoot at the other one first. I didn't have much time to think it over. I glanced, shot, and hoped I made the right choice. I would have a sore and bruised shoulder and the side of my face would show it after a day at the skeet range. That was good training for us and we enjoyed it.

We were anxious to get to the machine gun training. We had some classroom teaching on them, but we looked forward to the time of shooting the guns at targets from planes. We were taken to the place where the machine guns were mounted on stands and shot at a white target mounted on a jeep that ran on a circular cemented path at a slow speed. The jeep's steering was fixed so a driver wasn't needed. There was a raised cement guide in the middle of the pathway to aid in keeping the jeep on track. The gun stands were mounted so they were flexible, but the main stand was stationary.

There were always several instructors at the gun stands for safety reasons when the guns were being fired. The target jeep track was in a deep pit and the target stands were mounted so the jeep wasn't seen when it was going around the track. When a group of four colors were through firing their guns at the target, the target would have to be changed. Two students were assigned to do that task. I was told to go on that task one time and that was enough for me. All guns were supposed to be off-limits when a target was being changed. The change went this way: Two students would go to the track and wait for the jeep to come by. The one who wasn't holding the new target would get into the jeep and stop it. Then the target was changed and one would take the old target and get out of the way, and the other would restart the jeep, put the transmission in low and hop off. I was the one who stopped and restarted the jeep, and everything went as it was supposed to, until we got to the top of the track pit. As our heads reached the top, one of the gunners started shooting. I suppose the jeep with the target had time to be on its first time around. That was some sound as the bullets came whizzing over our heads! We were at the top of the pit and the sides of the pit were cut at an angle (sloped), so it didn't take us long to get to the bottom of the pit. We were yelling as loud as we could, "Stop shooting! Stop! Stop!"

In a moment or two, there was one of the instructors looking down at us asking, "Are you fellows okay?"

One of us said, "Just scared - you didn't give us time to get out."

We had a close call and both of us were still scared. That close call was a great lesson for all. I have often thought about this and have wondered how close those bullets were at our heads. Another few seconds and we would have been killed.

Another day at the machine gun range, an accident happened. One of the flex connectors broke on one of the guns at the stand while the gunner was shooting at the target. The machine gun is very heavy, about 75 pounds, and the gunner was still shooting it. The barrel of the gun was pointed to the ground and on the ground. All the time, bullets were going into the dirt and sand, and the instructors were trying to get the gunner to let go of the trigger. It was only a short time before it was over, but for those of us who were there, it seemed like a long time.

The next week was our time to get in the air with our training. We had already been schooled on what we would be doing in the air. They had pilots flying AT-6 planes that had been in the Army for a long time. They were sergeants - just plain three-striped sergeants. The Army Air Corps later changed those flying sergeants to flight officer rank. They were good pilots but wild with their flying. These pilots had a reputation of trying to live up to that name of "Wild Flying Cowboys."

I had the same plane and pilot on the AT-6 flights. In the rear seat where the gunner was, a .30 caliber Browning machine gun was mounted on a track that allowed the gun to be moved from the left to the right side, depending on which side the target was on. The gunner would have to stand up. The gun would be locked down with the barrel of the gun pointed to the back of the plane. The pilot would say when he was going to get in position for us to get ready to fire at the target and we would tell him when we had finished shooting our ammo. I do not remember how many times we had the AT-6 plane flights, but I enjoyed them. The trips out over the Gulf to meet up with the tow target plane and the trips back to the base were always full of surprises.

When we left the base going to meet up with the tow target plane, all four planes stayed together as a group with the target plane by itself. The gunners had headsets on, and the pilots talked with the other pilots and the gunner in the rear seat. This group of "Wild Flying Cowboys" would do some of their flying tricks for us. They would tell us what they were going to do and then they would do it. They would "stack the deck". That's when all four planes would see just how close they could get on top of each other without causing an accident. Then they would do their "shuffle the deck" routine where they would move the bottom plane out of the "stack" up to the top position and then they would keep that up for some time. They would always find time to do a little "follow the leader," and they would really do some fast and reckless flying. By that time, we would be close to the target plane and could see the target coming out. I would get the gun in position to fire at the target. The instructors said to aim and fire, advising us that if we tried to improve our aim, we would mess up.

"Aim and fire"; I followed that and got into trouble by scoring too many hits on one of the targets. One evening, after the hits on the targets were counted, a GI came to our barracks and told me to go with him to report to an officer in a certain office. I went and the officer told me to sit down and started asking me about my shooting that day. This is the conversation he and I had:

"How did you score so many hits on that one target today? Did you get someone to help you? Tell me how you did this? You had as many hits as the other gunners had on that target together."

I replied, "I didn't know I had scored too many hits. How could I have gotten someone to help me? How many colors were on the target, and how many planes were there at that time?"

"There were four colors and four planes."

I told him I couldn't have gotten help on a target if I had tried to, and I hadn't tried to. This was the first time in my life I had gotten into trouble because I had made a high score. I told the officer to do what he wanted to, but I wasn't worrying about too many hits; I was concerned about too few. He told me to return to the barracks.

On some of the return flights back to the base, my pilot enjoyed scaring us, especially those on their first flight. Out in the Gulf from Fort Myers, there was an island with two palm trees on it and they were close to the water. He would ask the gunner if he thought we could fly between the two trees. Then, he would fly down close to the water and head to the trees. We knew he wasn't going to hit those trees, but if that happened to be someone's first flight with him, they would shut their eyes. At the last moment, he would dip one wing and bring the other wing up, and the plane would go through the trees. In all my Army life, I was never seasick or airsick at any time. I have seen others get in a really bad condition.

One of the AT-6 plane pilots was named Joseph. He was of Native American heritage and was known as "Indian Joe." He was a very good pilot, and he tried to live up to the reputation of that group known as the "Wild Flying Cowboys." The planes had a two-position propeller on them, and when the blades changed from one position to the other, the change would make a strange noise. When they were taking off, the AT-6 pilots would see which one could get in the air in the shortest time. I wasn't flying that morning, but I heard about what happened. Indian Joe wasn't high enough when he brought his landing wheels up, and his propeller blades touched the runway. He was able to get the plane in the air and back to the runway and land okay. There was a bad vibration from the bent propeller blade, and that was the end of the fast plane take-off contest. I'm sure they declared Indian Joe the winner. The propeller had to be replaced.

I had to make the flight from the Fort Myers Field out over the Gulf Pass, the Florida Keys and back to Fort Myers. On the flight down and on the return flight, we would meet up with a target plane, and we would take our turn firing at the target. We were told to look for German submarines in the Gulf waters, but we didn't see any. There had been some seen in the Gulf of Mexico and also off the east coast. About fifteen minutes before we arrived back at the base, the flight engineer, a master sergeant, came to the back of the plane and said he needed to give us some instructions before we landed. He said this was his second time to fly with this pilot, a second lieutenant, and he almost lost it on landing. We thought he was trying to scare us, and we told him so, but he assured us it was the truth. The plane was a two-engine AT-18 or AT-19 Lockheed bomber with a Martin top turret. The flight engineer told us to watch for a signal from him, and at the signal, we were to move to the rear of the plane as quickly as we could. That was what we did. What the master sergeant had feared happened. The pilot lost control of the plane when the wheels touched the runway. We wrecked, and I mean wrecked; the left wing and the left engine were damaged, and the plane came to a stop on another runway.

We gunners were tossed everywhere in the rear, and the crash crews were at the scene in a few moments. The ambulances had us all to the hospital in a few minutes, and they gave us a good examination, and then they got us to the flight line. None had been hurt, just bruised and scared. We had been through a lot in that accident but didn't have any bones broken. They said they wanted to get us back in the air as quickly as they could. That was the best thing to do for anyone who had been in an accident and had not received serious injuries. They did that and we were glad to get through the gunners' training. We would have our graduation exercise in a few days and get our sergeant rank and pay increase on our next payday.

Fort Myers had an old observation plane on the base that was used to carry Army students on Sunday afternoons on sightseeing trips to the Florida Everglades. I was about halfway through my stay at the school when I heard about it and I wanted to go. I was on a short list of names scheduled for the last Sunday we were at Fort Myers. I went to the flight line about one o'clock, got in line and waited for my turn to go. The plane would be gone about thirty minutes, and there was just one GI before me. It was about 3:00 p.m. when the plane returned for the GI in front of me. The plane left but didn't return. There were two or three GIs back of me and we wondered what had happened. No one knew. We stayed until 6:00 that afternoon, but the plane didn't return. The base sent some planes out, but night came before they could find the plane. The search had to wait until morning.

The base sent out planes early on Monday and they found the plane and the two men. I never talked to them, but I heard about the troubles they had. The plane's wings were covered with a fabric material, and they hit a large bird. The wing was damaged so badly that the pilot had to land in the Everglade marshes. They were not hurt in the accident, but they had a bad night with mosquitoes, flies, and other insects. I have thought about this a number of times - that could have been me. What a difference those thirty minutes made. The Lord was with me keeping me out of trouble, as always, and He is doing that today. For that I am and I will always be grateful to Him.

The last shooting instruction with the shotgun was the skeet shooting practice. We stood and shot while on the flat bed of an Army truck without any stand support to help us stay on the truck. There was an instructor on the flat bed with us to mark down our scores, and to be along if there was an accident. The skeet range was a road in the shape of a big "U" and the sides were about a half mile long, and the end road was about one-quarter mile. There were nine targets on each side and seven targets on the end road. The targets were released when wires lying across the road were triggered as the truck's wheels ran over them. The range was made in a large pine tree area and there would be only one truck on the range at any time. The first part of the range was the hardest part. The huts, where the clay targets were shot out of, were low to the ground and hard to pick up on, and the clay targets didn't stay in the air very long. The target huts on the short back road and the last long road were tall and taller, and these targets stayed in the air longer. On one of my trips to this range, I started off doing great on the hard to hit clay targets, and the instructor said, "Shiver, you are going to have a great score today. You have hit all nine of the tough ones, and all you have left are the easy ones."

From that moment on I missed all the other ones. I still don't know what happened.

I graduated from the Aerial Gunnery (Flex) School at Buckingham Field, Fort Myers, Florida, on April 5, 1943. We had graduation that morning and they gave us a buck sergeant's stripes for our uniforms. We were the first group to receive the buck sergeant's rank. I don't remember the number of men who were in the class with me, but it was over a hundred.

I had a surprise that morning. The officer conducting the ceremony began by congratulating us on finishing the school, and then he said he was going to call out the names of the top 20 gunners in the class. I finished number 16!

We got ready to leave Fort Myers and we left on Friday, April 9, 1943, at 6:00 p.m. Our orders were to a replacement center at Salt Lake City, Utah. We left in two old converted boxcars with a third one used as a mess car.

<u>Orders</u>
<u>Fort Myers to Salt Lake City</u>
HG – B.A.A.F.F.G.S. – Ft. Myers, Florida
April 9, 1943 – to C.O. Repl-Wing - Salt Lake City, Utah
Par – 7-S.O. #96 – April 6, 1943 & left April 9, 1943.

Chapter 3

TRANSFERS AND ADVANCED TRAINING

"Transfer to Replacement Center, Salt Lake City, Utah"

We arrived by rail at Salt Lake City to a replacement center where we would be reassigned to different bases. We arrived on a Tuesday night at 10:30 after four days of traveling from Fort Myers, Florida. We left Fort Myers on Friday, April 9, 1943, at 6:00 p.m. in an old boxcar that had been converted into a troop car. They had put some windows on the sides and made park benches for seats with no solid bottoms to sit on. There were two such troop cars and another boxcar made into a mess hall to feed us. All three rail cars were put on the end of a passenger train and that was where we stayed. We were told we could step on the ground when we got to Salt Lake City and not before. That was a very bad train ride. We had wieners three times a day, morning, noon, and night. After four days and nights on that train, we had to learn to walk again. We were glad to get out of that boxcar! We got on GI trucks and went to the base.

We arrived on April 13, 1943, and were told we were being assigned to squadron A, Barracks 1703, AAB SLC, 18th Replacement Wing. It was nice to get a shower, some clean clothes and a bunk to sleep on in place of the benches. They told us we would be at Salt Lake for only a few days, but we could expect to have a dress inspection on Saturday morning by the base commanding general. His pet "gig" (military slang for demerit) was haircuts. I went to the PX barbershop on Friday afternoon about three o'clock and got a haircut for twenty-five cents. I must have gotten a bad one because I got a haircut gig and one for not having my sergeant stripes on my shirt. Eugene Sanders from Mississippi also got a gig for not having sergeant stripes on his shirt.

The food was bad at Salt Lake. It was a consolidated mess hall that fed 10,000 GIs. At one meal, I got a bad piece of meat. I wasn't the only one. There were signs everywhere that said, "Take all you want, but eat all you take." Some of the men were trying to stick the meat to the underside of the table. The mess hall officer was checking the trays as we brought them back. I got up and walked over to him and asked if he had eaten a piece of the meat. He said no, and I told him I couldn't eat what I had. He told me to dump it in the can. I did and left the mess hall.

I enjoyed the few days at Salt Lake; we just waited on orders to leave for someplace else. As I lay on my bunk, I could see the Mormon Temple out the window of the barracks. It was a beautiful view. Our orders came and we boarded the train Sunday evening, April 18, 1943, at 6:00 p.m. We were on a rail coach car, but we didn't leave Salt Lake until 1:30 a.m. that morning. We were going to Tucson, Arizona.

<u>Orders</u>
<u>Salt Lake City to Tucson</u>
Grp. Hd. - 18th Replacement Wing - Army Air Base - Salt Lake City, Utah, April 16, 1943
To C.O. 71 B.C. Attached. 39th Bomb Grp. AA.B –
Davis-Monthan Field
S.O. 107 - HQ 18th Replacement Wing - Dated April
April 17, 1943

"Transfer to Tucson, Arizona"

We arrived in Tucson by rail Tuesday night at 10:00 p.m., April 20, 1943. We went by truck to Davis-Monthan Air Base. We were put in Barracks #605. Next morning, we were told we were in boot camp and would stay for three days. We were sent to 62nd Bomb Sqn. (H) Barracks 313. We were moved to Barracks 110, then to Barracks 310, and finally to Barracks 312. We didn't know what was happening to us. Then, on May 4th they transferred me to 676th Squadron - 444th Bomb Group. Soon after arriving at Tucson, I was told I was to be an engineer instructor. I went to the squadron commander and told him there had been a mistake. I hadn't been to a B-24 school. In fact, I had not seen one.

I asked, "How could I be an instructor?"

He answered, "That's your problem - I have enough myself."

I returned to the barracks and sat on my bunk. A sergeant line mechanic was on his bunk next to me and asked, "What's your trouble? You look sad."

I told him what had just happened.

He said, "I will help you. I work on the flight line on B-24s. I have been to B-24 school. In fact, I have an extra big manual I will give you, and I will take you to the flight line with me."

That's what he did. I felt better and I was relieved. He was a great teacher and I was eager to learn. I was very thankful for his help. I will always think of him and his manual. In fact, in 1989 I gave that manual to The Collins Foundation for their B-24 "The All American". I was on my way to becoming a flight engineer.

Flights from Davis-Monthan AAB - Tucson

My time at Tucson was short and fast. After I was checked out as a flight engineer instructor, I was used almost all the time, both day and night. I missed mess hall mealtime a number of times, so I would go to the PX and get a sandwich and drink. Davis-Monthan was a first phase flying school.

The pilot instructor and engineer instructor worked as a team to teach a new pilot to take-off and land a 4-engine B-24 bomber. That was a hard job. Some would have a little two-engine time, but not much. Somebody had to do it. I would go to the squadron operations office and check the blackboard for the next flight. If I was too tired to make it, I would ask the clerk to take me off and I would hit the sack and sleep. I did make notes on some of the flights but not all of them. The following are three of the most memorable ones:

One of the instructor pilots I teamed up with was a redheaded young man, 2nd lieutenant, a very good pilot but wild with his flying. A natural pilot, he did not worry about anything. He and I had a young 2nd lieutenant up for instrument flying late one evening. We put shades on all windows until it was dark. The lieutenant was doing a very good job. I was in the nose section of the plane. I had the headset and mike on and had been watching for other planes. The instructor pilot told me to come up to the flight deck. He wanted to talk with me. As soon as I got in the cabin he asked me a question. "Have we got any oxygen?"

"I don't know. I will check." I checked and got back to him. "We have plenty of oxygen on plane."

He asked me, "How high can this plane get to?"

I said, "I don't know."

He said we would find out. Then he told me his plans. We were going to cross over the border into Mexico and we would see how high we could go. He got in the left seat and told me to go to the front end of the plane and watch for any planes and to use the headset and mike. It was approximately 9:00 p.m. We went on oxygen and started to climb. About two hours later we couldn't go any higher. He said, "Now we know - 31,000 feet. That's it."

The engines had really been working hard. We returned to base and he told us not to tell anyone about what we had done. He told us he would fix the paper work. I didn't hear anything more about it.

We come to the second story:

A few days later, I was with this redheaded lieutenant instructor pilot again. We went with a full crew headed to a gunnery range. There was a proper time to go in and a time to get out. This gunner range was in New

Mexico. It was in a desert area. The range was fixed up for the plane's gunners to try to hit targets of plane mockups and old car bodies. The ground was marked off for the plane to follow. It was approximately twenty miles long and two miles wide. For the top turret gunner to be able to fire at the targets, the plane would have to fly at an angle. Everybody always wanted to fire at the targets. We had just got on the range when the co-pilot, hearing the guns firing, told the redheaded instructor he was not waiting until all the ammo was shot up. He got out of the co-pilot's seat and went to the rear of the plane. The instructor pilot told me to sit down. He and I were the only ones on the flight deck.

About ten minutes later, he told me to take the wheel. We were 100 to 125 feet off the ground. I took it and was looking at the flight indicator. He took his cap and covered it up and said, "When you are this close to the ground, you look out and fly by the seat of your pants."

We were coming up to where we had to turn, so I told him to take the controls. He said, "You fly it."

I told him. "NO".

As he was getting out of his seat, he said, "You got it whether you want it or not."

He left the flight deck and I was alone. It was about fifteen minutes before the crew pilot came back to the cabin. I have often thought about that - ten men on a team plus a gunnery instructor, pilot instructor, and myself, making a total of thirteen. When the redhead came back to the cabin, I told him off. He said I did a good job, but I said he and I were not working together anymore.

I went to the operations clerk and told him not to put us together again. I didn't tell operations staff about what he had done, but I did tell a friend who was working on the flight line. I met this friend later, in Pueblo, in April of 1945. He was still working on the flight line. He told me about what had happened to the redheaded pilot. He got in trouble with some of his flying. He was reported by a train engineer for flying head on towards the train. Someone got the plane's number and the engineer called the base. Later, the redhead was court-martialed for his train playing action. He was a good pilot, but foolish and wild.

And now the third story:

Operations C.O. wanted to check out a pilot for night flying and instrument checks. He asked me to go as flight engineer. He was a captain and I had been with him on flights before.

We left about 7:00 p.m. The captain was in the co-pilot's seat. Everything went well until we put shades over the windows. Then we got into trouble. I knew the pilot was not ready for this.

I was between the pilot and co-pilot's seats, leaning onto the back of their seats. I asked the lieutenant if he had been checked for day flying. He said no. Then the captain got mad and started cussing really bad. I told the captain to calm down. He was not helping the situation at all. He really got mad and was cussing more. He blamed the lieutenant; I knew I had to calm him and get him off the lieutenant. I told him someone in his operations office had made the mistake.

"Let us get back to the base," I said.

He said okay and told the lieutenant to change seats with him and he would take over. I know the lieutenant was happy, but he never said anything to me. We arrived at base approximately 9:00 p.m. and got into the landing pattern. The captain called for 1/4 flaps---1/2 flaps---3/4 flaps, and we turned on the final approach. He called for full flaps. I didn't look at the flap indicator; I was watching the speed indicator. On the final approach, the engineer called the speed to the pilot. I had already told the captain we were coming in too fast. At this time, I looked at the flap indicator and I saw we didn't have the flaps down. The lieutenant had not pushed the lever hard enough to activate the flaps. We were coming in too fast, almost on the ground. When I told the captain that we had no flaps, the lieutenant moved the flap lever all the way down, and we went up like an elevator. Instead of being on the ground, we were about fifty feet up. We bounced up and down about two or three times. We were on grass between two runways. I couldn't get to the magneto switches, but I could get to the fuel levers. I cut the fuel off to all four engines. We stopped on another runway.

The captain did do some real cussing then. He said he had it under control all the time. I told him he didn't, and all he had to do was tell the tower we were on the other runway. We had to restart the engines. That was what we did. We taxied and parked and checked the plane - no damage. The lieutenant didn't say anything. The captain and I walked to the operations office and he was still mad. He told me he was going to report me for cutting the engines off. I told him he wasn't going to do anything.

If we had a hearing, I was going to put him in a bad situation. I told him, "#1 - That was your office that made the mistake about the lieutenant not being ready for a night test. #2 - If I was caught in another situation like that, I would do the same again. #3 - You shouldn't cuss. You shouldn't get mad. You are no officer and no gentleman."

I never heard anything more about the incident. It wasn't long after this before the captain told me a request had come in to send an instructor engineer to El Paso, Texas, to join a combat crew going into third phase training. This person was going to miss first and second phase training. He had recommended me. I have often thought about that. Did he want to get me away from Tucson, or did he really think I was ready to skip first and second phase training? I will never know and I don't need to know. I left Tucson by train on Wednesday, May 26, 1943, at 1:30 p.m., but not before getting five shots at one time – three in one arm and two in the other, because they had lost my medical records.

I was at a number of places while I was in the Army Air Corps. I saw some of the beautiful natural wonders of these United States from the air and on the ground. Arizona has its share of them. First, would be the weather. While I was at Tucson only a short five weeks, the sun was shining every day. I think Tucson claims to have sunshine 300 days a year.

Soon after I got there, they had us standing outside in the sun at 10:00 a.m. in full dress uniform for an inspection by a general. It was a very hot day, and that inspection lasted until 11:30 that morning. We learned quickly how hot the sun could be in Tucson.

The Grand Canyon was something to see, especially from the air. Other interesting things to see were the Hoover Dam, the Colorado River, and the giant cacti all around Tucson. There is the Saguaro National Monument that is near Tucson and contains cacti that grow as high as fifty feet. I tell everyone that at Davis-Monthan Air Base, we had dry desert air, sunshine, mountains, giant cacti, and rattlesnakes. Also, we flew with the crews to

Albuquerque and Alamogordo, New Mexico. There was either a bombing range or a gunnery range at those places. I don't remember which one.

<u>Orders</u>
<u>Tucson to Tucson</u>
HQ - 39th Bomb Grp. (H) AAB Davis-Monthan
May 4, 1943 to C.O. 444th Bomb Grp. (H) D/M Field
Par. 3 S.O. #124 - May 4, 1943

<u>Flights from Davis-Monthan AAB - Tucson</u>
5/2/43 B-24 #250 (0815-1145) Take-offs and Landings - (3.5 Hrs. Credit)
Pilot - Wilson
Co-pilot – Cook; Co-pilot - Watters
Radio – Krivonak
Engineer - Vann
Asst. Engineer - Shiver
Gunner Kirkland
(We spent 25 minutes on runway)

5/3/43 B-24 #651 (1645 - 2115) - (4.5 hours credit)
Pilot - Reid (instrument flying time split between pilot and co-pilot)
Co-pilot - Halliday
Radio - Grimes
Engineer - Vann
Asst. Engineer - Shiver
*Armstrong
*Garany
*They did not show up before take-off.

5/7/43 B-24 #250 (3.7 hours)
(Take-offs and landings and some instrument time for Floyd)

Pilot - Wilmer
Co-pilot - Floyd
Radio - Zalinsky, J.L.
Engineer - Gidley, R.A.
Asst. Engineer - Shiver

5/8/43 B-24 (0900 - 1245) - (3 hours & 45 minutes credit)
Pilot - Staben (Instrument check for Lewis)
Co-pilot - Lewis
Co-pilot - Lynn
Radio - Alspaugh
Engineer - Gidley
Asst. Engineer - Shiver

5/9/43 B-24 #865 & #651 (0400 - 0800) - 4 hours credit)
(Co-pilot Checks)
Pilot - Wilson
Co-pilot - Hutchison
Co-pilot - Johnson
Radio - Raymond
Asst. Radio - Eliken
Engineer - Henley
Asst. Engineer - Shiver

5/10/43 B-24 #865 (1200 - 1600) - (4 hours credit)
(10 bombs at 6,000 feet DM & instrument training split for pilots)
Pilot - Hutchison
Co-pilot - King
Bombardier - Ghiorse

Instructor Bombardier - Miesel
Radio - Alspaugh, W.W., S/Sgt.
Engineer - Shiver

5/11/43 B-24 #830 (0845 - 1130) - (1.8 hours credit)
(Instruments training for 2)
Pilot - McCarthy
Co-pilot - Halliday
Radio - Gurney
Engineer - Shiver

5/11/43 B-24 #865 (2400 - 0400) - (4 hours credit)
(10 bombs at 6,000 ft. & instruments for Yoder – 2 hrs.) #26 for Yoder
Pilot - Hutchison
Co-pilot - Yoder
Bombardier - Strasburger
Radio - Labozzo
Engineer - Shiver
Asst. Engineer - Cumming

5/12/43 B-24 #651 (2045 - 0030) - (2.8 hours credit)
(Instruments for Martin #2)
Pilot - Essick
Co-pilot - Martin, A.O.
Radio - Raymond
Engineer - Shiver
(Scofield didn't report for radio operator)

5/14/43 B-24 #830 (0400 - 0800) Landing checks #5 - (4 hours credit)
Pilot - Staeben
Co-pilot - Bremner
Radio - Labozzo
Engineer - Shiver
Asst. Engineer - Porter
Furst

5/14/43 B-24 #830 (1645 - 2045) (Crew #329) – (2.2 hours credit) (Landings & 5 DM. Bombs #1 @ 6,000 feet)
Pilot - Van Wingerden
Co-pilot - Sims
Co-pilot - Parks
Bombardier - Shipp
Gunner - Hunt
Gunner - Murray
Radio - Lewandowski
Engineer - Moore
Asst. Engineer - Fowler
Instructor Engineer - Shiver

5/15/43 B-24 #865 (0415 - 0815) (Crew #335) - (3.3 hours credit) (Instrument Instruction for Waterman #12 and PB-2 Guns)
Pilot - Martin, R.J.
Co-pilot - Waterman
Co-pilot - Almlie
Bombardier - Spear
Radio - Anderson
Gunner - Bouder

Gunner - Fleenor
Instructor Gunner - Bailey
Engineer - Lawson
Asst. Engineer - Kling
Instructor Gunner - Ochda
Instructor Engineer - Shiver

5/15/43 B-24 #865 (#41 - 2365) (1215 -1615) - (3.6 hours credit)
(Instrument Instruction for pilot and co-pilot)
Pilot - McCarthy
Co-pilot - Derry Berry
Radio - Zalinsky
Gunner - Glasscock
Engineer - Holland
Instructor Engineer - Shiver

5/1543 B-24 #830 (2045 - 0030) - (2.3 hours credit)
(Instrument Instruction split for pilot and co-pilot)
Pilot - Lewis
Co-pilot - Pickett
Radio - Scofield
Gunner - Glasscock
Engineer - Holland
Instructor Engineer - Shiver
Asst. Radio - Reegan

5/16/43 B-24 #250 (0430 - 0830) (Crew #331) - (3.5 hours credit)
(Instructions check for pilot #4 check landings and take-offs - 9 total)
Pilot - Staeben

Co-pilot - Perron
Radio - Raymond
Instructor Engineer – Shiver

5/18/43 B-24 #250 (0500 - 0800) (Crew #323) - (2.3 hours)
(Instructions #2 check for pilot & co-pilot)
Pilot - Walters
Co-pilot - Johnson, E.T.
Radio - Rhodes
Asst. Radio - Zanni
Engineer - Davis, AJ.
Asst. Engineer - Mitchel
Instructor Engineer - Shiver

5/18/43 B-24 #250 (2300 - 0300) - (3.3 hours credit)
(Instructions for Co-pilot Martin)
Pilot - Buenting
Co-pilot - Martin, A.O.
Radio - Tejral
Instructor Radio - Alspaugh
Gunner Long, Wm. E., Sgt
Engineer - Balle
Instructor Engineer - Shiver

5/19/43 B-24 #830 & #865 (0300 - 0700) - (3.3 hours credit)
(Night check #5 and take-offs and landings - 4)
Pilot - Van Pelt
Co-pilot - Bremner
Co-pilot - Yoder

Radio - Keegan
Instructor Engineer - Shivert

5/19/43 B-24 #865 (2315 - 0315) (Crew #329) - (2.6 hours credit)
(10 P Bombs - 20,000 feet and insts. Split #26)
Pilot - King
Co-pilot - Senf
Bombardier - Shipp
Radio - Gurney
Gunner - Singleton
Gunner - Szepdin
Engineer - Long
Asst. Engineer - Oickle
Instructor Engineer - Shiver

5/20/43 B-24 #865 (0315 -0715) (Crew #321) - (1.3 hours credit)
(10 Bombs DM 6,000 feet PB2 - Guns #26)
Pilot - Allen
Co-pilot - Nixon
Bombardier - Brennan
Radio - Malkin
Asst. Radio - Leeseman
Gunner - Shook
Gunner - Ross
Engineer - Coughlin
Asst. Engineer - Czupich
Instructor Radio - Zalinsky
Instructor Engineer - Shiver

5/21/43 B-24 #651 (2315 - 0315) (Crew #159) - (4.0 hours credit)
(Insts. for co-pilot)
Pilot - Graham
Co-pilot - Almlie
Radio - Carpenter
Gunner - Bernre
Gunner - Emerich
Engineer - Greco
Asst. Engineer - Beazley
Instructor Engineer - Shiver

5/22/43 B-24 #250 (2315 - 0315) (Crew #323) (3.3 hours credit)
(10 bombs - 6,000 feet DM and Insts. #26)
Pilot - Walters
Co-pilot - Almlie
Bombardier - Spear
Radio - Rhodes
Asst. Radio - Zanni
Gunner - Crane
Engineer - Davis
Asst. Engineer - Mitchell
Instructor Engineer - Shiver
Observer - Musella
(Total flying time 5/2/43 to 5/22/43 was 70.3 hours)

Tucson to Biggs
HQ - 444th Bomb Grp. (H) AAF Tucson, Arizona
May 24, 1943 to C.O. 330th Bomb Grp. (H)
Biggs Field, Texas to Crowder Prov. Grp.
P - 3 S.O. #144 - May 24, 1943

"Transfer to El Paso, Texas"

I arrived by train at El Paso at 10:00 a.m. on Thursday, May 27, 1943. I was to replace the crew's assistant flight engineer, who was in the hospital with yellow fever. The crew was finishing second phase training and would be leaving Biggs AAB and going to Pueblo, Colorado, for third phase training and then they were to go overseas. The crew was 20-9 of Colonel Crawford's Provisional Group. I went out to the base about 2:00 p.m. The crew was expecting someone to come in to join them and had left word for me to join them in town. I guess they were anxious to see their new crew member. I went back into town to the hotel and met the crew and I was satisfied with what I saw. The following is a short review and some information on all the crew members.

Crew #20-9
Pilot - Mills, Raymond H. - Flight Officer #203
Co-pilot - Cobb, Allan J. - #0-676749 - 2nd LT
Navigator - Willis, Harry H. - #0-678805 - 2nd L T
Bombardier - White, Clifford F. - #0-736741 - 2nd LT
Radio - Thomson, Tommie M. - T/Sgt.
Asst. Radio - Birch, Veral J. #39829758 - S/Sgt.
Engineer - Miller, A.E. - T/Sgt.
Asst. Engineer - Shiver, John J., Jr. - #34335079 S/Sgt.
Gunner - Ballod, Robert P. - #13043004 - S/Sgt.

Some Information on the Men of Crew #20-9
Colonel Crawford's Provision Group

<u>Pilot - Mills, Raymond H. - Flight Officer:</u> Mills told me some things about his life, but not much. He grew up in Walla Walla, Washington, left home when he was 16 years old and joined the Army. He and I were about the same age and he shared a few things with me. After I joined the crew in El Paso, he said he and I had to have a talk away from the others. I told him anytime would be fine. Before we left El Paso, we had the talk.

The first thing he told me was about his eyes. He always had his sunglasses on. He told me the sunglasses were prescription, specially made for him and he would have them on all the time - day and night. The only time he did not have them on was when he was sleeping.

I had to ask, "How did you get in the Army Air Corps?"

He replied, "I always have someone to take my eye examinations for me." Mills had a friend his size, so he was able to get away with it.

He then told me about his Army life. He worked hard and got to be a staff sergeant in the regular Army. He was stationed in the Philippine Islands and he wanted to fly. He applied for cadet training, was accepted and got back to the United States before the war started. He was a good pilot and shared some of his flying experiences with me.

The best one was about a cross-country trip in an AT-9 plane with an instructor along. This was a two-engine plane, and the instructor had given him orders not to try any tricks with it while he got a little sleep. Mills said he just had to roll it. He did one roll and didn't wake his instructor, then another, and finally a third roll, which did wake the instructor, who asked, "What's wrong?"

Mills told him they had hit a little turbulence and he could go finish his nap. He never told the instructor about what he had done.

Then I found out the reason for the meeting with me. He asked me if I could synchronize the props. I told him I could. He asked me how I did it. I said, "I do it by sight and sound." He wanted an explanation. I told him I had trouble with that until I discovered my way of working the four toggle switches. I synchronized numbers one and two props together by sight and then did numbers three and four the same way. Then I took #1 and #2 switches together and #3 and #4 switches together and worked them as only two switches and brought them in by sound. That worked for me, and I got them all together that way.

Mills then told me he wanted me to be the engineer and let Miller take the top turret. I told him Miller had asked for me to swap places with him, and I would do what he wanted me to do.

"You are the commander of the crew, so you can tell them about the change." I told him.

He said, "That's done."

I was only a sergeant then and Miller was a T/Sgt, but that was okay with the crew. We worked together as a combat crew and that's what counted.

Mills went as co-pilot on a crew to a target on September 2, 1943. The target was R.R. Marshalling Yards in Sulmona, Italy. He was killed on his first mission. Lt. Hoover Edwards, the pilot of the crew, told me the plane was on fire and Mills left the plane before him and he was okay. Later, he was found dead on the ground.

<u>Co-pilot - Cobb, Allan J. - 2nd Lieutenant:</u> Cobb was a very good pilot, but he didn't enjoy being a four-engine co-pilot. He had finished his training as a fighter pilot and was given a co-pilot position on a crew in place of being sent to a fighter group. But, he accepted his co-pilot's job and did a good job at his assigned position. He was from New Hampshire and went to Dartmouth College in Hanover. He played on the hockey team, and he told us the hickory stick was really hard when you played the game and got hit with it. He was not happy with his flying on the B-24, because it was too slow. But he never complained even though his heart was in flying a fighter plane.

Colonel Kane had a P-40 plane he used to fly around the bombers while they were getting into the proper place in the formation. When we moved to Tunisia from Benghazi, he asked Cobb to fly his P-40 to Tunisia for him at a later date. That made Cobb happy. The plane had to have an extra gas tank installed underneath. We called it the belly tank. He would have to stop at Tripoli and re-fuel. One day when we didn't have a mission, we were in a large two-center-pole tent we used for a day room, when we heard the P-40 coming. We ran outside as Cobb buzzed the area. He was flying low and fast. He just cleared the belly tank over the tent poles. Someone went out to the landing area to get him. We were waiting for him to arrive. We were glad to see him, and he said, "How did you fellows like that buzz job?"

I said, "You missed the tent poles by one or two inches."

He replied "Boy, I'm lucky, I forgot about that belly tank."

Navigator - Willis, Harry H. - 2nd Lieutenant: I don't remember much about him. He was a very good navigator and that was a plus with me. He was from Macon, Georgia, and he was very good with a deck of cards or rolling dice. He refused to gamble with the crew members or his friend. He was somewhat a ladies' man.

Bombardier - White, Clifford F. - 2nd Lieutenant: I don't remember anything about White, except he was a small man and a very good bombardier.

Radio - Thomson, Tommie M. – T/Sgt: Thomson was from Texas and he was a true Texan. He was always bragging about Texas. He had a pair of pearl handled 45 pistols his grandfather had given him before he left Texas for the service. He was proud of them. He was killed on his first mission to R.R. Marshalling Yards in Sulmona, Italy, on September 2, 1943.

Assistant Radio, Birch, Veral J. – S/Sgt: Birch was from Utah and a friendly person, but I didn't get to know much about him in the short time he was on the crew. He liked his whiskey. He would go to Pueblo and come back late at night. When he woke up one morning, he sat up in his bunk, and asked if anyone could give him a shot of whiskey.

One person said, "I have a little bottle of strong Mexican whiskey you have to use a lemon or lime to chase down. I'm going to teach him a lesson."

A few nights went by before Birch went to Pueblo. The next morning Birch called out as everyone expected him to do. Everyone got to where they could see Birch. Ballod and I came out of our room to watch. The person who had the bottle of whiskey let Birch ask about three times before he brought the bottle over to him. Birch took the cap off, emptied it and said, "Do you have some more?"

Everyone was surprised and couldn't believe what we had seen. Most of us believed Birch had a petrified stomach and no one could help him with his drinking problem but Birch.

We finished our third phase training and Colonel Crawford let us leave Pueblo on the evening of July 3, 1943, with an eight-day delay en route to Herington, Kansas. Almost all of the men had made plans to go home before going overseas, but Birch told me he was going to stay in Pueblo and join us later in Herington. When we all arrived in Herington on July 13, 1943, Birch didn't show up. No one knew where Birch was.

The next day, Sgt. Max W. Roach, #39829246, was located and assigned to the crew to replace Birch. We found out later why Birch did not come to Herington. He had been in jail in Pueblo for thirty days. He got on a drunk in Pueblo the first night and lost his orders. The MPs had picked him up and put him in jail, and that's where he stayed for thirty days. He said he pleaded with them all the time to let him make a phone call to the air base for them to check out his story. They wouldn't do anything but let him sit in jail. After they let him out, he checked into Herington and they found a position on a crew for him. I have forgotten how long he had to wait, but he did come by to see me. I was glad to see Birch and he looked great. I told him thirty days in jail certainly did wonders for him and it did sober him up. I never heard from him again, and I appreciated him looking me up. Sgt. Max W. Roach was promoted to S/Sgt. on special order No. 46 dated July 14, 1943.

<u>Engineer - Miller, A.E. – T/Sgt.</u>: Miller was from Nashville, Tennessee. He had been working as a clerk in a ladies' shoe store in Nashville, and he

wanted to be known as a ladies' man. He was tall and handsome. I don't know why he was ever made a flight engineer. He wanted to be a top turret gunner. That was when he was happy, sitting in the turret. When I joined the crew in El Paso, Texas, he asked me if I would be the flight engineer and let him be the top turret gunner. I told him that would be okay with me, if it was what the crew wanted. I told him I would talk to Mills about it; I did and it was okay with everyone. Miller was very happy with the swap and I was satisfied. He and I became close friends after that.

The group would not let a new crew go on a mission alone. They would let a part of the crew go with part of an experienced crew and then the other part of the crew would go on a mission with another experienced crew. After this, the new crew would be ready to go as a combat crew on a mission on their own.

Before the September 2nd mission, Mills got the crew together and told us he and three others were all who could go on the next day's mission. He told us to decide which three would go. Miller and Thomson said they were going and it was their right to go, because they outranked the rest of us. That left only one more to go, and we four remaining crew members decided to draw straws. We didn't have straws so we used matches. All of us wanted to go, but Ballod won. I met and talked to the navigator of the crew that Mills, Miller, Thomson and Ballod joined on that September 2, 1943, mission trip where all four new men were killed. All of the members of the original crew of the plane "Sad Sack" survived. The navigator, John Fontenrose, confirmed that our crew members who had gone as the top turret, two waist gunners, and the co-pilot were all killed on their first mission.

<u>Gunner - Ballod, Robert P- S/Sgt</u>: When I met my crew in El Paso, Texas, I was happy to be a member of that crew. I liked what I saw. I met them at a hotel in downtown El Paso. They were there to celebrate finishing the second phase of training and going into the third phase at Pueblo, Colorado. I had been sent there to replace the crew's assistant flight engineer. At the base headquarters was a message to join them in town. They had a room at the hotel on the fourth floor. I introduced myself to them and was

immediately drawn close to Ballod. I think it was his speech. We became good friends and he needed a close, true friend.

Some of the crew was going to go across the river bridge into Juarez, Mexico. It was some city to see. We had to have all our money changed into two-dollar bills on the U.S. side of the river. We could carry only silver coins and all paper money in two-dollar bills. It was no big deal with us, because we didn't have much money. The Germans were trying to get U.S. money for their spies, and our leaders thought two-dollar bills would be too much of a telltale sign for the spies to have. A few of the crew were going to go, so I joined them. Ballod and I paired up and we walked over to Juarez. Some wanted to see the bullfighters, so we went to an arena. The noise of the crowd was something to hear. It was very loud. Ballod and I decided we would not go inside, but the others went. We left them and went walking and looking at the small shops.

About 8:00 p.m., we had seen enough and we walked over the bridge back to the U.S. We got on the base bus and went out to Biggs Field to the barracks and hit the sack. The rest of the crew came back the next day. That was when they were supposed to be back from a three-day pass.

The crew had to make two more flights to complete the second phase training, so I had a chance to join them before we left Biggs for Pueblo. Ballod and I had some time together before we left for Pueblo. He shared with me some things about his life. He was born in Latvia. His father was a Russian and his mother was a German. His father was in the Russian Army and the family hadn't heard from him in a long time. They assumed he was dead. His maternal grandmother must have had money, because she came to the United States in 1937 and lived in Baltimore, Maryland. Ballod had one sibling, a brother.

He was a good friend and a very good gunner. He had his name changed from Ballodestie to Ballod when he came to the U.S. He was about a year younger than me and was having trouble with our English language. He was handsome, a very athletic type young man and good at anything he did. His grandmother brought his mother, his brother and Ballod to her home in Baltimore in 1939. They applied for U.S. citizenship as soon as they got here, but Ballod had trouble with the English language requirement. I tried to help him any way I could. He asked me to read the short letters he received from his grandmother and then to write short letters for him back. All this time, I was helping him with the citizenship book he was using to prepare himself for the test. He wanted to get his citizenship papers before we went overseas.

Ballod told me about his school life in Latvia. The country was on the Baltic Sea and it was very cold in winter. During the winter, he and his brother skated six and a half miles on a frozen stream to school and six and a half miles back home each day; that explained his athletic body. He never said much to me about his life in Latvia, but he was always telling me about his life in America. I didn't question him.

He told me he got his first job at the shipyard in Baltimore and liked working there. That didn't last long. He was fired when they discovered his mother was German. He got his next job at a barbershop, cutting hair. He was a good barber. He was good at anything he did. He cut my hair for me and did a very good job. He said he would need only six to eight minutes on a man's hair, but found that he had to take twelve to fifteen minutes on a woman's hair. He didn't get fired, but because he couldn't speak very good English, the word was out that he was from Germany and no one would sit in his chair.

He went to New York City and took a job as a teacher at a dance studio. He was a handsome young man and told me he was a good dancer, but was always in trouble with his English words. He had to quit and he went to a recruiting station and they signed him up. He was amazed he wasn't wanted at the shipyard, but was okay for the Army Air Corps. I told him we always had to play with the cards we're dealt in life and always do the best we could with them. I told him we had a lot of work to do concerning his citizenship test and for us to spend as much time as we could on his book. He agreed and we did just that. He wanted citizenship so bad and he was a good learner. I would read and explain each part and let him see the words as I read them.

When we arrived at Pueblo, we were assigned to our barracks. I was told our crew was to be on the second floor. I told Ballod to follow me. I ran up the stairs and claimed the room at the front of the barracks. That was the floor our crew was assigned to. Ballod and I had a private room all to ourselves. We could shut the door and not have to put up with the noise from the open floor area. There were two cots in the room and it was an ideal place for us. We used all of our spare time on Ballod's project. We found out there was a U.S. Customs office in Pueblo. After about three weeks, I told Ballod I thought he was ready. He went to the office and they gave him his test. He passed and they had him sworn in as a citizen of the U.S.A. That was what he had been wanting. He was a happy person and I was happy for him. He gave me a good handshake, a smile and a big thank you.

I Always Wanted To Fly

<u>Gunner - Charron, Arthur A. - S/Sgt.</u>: After our crew lost its pilot and three other members (Mills, Miller, Thomson, and Ballod), the remaining crew went separate ways. We were used as fill-ins where needed and as spare crew members. I was never on a crew with Charron, but he and I were together as tent mates in a two man tent in Tunisia. Charron and I never did see eye-to-eye on anything. He did just what he had to do and no more. He was from Vermont and told me he and his father were in business breeding dogs and selling them.

While we were in Tunisia, the operations clerk came in the tent and woke me up about four o'clock one morning. I asked Charron if he had a mission that day. He said no, and I left the tent. When I came in that afternoon, he was still sleeping. The next day, he was still sleeping. I checked with the clerk and he told me Charron had told him to leave him alone. I checked with the mess personnel and they hadn't seen him in three or four days. I went back to the tent and tried to wake him, but I couldn't get him awake. I went to the squadron office, got one of the clerks to come back to the tent with me, and we still could not wake him up. The closest hospital was a British field hospital about forty miles away. The clerk got a GI ambulance to come and they carried Charron there. The next day the clerk told me the hospital had called and told him Charron had sand-fly sleeping sickness and he would be back to the base in a week or two. Charron finished his fifty missions on June 13, 1944.

To get to Biggs Army Air Base from El Paso, we had to go past Fort Bliss, an Army base. The highway to Biggs AAB went by that Army installation. There were small tents as far as you could see. Later, I checked on the size of that post, and the book had Fort Bliss at 1,182,379 acres. I lost some of my notes, but I'm sure Mills's crew wasn't through with their second phase flights. They thought they had finished, but they were two flights short. I remember the flights out of Biggs and the mountains close by. Miller took the top turret post, and I was the engineer. Before we left Biggs we made the remaining two flights on May 30 or 31, 1943. We were being sent to Pueblo by train.

<u>Orders</u>
<u>Biggs to Biggs</u>
459th Bomb Sqn. (H) 330th Bomb Grp. (H) AAB Biggs Field, Texas - May 30, 1943 -
To C.O. 460th Bomb Sqn. - 330th Bomb Grp. (H) Par. 17 - S.O. 128 - May 29, 1943

<u>Biggs to Pueblo</u>
460th Bomb Sqn. (H) 330th Bomb Grp. (H) May 31, 1943 to C.O. 471st Bomb Grp. (H) Pueblo, Colorado - S.O. #150 - Par - 16
Left June 1, 1943

"Third Phase B-24 Training - Pueblo, Colorado"

The crew arrived by train at Pueblo at 10:00 a.m. on June 2, 1943. We were Crew #20-9, Col. Crawford's Provisional Group. We were in the 804th squadron - 471st Bomb Group. We were there to get third phase training as a B-24 crew, and when we completed the training, we would leave as a crew ready to be sent overseas. We were told we would be in Pueblo approximately one month and a busy month was planned for us. We would be on some long flights, day and night.

Near the end of our training at Pueblo, we had to go on a three-day training mission. One of those flights would be over the Gulf of Mexico. This was the final phase of training and every day was important. Some flights were from 4:00 a.m. until noon and other flights were from 4:00 p.m. until midnight or later. On some of the flights the wing tanks were not filled and the plane had an extra 500-gallon tank mounted in one of the bomb bays. It was full, and the crew had to transfer that fuel into the wing tanks. The flights were made to the bombing range and to the aerial gunnery target range. Both were in New Mexico. One was located at Albuquerque and the other one at Alamogordo.

There were a lot of interesting things to see while flying over Colorado. First on the list were the mountains. From my barracks room I could see Pike's Peak. That mountain was 14,110 feet high, but I read Colorado has a mountain 29 feet higher than Pike's Peak. Mountains and more mountains. There are approximately 1,500 peaks higher than 10,000 feet. There is a lot of farmland in certain parts of the state, especially large, flat wheat fields. Sometimes, we would fly over some of them and get close to the ground. There was a large iron and steel manufacturing operation not far from Pueblo. A canyon of the Arkansas River extending about ten miles from Canon City, Colorado, is more than 1,000 feet deep. It is the most remarkable chasm in the world, and a railroad was built through it at the bottom next to the river. At some points the canyon is only thirty feet wide. Many bridge-like structures had to be built along the walls of the gorge in order to put the railroad tracks through. The highest suspension bridge in the world, 1,053 feet above the water, spans the gorge at the top. Its name is the Royal Gorge Bridge, and I saw it when we flew in the gorge while we were in training at Pueblo.

One day in training we were flying up out of the gorge when Mills and Cobb got into a discussion about whether to go under the bridge or over it. We were headed straight toward it, and it was getting close fast. I told them to do one or the other now - and I meant now! We didn't want to hit it. Mills pulled the control wheel back and we went over it. I told them I didn't appreciate such things as that. There is a time and place for all things, but what they had just done was uncalled for. They didn't say anything more to me about the near-hit on the bridge, and I didn't say anything more to them about it.

On the way to Denver from Pueblo, we went through Colorado Springs. On one of our off days, another GI and I would hitchhike toward Denver and back to the base. On one of the trips back to Pueblo, we got a ride in a big truck pulling two trailers. We needed a stepladder to climb up into the cab, but we made it. That was the largest rig I had ever seen. The driver was such a friendly person and we enjoyed talking to him. He told us he had the run from Denver to Chicago, and the refrigerated trailers of vegetables had come from California to Denver. He would hook the trailers on as soon as they arrived. We were amazed at his driving that big rig. He was always shifting gears. It had an extra large steering wheel with one shift lever on the left and two on the right. The rig would go up those climbs as fast as it would go down them, and he was moving those three levers with his arms through the steering wheel. It was a good ride back to Pueblo. I will always remember seeing a very good truck driver doing his job.

Another interesting thing in Colorado was a six-mile tunnel through a mountain forty miles west of Denver. It's named the Moffat Tunnel after the man who was in charge of that big project. It's a railroad tunnel, and I was on a train one time in the service and went through it. It was very dark as we went through it. It is wonderful to recall things I did when I was in the service so many years ago.

"A Training Flight to Gulfport, Mississippi"

We left Pueblo in plane #145 at 6:00 a.m. on the morning of June 27, 1943. We had an extra man on the plane with us. He was a captain and was going with us as our co-pilot, but I found out the next day the reason he was with us. He had a brother stationed at MacDill AAB at Tampa, Florida, and he wanted to visit him. He was Colonel Crawford's operations officer, and he was a very good pilot and a friendly person. The crew was glad he joined us for the trip, and our co-pilot flew some of the time. We left Pueblo with another plane going to the bombing range in New Mexico, and our pilot got some formation flying training time. We weren't due into Gulfport until four o'clock that evening, so we had a few hours of nothing to do except fly and sightsee.

We flew down to the Rio Grande River, turned left, and followed the river to the Gulf of Mexico. I had checked on our gas and we were getting low. I told the crew about it and said we were too low to take a chance on getting to Gulfport. The gas tubes can be off as much as a hundred gallons. We need not risk getting to Gulfport. We saw a Navy field on a little island close to New Orleans. It was a short runway and it had a seawall around it. It had been raining, and I asked if we could land and take-off on such a short runway. The pilot and co-pilot said, "Yes, no problem."

We landed, got some gas and maneuvered on the runway to take-off. That runway got shorter every time I looked at it and the seawall got higher. I told Mills we were in trouble. He looked at me and said for me to quit worrying. I always called the airspeed to Mills on take-offs and landings. The strip was wet and slippery and when he released the brakes we lost some of the runway. I didn't think we were ever going to make it, but we had gone too far to abort the take-off. The seawall was coming up to us fast and it appeared higher. I didn't know what we could do. Someone said, "Bounce it over the wall!"

Mills asked me, "Can we do it?"

I replied, "Try it! Anything is better than hitting the wall." Mills pulled the control wheel up and down at the right time and we bounced over the wall. There wasn't time to be scared. I think we were at the edge of flying speed, because as we came down to the water outside the wall we got airborne. The tail section touched the water and someone came on the inter-phone and said, "Praise the Lord." We were thankful we hadn't hit that wall.

We arrived at Gulfport on time, found our barracks for the night and went to the mess hall for our evening meal. After supper, we were told about our over-water flight the next day, June 28, 1943. We were to get up at 4:00 a.m., attend two meetings at 5:00 a.m., and take-off at 6:00 a.m. There was a weather officer who gave us a report for the day. He told us we could expect a beautiful day for our trip over the Gulf of Mexico. We would fly south for two hours and then turn left and head toward Florida. We would make radio contact with a tow-target plane and the gunners would get some shooting time. The bombardier would drop flasks of dye in a large circle in the water, and then drop the practice bombs at the targets. We would fly to Orlando Navy Station, fly around the base, and report our plane and crew numbers to the tower. Then we would fly to Brookley Field at Mobile, make contact with the tower and return to Gulfport.

We had plans for the day, but plans are made to be changed. We were on the flight south from Gulfport when the beautiful day turned into a bad storm - wind and rain - it was difficult flying. We tried all altitudes, but it was bad. It was a bad storm we were in, and I told everyone on the plane I lived in south Alabama, where the Gulf weather is impossible to predict. We say "If you don't like the weather now, just wait a little while, it's going to change."

We found the best altitude to fly was a few feet above the water. That's where we flew until we made the left turn toward Florida. After a short time, we were out of the storm and we climbed up off the water and tried to make radio contact with the tow-target plane. No luck. We all agreed to forget the tow-target plane. We said we had had enough target shooting, and we would let the bombardier do his practice now. That we did, and we flew to MacDill AAB at Tampa, instead of flying around the Navy base at Orlando as we were told to do. We landed at MacDill and the officers got off, but the rest of the crew had to stay on the plane. About two hours later, they returned and I'm sure they all had a meal at the officers' club. The captain told us he and his brother enjoyed their time together. We got the plane in the air and started on our flight. We made contact with the tower in Mobile and headed to Gulfport. We landed at Gulfport and the crew got to the mess hall for the evening meal. We were told our plane would be serviced and ready for us to leave Gulfport early the next morning.

On June 29, we left Gulfport at 6:00 a.m. on our return flight back to Pueblo. Another plane left at approximately the same time we did, so the pilots and co-pilots could get some formation flying practice time on our return trip home. That's what we did. I knew the pilots and co-pilots needed to have formation practice time, but they didn't need to push it so close to accidents. As we arrived over Pueblo, the other plane was flying close to us on our right side with his left wing stuck in between our right wing and our right vertical stabilizer. Some of the crew in the rear section of our plane called us on the inter-phone, and they were scared. They had been making movements with their arms trying to warn the other plane away from us, but the pilot wasn't doing anything except making things worse.

About that time, we hit some wind currents over Pueblo, and I thought the two planes would come together and fall all over the city. The pilot of the plane flying too close to us made the right move to avoid a collision. He brought his left wing up and the right down and immediately banked to the right. That was the right move at the right time, and I thanked the Lord for it. We landed at the base, and we were happy to be home and near the end of our third phase training.

"Colonel Crawford Visits our Pueblo Barracks"

One evening at about 4:00 p.m., Colonel Crawford, our group commander, paid a visit to us in our barracks. He didn't let anyone know he was coming. It was a few days before we were to finish our third-phase training and our crew was on the second floor of the building. Ballod and I lived in the room at the front of the second floor stairway. Our room was in order, but the barracks were a mess. The floor had old newspapers all over it. It was something to see. Just as Ballod and I came out of our room, we heard someone call out "Attention!" in a loud voice. We were surprised to see our commander in the middle of the room looking over the mess. Everyone was standing at attention and no one was saying a word.

Finally, the colonel spoke. He said in a soft voice, "At ease, fellows. In a few days, you will be leaving Pueblo. I am proud of your accomplishments while I have been your commander. Enjoy your last few days here at Pueblo, and men, before you leave your barracks, PLEASE CLEAN IT UP! I know you don't want anyone to see how you live. This is a big mess - CLEAN IT UP!"

The colonel left the building and the men cleaned the barracks.

"One Bad Night Training Flight"

On one of our night training flights, we got into a bad situation and didn't know what to do about it. It was one of the long navigation training flights. We had the left 500-gallon bomb bay tank full of gas to use on the flight. We could transfer it into the wing tanks and get some training in transferring the fuel. That's what Miller and I chose to do.

We didn't know it then, but our radio operator wanted to get some time in the co-pilot's seat, so he and our co-pilot, Cobb, had swapped places for a little while. At the time we turned on the transfer pump switch and set the fuel selector valve to the desired position, there was a little momentary drop on the engine fuel pressure gauge. Sergeant Thomson flipped the auxiliary fuel pump switch on and a fuse blew to our transfer pump circuit. At the time our pump wasn't working, the engine fuel pump pressure gauge was showing a normal reading. Thomson flipped the auxiliary pump switch off, but the bomb bay tank was receiving gas from the wing tank. We looked at the auxiliary switches and put the selector valve back to the normal position and asked if anyone was flipping any switches on. They told us "No."

We replaced the pump fuse and tried again – same thing over and over and over again.

Our tank in the bomb bay was leaking at the large filler cap and all our fuses had been used. We had to return to Pueblo and report the problem. The transfer pump wasn't strong enough to pump fuel against the engine and the auxiliary pump combined. Thomson should have told us what he had been doing, but he didn't. The engineer officer told us about it the next day, and Mills, our pilot, told us not to say anything to Thomson about it. That was the end of that episode. We were in a bad situation that night with gas fumes all over the bomb bays, and the hot exhaust fire coming out of the #2 and #3 engines not far from the bays. We were glad to walk away from the plane that night.

"Another Crew at Pueblo"

When we were training in Pueblo, there was another crew in Colonel Crawford's group close to us, and we spent our free time with them. They told us one of their gunners always wanted to sleep on the flights when he wasn't busy. He was their ball gunner and when he wasn't in the ball turret, he was sitting down with his chute on, with his back against the rear bulkhead wall. He wouldn't wake up when they landed and taxied to their parking space. They had to shake him and keep working with him to get him up, and they were tired of that.

They came up with a plan to change him and they told us about it. They would make the gunner think the plane was crashing after it had landed and before the engines were cut. The B-24 had a nose wheel and it was tail heavy. It wasn't unusual for the plane to fall to the rear, especially when all engines had been run up to a high RPM to clear the cylinders and the switches were cut off. The timing of the plan had to be right for it to be effective and executed perfectly. When the switches were turned off, the engines backfired and black smoke came out of all the engines. The rear section of the plane came down and the tail section skid hit the cement parking ramp with a loud noise.

At the right moment as planned after a night flight landing, the crew caused the engines to backfire. The crew member, who usually woke the gunner up by shaking him, instead yelled loudly to the gunner as he hopped out one of the waist windows, "This is it!"

The gunner jumped awake and went out the other window, headfirst, pulling his chute handle as he went. He was only a short distance from the cement ramp, and he landed on his face with his parachute opened all over him. His face was scratched and cut, but he didn't break any bones. That was a bad way to get him used to staying awake, but I'm sure it was a lesson the gunner never forgot. We didn't joke with him about jumping out of the plane headfirst - we left that to him and his crew members.

Pueblo Army Air Base

804th Bomb Squadron-471st Bomb Group

3rd Phase Training Flights

June 1943

June 3rd - Local- Familiarization Flight - Day
Plane 991   2:00 Hours
This flight was made for the crew to get familiar with the area and the base as seen from the air.

June 4th –Navigation Flight - Night
Plane 991 2:30 Hours

June 5th - Navigation Flight - Day
Plane 993 2:00 Hours

June 6th - Navigation Flight - Night
Plane 993 4:00 Hours

June 7th - Bombing & Gunnery - 300 feet - Day
Plane 993 4:30 Hours

June 8th - Skip Bombing - This was the start of our 3rd phase training - Night
Plane 426 4:00 Hours

June 10th - Skip Bombing - Night
Plane 426 4:00 Hours

June 12th - Bombing - 14,000 feet - Night
Plane 426 6:30 Hours

June 14th - Bombing & Navigation - Night
Plane 426 6:00 Hours

June 15th - Return to Base - Engine trouble - Day
Plane 426 1:30 Hours

June 20th - Bombing & Gunnery - Day & Night
Plane 426 7:00 Hours

Bombing - 10 Bombs @ 24,000 feet
Gunnery - 3,000 Rounds

June 22nd - Bombing - 10 Bombs @ 24,000 feet - Night
Plane 065 6:30 Hours

June 25th - Navigation (From Pueblo to Kansas City to Sioux Falls back to Pueblo) - Night
Plane 026 8:15 Hours

June 26th - Night Formation Flying & Navigation
Plane 268 9:30 Hours

June 27th - Formation & Navigation to Gulfport, Mississippi - Day
Plane 145 9:45 Hours
(This was a flight to Gulfport - we spent the night there.)

June 28th - Over-water navigation training - Day
Plane 145 6:00 Hours

We had a flight south of Gulfport and then took a left turn to Tampa, Florida and landed at MacDill Air Base for two hours.

June 28th - Navigation - from MacDill Air Base back to Gulfport, Mississippi - Day
Plane 145 4:00 Hours

June 29th - Navigation & Formation Flying - Day
Plane 145 - 8:00 Hours
Back to Base at Pueblo from Gulfport, Mississippi

July 1943

July 2nd - Returned to base at Pueblo - Day
Plane 993 - 0:45 Hours
Engine trouble - prop. - gov. trouble

July 2nd - Returned to Base at Pueblo - Day
Plane 007 - 1:30 Hours
Engine trouble - prop. - gov. trouble

July 2nd - Final flight of our third phase training at Pueblo, Colorado - Day
Plane 007 - 4:15 Hours
Bombing and gunnery - five demos, three incendiary bombs and several boxes of 50-caliber machine gun ammunition.

We dropped bombs in a lake somewhere in Colorado, blew out a city's water reservoir, and killed some horses. The ammunition boxes were tossed out of the plane somewhere in a mountain area.

Pueblo Army Air Base
804th Bomb Squadron 471st Bomb Group
Third Phase Training Flights

June 1943	Plane #	Day Time	Night Time	Description
3rd	991	2:00		Familiarization – Local – This flight was made for the crew to get familiar with the area and the base, as seen from the air
4th	991		2:30	Navigation
5th	993	2:00		Navigation
6th	993		4:00	Navigation
7th	993	4:30		Bombing & Gunnery – 300 feet
8th	426		4:00	Skip Bombing (Start of 3rd phase night training)
10th	426		4:00	Skip Bombing
12th	426		6:30	Bombing 14,000 feet
14th	426		6:00	Bombing & Navigation
15th	426	1:30		Returned to Base – Engine Trouble
20th	426	Day/Night	7:00	Bombing – 10 Bombs – 24,000 feet Gunnery – 3,000 Rounds
22nd	065		6:30	Bombing – 10 Bombs – 24,000 feet
25th	026		8:15	Navigation to Kansas City to Sioux Falls – back to Pueblo
26th	268		9:30	Night Formation flying and navigation

27th	145	9:45			Formation and navigation to Gulfport, Mississippi – we spent the night there
28th	145	6:00			South to Tampa, FL; landed at MacDill AFB for two hours; over water navigation training
28th	145	4:00			Navigation back to Gulfport, Mississippi
29th	145	8:00			Navigation and formation flying back to Pueblo
July, 1943					
2nd	993	0:45			Return to base – prop., gov. trouble
2nd	007	1:30			Return to base – prop., gov. trouble
2nd	007	4:15			Bombing and gunnery – five demos and three incendiary bombs – dropped bombs in a lake somewhere in Colorado, blew out a city's water reservoir, killed some horses and tossed the ammo out somewhere in a mountain area
Totals	Day/Night	44:15	58:15		
	Grand Total	102.30 Hours			

Third phase flight training - crew #20-9 in Pueblo, Colorado

Flights – June 3, 1943 to July 2, 1943
Day Flight Times   44:15 Hours
Night Flight Times <u>58:15 Hours</u>
Total   102:30 Hours

Chapter 4

AN EIGHT-DAY LEAVE

Home to Atmore and on to Herington, Kansas

"A Circuitous Route"

Colonel Crawford called the combat crews of his provisional group together early on the afternoon of July 3, 1943, to tell us where we were being sent. I was a member of Crew #20-9 (Mills's crew), and we were in "Section D" of the Crawford group. The colonel told us we were leaving Pueblo and were to get an eight-day "delay en route leave" to Herington, Kansas. Sections A and B were getting their orders that afternoon, and Sections C and D were to get theirs the following afternoon. He told us they were doing this to help prevent a bad situation at the train station. He said we had completed our training and were to be processed for overseas duty when we arrived at Herington.

After Sections A and B had received their orders and left the area, the colonel gave us our orders. They were dated July 4, 1943, and we were told if we left that afternoon we should avoid meeting up with any MPs. However, if we were stopped, we were to explain why we left early, and if the MPs didn't accept that, we were to tell them to call the base at Pueblo. The colonel was going to tell headquarters he gave us permission. He wished us good luck and said not to be late in arriving at Herington, Kansas.

I had checked on getting a flight home, and the only flight I could get out of Pueblo was one on Continental Air Lines through Dallas, Texas, through New Orleans and finally to Mobile. On top of that, I could only get a "D priority" and almost anybody at any time could take your seat at every stop. I went to the Red Cross office in Pueblo to get some help, and I struck out. I went in the office and was surprised at how I was treated. I only asked the lady if she could help me get a higher priority than a "D" status and her answer was, "We don't buy plane tickets for service men at this office."

I told her I hadn't asked her to buy a ticket for me, only for her help in getting a priority for me. She refused to help me. I was disappointed, but I let her know I just wanted to go home and see my wife before I left the U.S. for combat. She didn't say anything else to me; I walked out and went back to the base. My crew member, Ed. Miller, wanted to know how I made out at the Red Cross office and I told him about striking out. He told me he wanted to go home to Nashville and our best chance of getting home was through Chicago and Atlanta. We talked it over and decided to go to Denver and go from there.

We called the station that had a bus scheduled to arrive at Denver the next morning at six o'clock. I don't remember what time we left Pueblo, but we rode all night in an old bus and arrived in Denver on schedule. We got a cab to the airport and met a young lady who was working at the United Airlines desk. We told her our mission and she told us we were fifteen minutes late. The flight to Chicago was full, but she said she would have rolled two people off and the two of us would have been put on it. She had just teletyped the manifest of those now boarding for Chicago.

"I can't change it now," she said," but I will put you on the afternoon flight that leaves Denver at three o'clock and gets you into Chicago in time for you to catch an Eastern flight at eight o'clock tonight for Atlanta. I'm a part-time stewardess, and the days I'm not flying, I work at the United Airlines counter here at Stapleton Airport. You can count on the two of you having a seat on the plane leaving Denver this afternoon, and I will tell the stewardess on the flight to watch out and not to let anyone bump you off the flight when it stops at Omaha. Be back this afternoon by two-thirty and I will be here to see that you have a seat on the Chicago plane."

Miller and I thanked her and got a cab back to downtown Denver. We got out of the cab on the main street of Denver and asked the cab driver to tell us the best place to get breakfast. He pointed and told us we were almost at the best one in Denver. We walked a half block to the nice restaurant and placed an order for a full breakfast. We hadn't eaten anything since noon the day before. We asked the waitress where we could find a place to sleep for three or four hours. She told us to try the hotels, but everyone we called gave us the same answer, "No vacancies - full up."

The waitress came by and asked us, "Have you found one?"

"No." I remarked, "It's July 4th today - everyone's in town."

About that time she tossed a key on the counter and told us we could use her apartment. I thanked her and pushed the key back to her. She took a pad and wrote an address on it and told us to call a cab to go there and get a little sleep. She said she would call us at noon and we could catch a streetcar that came by the apartment at 12:10. "It will come by again at 12:30 coming back to town, and the trolley stop is close to the restaurant. You will be back here at one o'clock and that will give you plenty of time to eat and get out to the airport for your flight."

We did that, but I told the cab driver to wait until we tried the key before he left. The key unlocked the door and I waved to the driver and we went in. It was a strange feeling to go in and go to bed. The apartment was very clean. It had a sitting area, two bedrooms, a kitchen, and one bathroom. In a few minutes, Miller and I took off our clothes and hit the bed. We decided to use the same bed and we went to sleep.

The telephone on the night stand on my side of the bed rang and woke me up. I picked it up and the waitress was on the line. She told me it was the third time she had called to get us up. I thanked her and as I put the phone down, I heard the trolley bell ringing. I got up and rushed to the window to see which way the trolley was going. I didn't know if this was the first or second time it had gone by. It was the first time. We had twenty minutes to be at the street. Miller was still asleep. I went to his side of the bed to get him up, and I looked through the door to the other bedroom. I noticed a sailor's uniform on a closet door, but I didn't see anyone in the room. We hurried out to be at the street waiting on the trolley.

We arrived at the restaurant, ordered a noon meal and called a cab to take us to the airport. I told the waitress about seeing the sailor's uniform on the closet door, and she said it was her brother's clothes. He had left them there. We thanked the waitress for her help, and tried to pay her for the bed. She wouldn't accept any money but did try to get us to stay overnight in Denver. She told us she had a friend and the four of us could have a good time in Denver that night.

Miller asked me if I wanted to do that, and I said, "No way! I'm married and I'm going home to my wife. Miller, you can stay, but not me."

Miller said he was going to go with me. The cab came to the restaurant and got us to the airport on time. The United Airlines young lady was there to greet us. She had returned to make sure we got on the flight. We thanked her and it wasn't long before our plane landed and we got on the plane. It sure was a good feeling to be on the way home after the delays. Everything went okay until the captain told us we were going to be in a storm as we got close to Omaha.

In a short time, we were in it and it was a bad storm with a lot of lightning. The captain said we had to land, but not in this storm; he had received orders to go to an area northeast of Omaha and fly in a circle for a while until the storm passed. That's what we did for one hour, and then it was okay to land. We didn't stay at the airport very long before taking off for Chicago.   We arrived at Chicago, rushed to the Eastern Airlines counter and were told the plane had left for Atlanta ten minutes before the United plane arrived. The delay at Omaha was what made us have to stay overnight in Chicago. The next flight to Atlanta was the next morning at eight o'clock. We decided to go into the city and find a place to sleep.

"The Palmer House Hotel, Chicago"

The only transportation we could find was a Blue Bird Limousine, and the driver told us he could take us downtown. He was very nice to us; I don't remember if he charged us for the ride or not. That was some ride. He stayed on the horn all the time, from the moment we left the airport until we stopped in front of the Palmer House Hotel. He didn't slow up for anything. He ran through red lights and dodged traffic at signal lights. He took the road, but he stopped at the hotel without an accident. Miller and I went in and realized we were in a high-class hotel.

We were in a very large lobby with one wall that had several large glass doors through which I saw people dancing. I told Miller we were in a classy hotel, and we were out of our pay range, but it wouldn't cost us anything to check it out. We went to the desk and asked if we could get a room for the night. The man told us none were available. We thanked him, picked up our bags and started for the door. A man coming out of an office walked toward us and asked us why we were leaving. We told him we had asked for a room, but were told none were available. He didn't say anything to us, but motioned to a bellboy to come over and take us to a certain room number. The bellboy picked up two of our bags; Miller and I had only one bag to carry. The bellboy told us to follow him and we went by the desk where a man gave him a key.

He went to an elevator with Miller and me following. I don't remember what floor we stopped on, but it must have been the top floor. He went to a door, unlocked it, set down the bags he had carried in the room, came out, and gave the key to me. I stepped inside, took one look and immediately came back out and told the man there had been a mistake. We couldn't afford that room and I tried to give him the key, but he refused to take it. He said he had done what his boss had told him to do. Miller and I looked at each other, and then we gave the man a tip. He left us and we went into the room.

The room was extra-large with big couches and several chairs in it. There was a bedroom on each side of a large center room. One was green and the other was pink. The carpet in all the rooms was very thick and extra soft. I told Miller to take the room he wanted and I would take the other one. I said we could take a quick bath and go some place to get something to eat. He agreed and we left the suite in about thirty minutes. We noticed on the floor close to our suite a lady sitting at a desk. I told Miller we would tell her to give us a call in the morning at five o'clock when we returned.

We went to the elevator and then to the outside of the hotel, got a cab and told the driver to take us to a place where we could get something to eat. He drove a few blocks, stopped at a place and told us we would enjoy eating there. We tried to pay the cab driver, but he said in Chicago there was no charge by orders from the mayor. He said, "There is no charge for cabs in Chicago for service persons."

Miller and I went into the restaurant and ate a little food and went to pay for it, but the man told us our ticket had been paid. The man who had just left had taken care of it. When we walked outside, we heard and saw our first elevated train. It scared me. It was right in front of us and I didn't see it until it went by.

We got another free cab and returned to the Palmer House. We went to our floor, stopped at the desk and asked the lady to give us a five o'clock call in the morning. We entered the suite and I told Miller I didn't know how expensive our room would be, but we were really living it up in style that night. The large room had a glass wall area in the center section that gave us a beautiful view of Chicago's loop area at night with all its lights. We went to our rooms, each with its own bathroom. Then we hit the beds.

I woke up when the phone call came at five o'clock and got dressed. Miller was ready to go also. I told Miller we might as well eat a good breakfast at the hotel instead of hunting another place. "We slept in style last night, so let's continue this last fling at living like big shots."

He agreed; we took another look at the suite and walked out. We thanked the lady at the desk and took the elevator to the lobby. We saw the dining area and went in and asked if we were too early for breakfast. The waiter said no. We ordered a full breakfast and enjoyed it. The waiter gave us our tickets and told us to pay at the front desk when we checked out. We went to check out and received a big surprise. The man asked us if we had enjoyed a good night at the hotel and we said we had. He looked at us with a big smile and told us our bill was $3.30 each. "You owe for breakfast; the rooms are on the house."

What a surprise! We thanked the man, picked up our bags and went outside to get a cab to the airport. We saw the Blue Bird Limousine parked at the curb. We asked the driver if the limousine was going to the airport, and he said it was. We had timed our checkout at the hotel just right. We got in the limo and left the Palmer House Hotel. Once again the driver got on the horn and ran through all signal lights both green and red.

We arrived at the airport in time for our flight on Eastern Airlines to Atlanta. The plane had a male attendant instead of a female stewardess. We arrived in Atlanta about midday, and Miller got a bus to Nashville and I got one to Montgomery where I would get a connecting one to Atmore.

It was great to see Myrtle for a few days. I had received an "eight-day delay en route order" from Pueblo, Colorado to Herington, Kansas, on July 4th and I arrived in Atmore late on the evening of July 5th. I got a plane ticket to leave Mobile early on the morning of July 11th. I had to report to Herington, Kansas by twelve o'clock noon on July 12th. That gave me a short week at home before leaving the USA for combat flying. I couldn't tell Myrtle I would be leaving for combat duty. I asked my father to tell her after I left Mobile.

"A Wild Ride to Herington, Kansas"

I left Mobile on July 11th on a DC-3 plane to St. Louis, Missouri. There, at Lambert Field Airport, I got a flight to Wichita, Kansas. The flight arrived at the Wichita airport about 7:00 a.m. When I first arrived, I couldn't find a cab to take me into Wichita to the bus station.

About 7:45 a cab came up. I got to him and told him I needed to get to the bus station. The driver asked me where I was going. I told him I had to get to the Herington Army Air Base by twelve o'clock noon that day. He said Herington was ninety miles from Wichita, and the bus to Herington would be leaving the bus station about 8:00. He was very nice to me and said we might make it. I remember the sign on the cab---it was the Black And White Cab Company. He told me his shift was over at eight o'clock that morning. As we got about a block from the bus station, I saw the bus leaving. I told him to catch it for me. He said he couldn't go any faster. "There is a governor on the cab, and I have the pedal on the floor now. The only chance we have is if a red light stops it, and then I can get in front of the bus."

We were about a city block behind the bus, but the bus caught all green lights. We trailed the bus all the way to the city limits, and then the cab driver stopped. He told me he couldn't go outside the city. "I'm sorry; we will have to go back."

I asked him if he could take me to Herington in his personal car. He said his car tires were bad, but his former boss, who had owned the cab company for a long time and had sold out the year before, would take me there.

"I'm sure, because he has a son in the service now," he said. He told me to go with him to the cab company; he would leave the cab, take me to his former boss and tell him about my problem. That's what we did.

He told me some things about his former boss. "He's got plenty of money, is a heavy drinker, has built a large home, and has two new cars. He's probably still in bed now getting over a drunk, but he can hold his liquor and drive with anyone. I know him; he's a good man and I worked for him a long time."

We arrived at the man's home. At the back of the house was a two-car garage. One door was open and the car was gone. The man got out, looked, came back to me and said, "His car is gone. His wife's Lincoln is there. I will see if anyone is home."

He went to the back door and pushed the doorbell a number of times. I could hear some talking being done. The cab driver came to me and told me the man was still in bed. He was told to get the door key from under the mat and to bring me to his bedroom. The man was sitting up in bed when we entered the room. He heard my story and told me he would get me to Herington by noon that day.

Then, he told his friend to go to the kitchen and look in a certain cabinet and bring him one of the bottles. The man returned with a full bottle of whiskey and handed it to him. He sat on the side of the bed and started drinking out of the bottle. I didn't know what to say. After awhile the man said to his friend, "I'm waiting on my wife to return with my car. I will get dressed now."

He hit the bottle again. I looked at the bottle when he capped it and gave it to his friend telling him to put it back in the cabinet for him. That man had drunk about a pint, and he seemed to be okay as he put his shoes on. He got up and asked what time it was. I said, "It's almost ten o'clock and we need to be on the way."

He told his friend if his wife wasn't back with his Chevy when we got outside, he would drive her Lincoln to Herington. That's what he did, and I mean he drove fast. We left Wichita fast, and he didn't slow down for anyone.

As we left Wichita, we were going up a high bridge over a number of rail tracks when he told his friend he hoped "old so-and-so", a friend of his who was a highway patrol officer, was at his usual spot at the bottom of the bridge. As we got on top of the bridge, we saw the patrol car there. The Lincoln had a V-12 engine, and we were doing about 100 mph, and he pushed the pedal more, got on his horn, then waved at the officer as we went by. He looked in his rear-view mirror and told us, "He's pulling out after us. We are going to leave him behind."

After about thirty minutes, he asked his friend about a cut-off road we could take and save some time. His friend said he didn't know about the condition of the road, but it would save some miles and time. So he decided to turn off and go that route when we came to it. I was in the back seat and holding onto the back of the front seat as best I could.

The short, cut-off road was a narrow, rough dirt road. He was going extra fast on the country road when we came to a corner turn spot on the road. He slammed on the brakes. We made the turn on the corner and came to a barricade across the road. He couldn't stop in time, so he left the road, missed the barricade, and then got back onto the road. The road had just been oiled for paving and the oil was all over the car. The driver said, "We can't stop now - we'll keep on going."

After a few miles, we passed a work crew who began shouting and waving their arms at us. Soon we were on the regular dirt road, off the cut-off and back on the highway to Herington. At ten minutes to twelve o' clock, we were at the gate to the Army Air Base. I made it! I showed my orders to the attendant and went back to the car to get my bags and pay the man for the trip from Wichita.

I asked the man, "How much do I owe you?"

He asked his friend, "Have you any money?" His friend said no.

The man said he forgot his wallet and he would have to get the car cleaned before he got home. "I wasn't going to charge you for the trip, but how about $25.00?"

I said, "That's okay with me. Here's $35.00 and I thank both of you."

As they drove off, I saw a new Lincoln with oil all over it leaving Herington Army Air Base. I was glad to be at the base on schedule and I appreciated their help.

Chapter 5

FINAL TRAINING AND DEPLOYMENT TO THE WAR IN EUROPE

"Training at Herington, Kansas"

I arrived at the Herington Army Air Base at the front gate on July 12, 1943. I was told to report to a certain building number, give them my name, and I would be told where to go. I did as I was told to do. I opened the door to a very large room with two desks and an officer at each desk. I was told to sit down at one of the desks. The officer at the other desk came over and started taking notes of the conversation between the officer and me.

The officer didn't explain anything to me. He started off by asking me, "Where were you on July 2nd?"

I replied, "I don't know."

"You don't know? I will tell you where you were. How high were you when you dropped those bombs in the water? How many bombs did you drop on your first pass over the lake? How many on your second pass? How high and where were you when you tossed out the chutes?" He asked question after question.

"You need to ask the pilot - the navigator - the bombardier - that's their job - that's not my job," I answered.

On and on and on it went for about two hours of one question after another. Repeats and repeats. Sometimes I would tell him, "You have asked me that same question, don't you remember?"

After awhile, I told him, "We aren't getting anywhere, are we?"

The officer taking notes was busy tearing page after page of notes out and tossing them on the floor. At last he asked me, "Sergeant, what is your job on the crew?"

"Sir, my job is flight engineer."

"What does a flight engineer do?"

"Sir, I pre-flight the plane on the ground and I call the speed of the plane to the pilot during take-off. After we are in the air and get the generators on, I check other things and if everything is okay and everybody else is settled down, I lie down on the flight deck and get a little nap."

He raised his voice, "You go to sleep while you are in the air?"

"Yes, sir."

"What if there is trouble and you are needed?"

"Sir, if one of those engines makes any unusual noise I wake up, and if anyone needs me, they call the radio man and he lets me know I'm needed."

"I don't believe you can sleep with all that noise."

"Sir, I don't care whether you believe me or not, but those little naps are wonderful."

Then the officer told me two members of the crew had already told him about what our crew did.

I said, "If you knew already, why did you spend two hours questioning me?"

He didn't answer me, but he told me I could leave. I got as far as the door, and the officer called my name; as I turned to face him, he said, "Sergeant, I want to give you some advice. You are going to be in combat in a few days. You will live longer if you stay awake."

I said, "Thank you, sir." I had my hand on the doorknob and I opened the door and left the building.

I went to find my crew and I found some of them, but two members hadn't made it in yet. All had been questioned by the officer in that building, and they told him all about what we had done on July 2nd. We weren't aware of it when we dropped the bombs, but we had damaged the city's water supply and killed a number of horses nearby. We didn't know what we had done, but the crew was to be punished for it.

Our crew, as well as the other crews of Colonel Crawford's Provisional Group, was supposed to get our new B-24 plane at Herington – the planes had been here for us, but they left the day before to be taken to Salinas, California, to a group going to the Pacific Theater. Our pilot, Mills, had already signed for our plane, but plans were changed. The original plans were for the Crawford group to be processed for duty with the 389th bomb group of the 8th Air Force in England.

The 389th, the 44th and 93rd groups had been sent from England to join the 98th and 376th groups of the 9th Air Force stationed in the desert south of Benghazi, Libya. These five groups were training for the big attack on the oil field at Ploesti, Rumania, on August 1, 1943. I was told, if we had gotten our plane on schedule, we would have left Herington and stopped off in South Florida for fuel and then landed for a day's rest in Trinidad - an island in the West Indies. We would have crossed the Atlantic Ocean to Africa and joined the group in the desert. But our plans were changed and we were going to be court-martialed.

Our pilot, Mills, didn't tell anyone about his plans. After a day had gone by, he called a crew meeting. He told us a general had been flown in to conduct the court-martial and none of the officers knew how to conduct it. Mills had been a staff sergeant in the regular Army before he became a pilot, and one of his men was court-martialed in the Philippine Islands. Mills had been there to help him. He knew how a court-martial should be conducted and he had told them how. The two crew members who told about what had happened would testify against the crew in the court session the next morning. There were no ill feelings toward the two crew members for what they were going to do - Mills's crew was a good group. We just wanted to get through the trouble we were in.

Mills told us he was going to let them have their court-martial, and after they had heard the testimony of the two crew members, he was going to make this statement: "I was and I am the commander of the crew and I will take full responsibility for the actions of the crew."

The result of the court-martial was the postponement of promotions of all crew members for a period of six months. Mills was already up for promotion to first lieutenant from flight officer rank. The crew thanked him, and we were happy to get the episode over. The fine was $300. Since there were ten crew members, each member gave $30.00 to take care of the fine, but there was nothing we could do about the promotion part. We were really glad to get this over with. We also thought – had we not been scheduled to be sent overseas, we could have been sent to the federal prison at Leavenworth, Kansas.

A number of things happened to the crew in the short time we were at Herington. The first thing was the general court-martial, and then our assistant radioman, Veral J. Birch, didn't report to Herington. On July 14, 1943, by special order #46 - Sgt. Max W. Roach was assigned to our crew and was promoted on the same order. Roach joined the crew and went overseas with us. He was from Utah, the same state Birch was from. Roach seemed to fit in well with the crew and after a few days, he and I became good friends.

We had arrived at Herington on July 12, 1943, with the expectation of getting our own B-24 plane, but that was not to be. They would process us for overseas duty and send us to Europe by an ATC (air transport command) plane. We were in the Sixth Heavy Bombardment Processing Headquarters Army Air Base at Herington, Kansas, and they had us busy all the time. Sometimes they would have us going to two places at the same time.

They sent me over to the medical building without telling me why I was being sent there. I arrived and they told me my immunization records had been lost, and they had to give me all the immunizations that day. I said, "I didn't lose them. I'm up to date on all my shots, and neither you nor anyone else is giving me any shots today. Do you understand?"

The GI medic went and got a lieutenant who told me I was going to get all those shots that day. I told them in plain words I wasn't, and they said again I was. By this time all eyes were on us and a captain came up and asked, "What's all this trouble over here?"

Before the medic GI or the lieutenant could say anything, I told the captain my shot record had been lost, and I was not going to get all those shots again, but they keep insisting I am.

"I am up-to-date on my shots. This same thing happened less than three months ago, and I had to take five shots at one time,"

The captain asked me, "Where were you?"

I told him I had to take those five shots before I could leave Tucson.

He immediately told the GI medic to give him one of the immunization records and he would make a record. "I was at Tucson and he is telling the truth. If anyone leaves Tucson, he has gotten all shots, even if his record was lost."

I told the captain, "Thank you sir, and will you make two copies?"

He did and I carried that copy with me all the time I was in the Army. A number of times later, the Army lost my immunization record, and each time they tried to keep my copy of the record, I would tell them "No way!" They could make a copy, but my copy stayed with me. I still have that record today.

We were issued a Colt 45 pistol with a choice of either a shoulder or belt holster to use in carrying it on the body. I chose a shoulder-type and carried it all the time I was overseas. While I was standing in the line to get the 45, I saw a GI I recognized. He was Aubrey Kearley, who lived in Robinsonville near my hometown, Atmore, Alabama. I went to high school with him and his brother, Julian. He later retired from the Air Force and moved back to the Atmore area to live.

A sergeant found me the next day, and informed me I had never been taught how to shoot the 45. He and I went out to the firing range for some shooting instruction. After shooting for about thirty minutes, he said to me, "Sergeant, I give up on you. I believe I could put you in a barn, close all the doors, and you could not shoot this 45 and hit a wall. Do you know what you are doing wrong?"

I replied, "I'm pulling the trigger instead of squeezing it."

"You are right. I don't have any more time to be with you. I checked on your gunnery school records, and I don't know how you made good grades there. I cannot teach you to shoot this 45 here. I'm out of time with you, so I'm giving you a qualifying score on the 45. Maybe you won't have to use it while you're overseas."

I never shot the 45 anymore. I turned it in before I left the squadron to come back to the States in May, 1944.

We were ready to be sent overseas. We left Herington by early morning train going to Presque Isle, Maine. We were put in a coach rail car and we stayed in it all the way to Presque Isle. They would shift our car from one rail line to another at different cities. We left Herington on July 18, 1943, and arrived at Presque Isle on July 20, 1943.

Orders:
Herington, Kansas to Presque Isle, Maine
Herington, Kansas – July 16, 1943 to C.O.A.T.C.A.A.B.
Presque Isle, Maine - S.O. #124 - Par. I – HG. -
A.A.B. and left July 18, 1943
3rd Airport of Embark at - HG - Air Transport Command
July 18, 1943 - to C.O. - S.O. #124 - Par. 1 - HG. A.A.B.
- Herington, Kansas

"Pre-Deployment at Presque Isle, Maine"

We arrived at Presque Isle from Herington on the afternoon of July 20, 1943, and were told we would be there a few days because of storms in the northern route to Europe. The Air Transport Command would fly us to Prestwick, Scotland, when the storms passed. There was nothing to do but wait. Time passes slowly when there is nothing to do to keep busy. We couldn't leave the base because we could be leaving at any time.

One morning some of us were outside our barracks when a young boy came by. We asked him where he was going. He told us he was going fishing. We asked him where. He pointed and told us there was a small stream that flowed through the base and he always caught some fish out of it. About an hour later, he came back and had two or three trout on a short stick on his shoulder. The fish were a nice size and a wonderful thing to see. The boy was about ten years old and was wearing overalls, a straw hat on his head, and a big smile on his face. He was bare-footed, and carried the fish on a stick. We caught the "fishing fever".

The first thing after the noon meal, two of the crew and I just had to go fishing. We went to the PX and bought a package of hooks and some fishing line. The young boy had given us his can with some worms, so off we went in the direction he had pointed out to us. It was only a short distance away in a wooded area where we found the small stream. It was a very narrow stream, only four to six feet wide, but it was cold and flowing. We got tree limbs for fishing poles, baited our hooks and got busy fishing. We were told the Canadian border wasn't too far from where we were, and that was the reason for the water being so cold. It was cold, very cold, and I should know because I fell in it!

We fished and fished but didn't get a bite. We went up stream and down stream. One time, I decided to cross over to the other side and try my luck there. I found a narrow spot about four feet wide to jump across, and as I made the leap my foot slipped. I fell in the cold water. That was the time to go. The stream wasn't very deep, only four or five feet, but it was cold. We returned to the barracks and I got a hot shower and some clean clothes.

<u>Notes from my Notebook:</u>
<u>From Presque Isle to Reykjavik, Iceland</u>
July 31, 1943 - C-54 Plane A.T.C. (Air Transport Command)

Presque Isle to Reykjavik, Iceland – 19 Hours
Transferred to 8th Air Force
From Reykjavik, Iceland to Prestwick, Scotland
August 1, 1943 - C-54 Plane A.T.C – 5 Hours

We got word on July 31, 1943 - the day we had been waiting for had arrived. The North Atlantic route was clear for flying to Europe. We were to leave Presque Isle late that day. We left about six o'clock that evening on a DC-4, a four-engine ATC plane (Air Force plane - a C-54). The captain told us we would stop at Newfoundland, Canada, long enough to top the fuel tanks with gas. The next stop to re-fuel would be Reykjavik, Iceland, the next afternoon. The last leg of the flight would be to Prestwick, Scotland. The captain told us we would be south of Greenland, and if we had any trouble on the flight to Iceland we could go to Greenland.

We had our regular eats with us – "K-rations". When we were moved by rail or plane, most of the time we would be fed "K-rations." Someone would always say, "Well, as long as it hasn't been opened, it's okay."

On the flight to Prestwick with us were six glider pilots. All were master sergeants and regular Army guys. They were on their way to England to start a glider school. We enjoyed them on the flight and told them we didn't want to be on flights over Europe without an engine.

We stopped for fuel at Reykjavik, Iceland. It was some time in the afternoon and we were allowed to leave the plane but not leave the area. We walked to get some exercise after sitting for so long. It was a very cold day and the wind was really blowing hard, but the sun was shining. The GI servicing the plane told us this was one of their better days. I was glad I wasn't stationed there like they were.

After the plane was re-fueled, we were off on the last leg of our flight to Prestwick, Scotland. We arrived there and were told we would be going by train to London that night. We checked the schedule and found out the train would be leaving the station at eight o'clock. Everyone was hungry, so we decided to split up. A few of the men stayed with our bags and guarded them, and the rest of us tried to find something to eat. We couldn't find anything in the short time we had, so we decided to come back to the station without any food.

We left Prestwick at eight o'clock on a train with little compartments. Each seated four persons and had a door which opened to the outside of the rail car. The rail cars had these types of compartments in all their trains. We traveled south all night and arrived in London at about 8:00 a.m. the next morning. We came into London Station through an underground rail system on August 2, 1943.

"Combat School in England"

We arrived in London's train station early in the morning about 8:00 a.m. on August 2, 1943. We stayed at the station while our pilot, Mills, checked with those in charge to see where we should go. In a few minutes, he came back and told us we had to be back at the station at six o'clock that evening. We would be leaving London at about eight o' clock that night for a little town about forty miles from London. We could take in London. We were told, "Go where you want to go, just be back here at six o'clock."

We didn't have any breakfast, and we didn't know anything about London. We started out to find an eating place. We had no place to leave our bags. We had to carry them with us. The crews split up into groups of six to eight each. The group I joined was made up of about four from my crew and two or three from another crew. We walked two or three blocks and saw a British Sergeant's Club sign on front of a building. There were about six or eight steps up to a closed door with a British sergeant standing outside. We asked if we could go inside and he said we could. One of the boys from the other crew had been demoted to a private for thirty days and his time was up. He didn't have his staff sergeant's patch on his sleeves yet, and the man at the door said he couldn't go in. We explained the situation to the sergeant, but he didn't believe us. After a few words, we told the Sergeant we had told the truth. We told him we were all going in together and he wasn't going to stop us. He told us to enter, and we did.

We had our first cup of British tea and one of their hard cookies. We appreciated their hospitality and we told them so. They told us about an American Red Cross building where there were beds for us to spend the night, but we told them we were leaving London early that evening. We decided to check out the Red Cross place and maybe get a cup of coffee and a donut. We found it and it was a nice place and we did enjoy the coffee and donuts. They didn't ask us to pay for the service, but we did and we were happy to.

We found out we were not far from a section of London known as Piccadilly Circus. We had heard some bad things about that area and some of the boys went to look it over. Three of us went elsewhere and saw another part of London.

We were surprised to see so many large balloons over London supporting steel cables hanging from them. That night we saw a number of large searchlights, with their beams of light scanning the sky. Of course, this was wartime; we could see the damaged and burned buildings everywhere in London.

Time passed quickly, but we made it back to the train station on time. Mills told us to stay with our group, and soon we were told to put our bags in a baggage rail car and get on a car for the forty-mile ride to a small place named Appleton. At Appleton, there would be an Army truck to take us to an air base close by. The base was close to a place named Chittington.

At Appleton, our bags were all put in rows at the station. We had name tags on the bags, and I was short one barracks bag. All of my bags had been put in the baggage car, because I had put them there myself. The missing bag contained a hundred dollars' worth of things I had bought at the base PX before I left the States. The train had already left the station before I discovered my bag was missing. The baggage car man had time in those two hours from London to untie and find a bag he wanted. I'm sure that wasn't the first or the last bag he had gotten. I'm sure he emptied the bag and threw it out of the rail car.

We got on the truck and soon arrived at the air base. We were told to find a cot in one of the small Quonset hut metal buildings and get some sleep. That we did, and it was a good feeling to get to sleep on a cot again. When we got up the next morning, we were taken to the mess hall for breakfast, and then we were told what the plans were for us. We were at combat school and we would have approximately two weeks of school. Then we would be sent to the 389th bomb group. The 389th group's base was at Hethel, England, but they had been sent to Benghazi, Libya, to join the four other bomb groups (44th, 93rd, 98th, and 376th) for the August 1st raid on the Ploesti Oil Fields. We didn't know when the 389th would be returning to England.

We started combat school. Our instructors were combat veterans, but I didn't know if they had finished their tours of missions or not. They showed combat films and told us how it was in combat. We had a number of hours of instruction regarding plane identification, specifically wing spans of enemy planes - things that would help us on the long hours to the target and returning to home base. The one thing all the instructors tried to get over to us was – "Take care of your guns - keep them clean and in good working order at all times". We were told to oil all moving parts, but not to use too much oil. Too much oil would cause trouble in the cold temperatures.

Lieutenant Cobb, our co-pilot, got sick with a high fever and was put in the base hospital. Several days went by and he wasn't responding to the medications the doctors were giving him. He was put into an isolation ward in the hospital where no one could talk to or visit him. Things started to look bad for Mills's crew. Word was out that we were leaving England in a few days. We were going to be sent to the 389th group in Benghazi, but we didn't have a co-pilot.

Mills told me he wanted to talk to me. He and our navigator, Harry Willis, had been working on a plan to get Cobb out of the hospital. One of their grandmothers had told him about an old home remedy of placing a bar of soap under an armpit to lower the fever of a sick person. They were going to get in to see Cobb the next day, if possible. This was about mid-afternoon on a Saturday and we were possibly going to be leaving England sometime on Monday.

Mills asked me if I would go with him and Willis into a little village and watch over them that night. They had heard about an inn named "The White Horse Inn," and they wanted me to keep them out of trouble and get them back to the base and their cots. He said they trusted me and would appreciate it if I would go with them and keep them out of trouble and let them enjoy themselves. I told him I would and I did.

They drank mugs of strong ale and enjoyed throwing darts at the only dart board in the inn. Some of the old men from the village got mad at Mills and Willis for keeping the dart board to themselves all the time. I couldn't stop them from playing their dart games, but I did get them to keep buying drinks for the inn's regular customers. The inn was about three blocks from where the truck spot was that would take us back to the base. The last truck was leaving at ten o'clock that night, so I knew I had to get them to leave the inn about nine-thirty.

I got both of them outside the inn and started toward the truck, when they told me they had to stop and sit a little while. I told them we had no time to rest. We had to keep moving. We got about a block from the truck when both of them got rubber legs and said that was as far as they could go. I got in the middle of them, with my arms around them, and I carried them toward the truck. It was a very dark night and I had gotten close to the back of the truck when an officer came in front of us. He started laughing and making some ugly remarks about us. I told him I didn't appreciate his laughing or his comments, and asked if he would help me get them in the truck. He gave a big loud "NO!"

I gave him an answer. I don't remember what I said to him as I got ready to load my two crew members. I had to lift them up one at a time. I got the job done, and while I was doing it, two things went through my mind. First, it was going to be easy to get them out of the truck body. Second - this would be the first and the last time I would ever be responsible to look after someone who goes off and gets drunk. We got back to the base and I got them to their cots. I just put them on their cots with their clothes on. I did take their shoes off.

Mills and Willis didn't get up until mid-morning, and after they had their noon meal, they called a crew meeting and told us about their plans. The two of them were going to get to Cobb somehow and get that bar of soap under his armpit. They went to the hospital and said the crew was being sent to Benghazi the next day and they had to explain it to Cobb. The nurse led them to Cobb and left them with him for a short time. They left the bar of soap with Cobb.

The nurse had assured them Cobb could leave the hospital the next day if his temperature was normal. We all had high expectations for Cobb to join us the next day and he did. He left the hospital before noon on Monday with a normal temperature. Did the bar of soap or the medicine get Cobb out? We didn't know and didn't care. Cobb joined us in time to leave for London early that night. I do know "the Lord works in mysterious ways" and "His wonders to behold."

We took a train from London to Prestwick, Scotland. We left Prestwick on August 16, 1943. We were given a little talk about our trip before we took off on our flight to Africa. When we left Prestwick, we were told we would fly west, and then turn south to make a big swing away from Europe to avoid detection by our enemies. We would be our own escorts. We would stop for gas in Marrakesh, Morocco, and go on to Algiers. When we were re-fueling, we could leave the plane, but we couldn't leave the area.

<u>Orders</u>
<u>08/16/1943 C-S4 A.T.C. - Prestwick to Marrakesh, Morocco, to Algiers, Algeria - 18:00 HRS.</u>

"In Algiers and On to Benghazi"

We arrived in Algiers on August 17, 1943, and were told we would be leaving for Benghazi in a couple of days. We were taken to a barracks and given permission to go into the city the next day. We didn't have to have a pass. They just told us to stay out of trouble and to be back at the base by six o'clock on the morning of the 19th. Our orders were already cut for us to leave Algiers early that morning.

I got with three or four others and we went into the city of Algiers. When we were at a new place, it was best to check with the GIs who were stationed there to find out about the places to see and the places to avoid. The GIs we checked with in Algiers told us to spend some time at the big public square, but not to buy or eat anything because it could make us sick.

We arrived at the city and went on a sight-seeing tour. There were plenty of older men and boys of all ages wanting to be a guide for us for a fee, but we were told not to use them. All women and girls wore veils on their faces and their heads were always covered. When we were walking in the narrow alleys and streets, we had to keep watching our backsides for someone coming at us from the rear.

We went to the square in the center of the city. It was a large area with tables and little booths all around the sides. One barefoot, old woman, who was sitting on the ground, had a small chicken with one end of a string tied to the chicken's leg and the other end of the string tied to one of her big toes. It was interesting to see her; she wore a big hat and appeared to be asleep. She seemed to be content with her life and she certainly wasn't worrying about the war.

One of my friends told me, at a later time when I was overseas, about what happened to him when he was in Algiers. He was by himself in a large cafe waiting for his meal when a man came to his table and asked if he could join him. The cafe was crowded and my friend told him he was welcome to join him. The man sat down and, after he had ordered his meal, began a conversation with my friend. He told me the man had just returned from Madrid, Spain, for the United States government. He had just completed negotiating a deal for a raw material swap between Germany and the United States. He had met an agent in Spain several times before the agreement was reached. The man told him that strange things take place in times of war. The man never told my friend the names of the materials.

Early the next morning, they called us together and informed us we would be leaving Algiers on a C-47 plane to Benghazi, where the 389th group was stationed. We would stop at Tripoli for fuel. The 389th group was on detached service with the 9th Air Force.

<u>Orders</u>
<u>August 17, 1943 - C-47 A.T.C. – Algiers to Tripoli (Castel Benigo Airport) 4 Hours</u>
<u>August 19, 1943 - C-47 A.T.C. – Tripoli to Benghazi (Benina Airport) 5 Hours</u>

———

At Algiers, we were put in a C-47 plane to take us to Benghazi Benina Airport. The 389th group was stationed approximately sixty miles south of Benghazi in the desert. The C-47 had two fold down wooden slat benches in it for us to sit on – the type of seats paratroopers used. They were not comfortable at all, especially for a long time. We had to sit on those seats for nine hours that day. We flew close to the ground at all times and it was a rough flight – up and down. I have often thought about those flights. We never had parachutes. I would say that flight was the roughest ride I ever had.

Part of the flight was over the Sahara Desert. That was something to see, especially from the air. Sand and more sand. I have read the Sahara is sometimes called the "Great Desert" because of its size, estimated to be three and a half million square miles. There were great sand dunes everywhere. We weren't very long at Tripoli. We left the plane and walked around while the plane was being fueled. We always had our K-rations to eat and our canteens of water to drink.

Chapter 6

BENGHAZI, LIBYA

"The Base at Benghazi"

When my crew left the States on July 31, 1943, we were assigned to the 8th Air Force 389th Bomb group. On August 28, 1943, we were transferred to the 9th Air Force 98th bomb group, 344th squadron. When the 389th was leaving Benghazi to return to England, they transferred some of the new crew members to the 98th bomb group. The 98th had lost so many crew members on the August 1st raid on Ploesti, Romania, that they needed new crew members. Mills's crew was one of the crews transferred. I stayed with that group all the time I was overseas. One of the good things I remember was I didn't have to worry about anyone in my group taking anything from me.

When we arrived at Benghazi, there wasn't anyone to take us to the base. We had to wait for transportation. We walked around parts of the city while we were waiting, and after two hours we were on our way to our group. We were assigned to little two-man tents. Max W. Roach and I were to be together in a small white tent and were given nets to cover our cots.

They told us some things to do to improve our living conditions. We had to keep the tent's rope pegs in the sand and that meant the pegs would have to be driven into the sand a number of times each day. We had to use the nets over our cots, because the flies and other insects were so bad.

Roach liked to sleep late when we didn't have to get up early. I would get up and try not to make too much noise getting the sand and scorpions out of the tent. I don't know if I was ever on a mission with Roach or not, but we stayed in the 98th bomb group. He finished his fifty missions on May 13, 1944, and I finished mine four days later on May 17th.

<u>Orders</u>
<u>August 28, 1943</u>
<u>Transferred to the 9th A.A.F. – the 98th bomb group - 344th squadron from the 8th A.A.F.</u>

Three B-24 groups from England (44th, 93rd, and 389th) had joined the two groups (98th and 376th) that were stationed in the desert for the Ploesti low-level bombing. The three groups from England were preparing to go back to England. My crew had arrived from England to Benghazi on August 19th, but they didn't tell us what they planned to do with us. However, we had to help get the groups ready to leave.

One day we were loading 55-gallon drums on a flatbed truck and trailer rig. The drums were used to mark off safe walkways and roadways in the group. Engineers had gotten all the landmines out of the sand and the drums had to be moved. The trucks and trailer rigs were extra big, so we could move a lot of them in a short period of time. Of course, we had a large number to load. We had four men on the trailer to stack the drums. There was a driver for the truck who moved it as we loaded drums on both sides of the road at the same time. We had just two men on each side. We would reach down in the sand, lift on signal, toss drums up to the trailers, and then the two on our side would stack.

Every so often someone would call "time out". We would do that so we could catch a little rest. Someone said, "We should kick the drums over so we don't pick up a scorpion."

The first drum we kicked over had a little snake under it. We killed it and then looked it over. It was about a foot long and had two little horns on its head. Somebody said it was an asp, the kind of snake Cleopatra used to commit suicide.

"Episodes at Benghazi"

I was asked to go on missions when someone was sick or wanted a rest or, as we said, just wanted to "sit one out." I was used as a replacement because my original crew had lost our pilot and 3 other crew members when they were killed on a mission on September 2, 1943. Because my remaining crew was split up, I went to the squadron operations' office and told them I wanted to make my quota of missions as fast as I could so that I could return to stateside duty. I offered to go as a top turret gunner, a waist gunner or as a flight engineer. I wanted to have the privilege of refusal if I wanted to because of a crew's reputation. So, that was our agreement. It worked out well for me and for operations.

Benghazi, Libya, is a port city on the Mediterranean Sea in North Africa between Tunisia and Egypt. The 98th group's base was at a spot approximately sixty miles south of Benghazi. We were at the edge of the Sahara desert and west of the Nile River. It was hot and dry. We got one quart of water a day. That was it - nothing more, nothing less. The water was brought into base in a tanker trailer by truck from a place about forty miles away, and each squadron had a large canvas bag which hung under a tripod. We called it a "lister" bag.

The bag was tended by a clerk from the squadron office with a list of the 344th's names on it and a guard was posted by it on the ground. The whole set-up was guarded by another armed soldier on an elevated tower. When you got your daily canteen of water, your name was checked off and that was all you were allowed until the next day.

The water was treated with iodine and plenty of it. It had a smell and taste to it, but it was wet and we got used to it. When the water truck arrived, a group medic got on the tank and started to empty bottles of iodine in, and the tanker would drive around the area to mix it up. But, it was wet and we always appreciated it.

The desert was something to see. Sand and more sand. Hot in the daytime and cold in the wee hours of the mornings. The winds would get the sand going about mid-day and dunes would form on ground. Some piled up to about fifty feet high.

We used white two-man tents at the camp. We dug out the sand about five or six feet deep, got boards from the bomb boxes and stood them up for the walls. We laid boards on the bottom for the floor. Then we put the tent over it and tried to keep the tent pegs in the sand. We dug a walkway out for the entrance with a ninety-degree turn in it to keep the wind from blowing sand straight into the tent. We had to tie the tent's entrance flaps together to try and keep some of the sand out.

The sand flies were really bad. We had to use nets over our cots. The cots were the cross-legged wooden type with canvas bottoms. We used paper on the canvas first and then folded one of our woolen Army blankets for a mattress. We used a second blanket for cover. We slept on the cots with our clothes on. We always had to have our flashlights handy. The sand scorpions and the kangaroo rats would come out at night. The rats would run and play on the floor boards and chase one another around and around. Everyone had a Sahara type hard hat to wear when we went outside during the day and we would keep it under our cot at night. I have seen the rats playing and sliding off the hats. They would run on the floor with their back legs only and hop on the hat then slide off and go back and do it again. They would make a patty-pat noise on the boards.

The scorpions were very bad and would get in the sack with us as well as cling to the underside of the tent top. When we woke up, there were two things we always did. We shined our lights at the tent top above us to check for scorpions. Next, we hopped out of the sack, grabbed our top blanket, shook the scorpions out and then checked our bottom blanket. I was never bitten by one, but I was told it was bad. I am sure that always sleeping with my clothes on kept me from getting bitten. I was awakened by a scorpion crawling on me during the night a number of times and I had to move fast.

I woke up in the wee hours of the morning one time about to freeze. I slept with my face up, and when I opened my eyes, I saw the stars. My tent had been cut open and my flight bag was gone. We had been warned about this, and we had been tying our bags with a small rope attached to our cots by our heads. An Arab must have had a very sharp knife to get that bag and not wake me up. It had all my flying stuff in it, even my chute, which was what he wanted. But, I could have had my throat cut.

Those Arabs were some kind of people. They would come into our area while we were on a mission and raid a tent or two, until someone spotted them and ran them off. We soon learned to tie the tent flaps together very well so they couldn't just walk in. They would come into our area and sell eggs to us. The going price was twenty cents per egg. About once a week, two or three of us would go together, pool a little of our water and buy an egg for each one of us to boil. We always had a little Coleman gas stove around. There was one in every plane that came over and we would get some gasoline to use for washing our clothes and for the stove.

One afternoon at about six o'clock in a tent close to mine, one of the gas stoves exploded and one of the men caught fire. I was looking at the explosion when it happened. The man on fire started to run. There was an Arab on a donkey close by. As the man on fire came by the Arab, the Arab jumped off the donkey and fell on the burning man, knocking him onto the sand, and putting the fire out in just a moment. I saw both the man and the Arab get up off the ground and neither of them was hurt. The Arab was in the right place at the right time and knew what to do.

There were a lot of stories about the Arabs and the Air Corps. The Arabs would claim that a camel or donkey they owned had been killed by a fighter pilot or a bomber gunner. If the group didn't pay up, the Arabs would cut some telephone cables. There were no poles used for the phones; the wires were put on the ground. I am sure they collected for some camels and donkeys that were never really killed.

———

While we were at Benghazi and going on missions, we had to cross the Mediterranean Sea going to and from the targets. We used an old sunken ship on our return for our landfall mark. One afternoon we made our landfall and no ship was in sight. The navigator had missed the ship. We talked it over on the intercom and we agreed to go left. We had missed our mark by a long way, because we began to think we should have gone right. But, at last the ship came into view. That old ship was a welcome sight because our gas was getting low. We didn't know how bad we could feel until we had to sweat running out of gas while flying and not yet home. But, we made it.

"A USO Show at Benghazi"

Early one September evening while the 344th Bomb Group was at Benghazi, we were entertained by a small, French USO troupe who put on a show for us. They had two or three French women and one French man who performed for us. The women danced for us, and the man ate some razor blades and a light bulb; then the show was stopped. Two GI's in a jeep drove up and told us the trouble. All lights were to be out and stay out. Two planes of German paratroopers were in our area to destroy our planes.

It was about 8 o'clock and it was dark. Our orders were to put two gunners at every plane, and the rest of the group was to get in their tents and stay there. We were told not to use flashlights or matches. There was to be total darkness and no noise of any kind. If we did not obey, we could get shot.

About 6 o'clock the next morning, we got the story. Hitler had made a speech at a factory a few days before, telling the workers they wouldn't be bombed because he planned to destroy the B-24's to prevent them from doing so. He knew the U.S. Air Force would want to bomb the factory after his speech, so he wanted to get those B-24s. He sent two planes of about thirty German paratroopers on a suicide mission to destroy the planes.

We heard the German officer in charge of the Nazi paratroopers had a rank equal to our major. He had two pistols on him, and there was a mad rush by the GIs to get those guns. They assumed they would be German Luger pistols, but that German had two American Smith & Wesson .38 caliber pistols instead. That was a big disappointment to the GIs who wanted the German pistols. All the paratroopers were captured before they could do any damage. I didn't get any sleep that night, and I don't think I was the only one who didn't. We were all glad to hear the good news the next morning, and we didn't think we missed much of the USO show.

"U.S. Congressmen Visit Our Bomb Group"

When we were at Benghazi, a congressional delegation paid us a visit. We all wondered what they wanted to see. No one was interested in them or what they thought. I didn't see them. After they left the group, we heard they didn't like what they saw. They left orders to have all the paintings or "nose cone art" taken off the bombers' fuselages. They said the image of the United States would be damaged by the paintings on the planes when they were shot down.

That's one order that wasn't obeyed. No picture was painted over or removed by their order or anyone else's. We were going on missions to help defeat our enemy by dropping bombs on them to kill them before they killed us. Why worry about what they thought of us? Those planes with the paintings on each side meant something to the crews. That's something the congressmen didn't know anything about.

As I think about this now, I wonder if times have really changed. It seems congressmen are pressured to spend time and money to get re-elected and make such trips to help them with that purpose in mind. I wonder if they know any more about what goes on overseas today than they did then.

"A Little Monkey Named Myrtle"

One day when the group was at Benghazi, a cargo plane from India stopped at the base. A GI on the plane had a small monkey he was trying to sell. The combat crews were always looking for a pet, especially a little dog. The GI with the monkey was asking $100 for it. I heard a lot of talk going on about the price for the monkey, but the plane left and the monkey stayed with the crew.

I never heard what they paid for it. The monkey was named Myrtle. She came with a collar and a small rope about twenty or twenty-five feet long. The crew would feed the monkey nuts of all kinds, especially peanuts. I never asked where the crew got the nuts. Myrtle's food may have come with her.

Everyone would come to the crew's tent and watch them feed their pet. Myrtle would put nuts in her mouth as long as they would give them to her. Then she would go up to the top of the pyramid tent, sit near the top and eat her nuts. Both sides of her jaws would be puffed out when she went up to the top of the tent. I don't know how long the crew had Myrtle. I told the crew my wife's name was Myrtle.

"The Bombs We Dropped"

We carried different bombs all the time. There were four squadrons in the 98th, and the bomb loads varied for all targets. The first bombers over the target usually dropped 500 or 1,000 pound demolition bombs. We had 2,000-pound demolition bombs, and I don't remember if the missions I was on used them. The second attack group dropped the incendiary bombs to start fires, followed by more demolition bombs to mix things up. Then an attack group dropped the "frag" (fragmentation) bombs designed to kill the men trying to put the fires out. The targets would get hit a number of times.

When I first started going on missions, we had a bunch of phosphorus stick bombs that were three or four feet in length and about the size of a big broom handle. These would be bound together with others by a steel band, which immediately came free when they were dropped from the bomb racks. This type of incendiary bomb was replaced by a thin, steel shell bomb of Napalm. These were highly incendiary bombs and we were glad to hear the bombardier cry "bombs away!" when they were dropped.

When the attack group of bombers reached the IP (Initial Point for the bomb run) and started the run, the plane had to fly in a straight line until the bombs were released. Napalm bombs contained a highly incendiary jelly-like substance like that used in flame throwers. We knew they had aviation gas and rubber in them. When we had a load of those bombs, and the ack-ack blasts were all around us, we were really glad to unload them. When you have seen a plane and ten men disappear in a big ball of fire, and you know it takes just a small fragment from one of those blasts to set that load of bombs off, you are glad they have been dropped.

When those flak blasts were close enough to shake the plane and we could smell the blast, then we wanted to leave the target area as fast as possible. It was amazing whenever we completed a combat tour without being injured or killed. I didn't get a scratch or any damage to my body or my mind in my combat tour. For that, I thank my Lord. He took care of me.

Chapter 7

HERGLA, TUNISIA

"Landing at Hergla – Back to Benghazi"

After landing at Hergla, the flying crews and planes were ordered to return to Benghazi to bomb air bases in Crete and Greece. The Germans had taken Crete over again. The 98th support group was still en route to Hergla when we returned to Benghazi. Because they were not with us, we had to sleep in the plane or on the ground and to help service the planes. Most days it was ten or eleven o'clock at night before we could get a little sleep. After flying on missions it was always good to get back to home base and sleep on a cot in a little tent again.

"The 344th Squadron Bus"

When the 98th Group was en route to Hergla from Benghazi they found a German bus on the side of the road. It looked new. The 344th had a plane line mechanic who had been a diesel mechanic before he joined the Air Corps. His name was Darrell M. George. Sgt. George checked the bus and knew he could get it running. Sgt. George and another mechanic were left by the bus and the 344th soon had its own squadron bus. Darrell and I became good friends. He was with me and the others who went to Naples on March 21, 1944, for a week of R&R. That bus was still being used when I left to come home.

"Our Time at Hergla"

When we arrived at Hergla on September 21, 1943, the 344th Squadron was assigned an area close to the Mediterranean Sea. We said we could throw a rock into the water from our tent, if we could find a rock. We were on a sand dune and dunes were everywhere. When we got there the officers claimed the flat areas between the sand dunes. We received a blessing by having our tents on top of the dunes when the rains started one night about midnight.

We had to help the officers get their things out of the water and into our tents until morning. We helped them move their tents to higher ground. We were using a large dry lake area for our planes' parking area. There was rain, rain, and more rain until our planes stood in two to three feet of water. There was nothing to be done until the rains stopped. The rains started on the night of November 5 and stopped about three or four days later.

An Army unit came in and got the planes out of the water. They used two large machines. One was placed on each side of the lake with steel cables fastened to each landing wheel support on the plane to be pulled out. The plane had a pilot running all four engines up at a high RPM with the plane's flaps down to give lift to the plane. They all had to work at the same time to get the plane to high ground.

The 415th Squadron's landing strip was used for take-offs. On November 10, 1943, the planes were flown to the 376th Group's field, a few miles from our base. The crews were carried to and from the planes by trucks.

While we were waiting for the rain to stop, I got diarrhea and didn't want to go to the medics for help. The talk was going around we would soon be leaving for Italy. If I went to the medics, they would send me to the British hospital which was about forty miles from our base. Then, when I would be released from the hospital, I would be on my own to get back to my outfit. I didn't want to take the chance of being left in Africa when the group left for Italy, so I didn't want to go to the medics.

Rector Long, from Arkansas, told me about his grandma's remedy - a good dose of cinnamon. I asked where I would find cinnamon. He told me we could try the mess tents. We did but had no luck locating cinnamon. Rector told me we should try the British cooks. When I asked why, he said they flavor their food more than we do. He told me to follow him. The first thing he did was go to the motor pool and check out a jeep. He checked the gas tank to be sure it was full of gas and it was, so off we went. We knew we had to stay on the trails where other trucks had been going because land mines were everywhere. The rains had washed the sand off the land mines. We could see the red fuse unit that would activate the mine if someone stepped on it or ran over it.

We stopped at a number of British units without finding any cinnamon. They would send us to another place and tell us how to get there. About three o'clock that afternoon, we came to a British refueling place. We fueled up the jeep, and I noticed the drums were marked "Lend Lease USA". I signed a paper for fifty cents a gallon and charged it to the 344th Squadron. I never was asked about that gas ticket. The men at the refueling place told us about a British outpost near there where they thought they might have some cinnamon. We thanked them and headed there. About thirty minutes later we arrived at the outpost. The mess sergeant asked how much we needed. Rector looked at me and asked how much. I replied that I didn't know. I had my canteen and cup with me. Rector told me to give my cup to the sergeant and told him, "Half a cup".

I got the cup back with the powdered cinnamon in it, and Rector told me to add water to it and drink it. I told Rector it was too thick to drink; I would have to eat it. He told me to get it down any way I could, so I did.

We returned to the base. The rains had stopped and the cinnamon paste worked. I told my friend, Rector, his grandma's remedy was potent medicine for me, and I thanked him for his help.

We didn't have anything to do the next day, so two of my friends and I decided to go to the town of Enfidaville. We started walking there and after about an hour, Capt. Huckleberry, our Operations Officer, came by and stopped. He asked us where we were going and we told him. He told us to hop in the jeep as he was going through there. He told us the group's water truck would be coming by about three o'clock in the afternoon, if we wanted a ride back. We thanked him, and he dropped us off in the town.

There wasn't much to see in the town, so we went back to the area where we had seen a large group at a railroad crossing as we came into town. There was a small railway building and close by there was a large group of men. We asked who they were, and one of them spoke to us in good English. The group was a company of the French Foreign Legion, and they had just finished slaughtering a large animal. We didn't stay there long. Big flies were everywhere. They were a rough-looking group of men. They were nothing like the Legion in white uniforms we had seen in the movies, but they were extra nice and friendly to us. We went away from them and sat down on the sand. It wasn't long before a big Army engineering truck came by and stopped to see if we wanted a ride. We said yes, and they told us to hop on. There were two GIs in the cab and two GIs with carbines sitting on the flat bed body. They told us they were shooting the land mines whose red caps were exposed since the rains had washed off the sand covering the mines. The truck driver was going at a slow pace and it was very noisy because there were red caps everywhere. After a few miles we came to a fork in the road; the driver stopped and told us they were going to go left, and we needed to go right. We thanked them for the ride and got off, then the truck left. When we got on we had not asked and they didn't tell us how far the truck was going. There wasn't anything to do except sit down, wait, and hope another truck would be by soon. We talked about how quiet it was without the noise of land mines exploding. There were so many of them. As we were sitting on the sand, we noticed small, yellow butterflies everywhere.

We didn't have to wait very long before another truck came by. The first thing we asked was how far they were going. The driver said they were going to the 98th Bomb Group. We got on the truck and in a short time we were at the base. It was good to be back.

"A Trip to Cairo That Never Happened"

When we were at Hergla, Tunisia, Lt. Keating's crew's name came up to go to Cairo, Egypt, on an R&R mission. The crew that had been there before had really enjoyed their time in Cairo. We were happy to be going. We were on the end of the runway, ready to start our take-off, when Lt. Keating received a call from the control tower not to take off. Orders had been received from General Jimmy Doolittle, Commander of the 12th Air Force, cancelling all flights to Cairo because there had been some fighting in Cairo between the GIs and the British.

Lt. Keating told us about this and said we were still going to take off and go as planned. He said he could tell them he didn't hear that message because he had turned it off. As he started to push the throttles to start the take-off, a jeep with a big red flag on it drove up, and our trip to Cairo was not to be.

"An Old Ammo Dump"

In the desert areas of North Africa there were what we called old ammo dumps. Engineers would go over the areas and collect all the explosives they could find. They had several large piles at certain designated areas. When I say large piles, I mean large. I saw a number of them from the air and also from the ground when Sgt. Rector Long and I were in a jeep going to the British mess units trying to find cinnamon for me. The engineers would post signs notifying us when the dumps were to be destroyed. A plane would fly over them and a bomb would be dropped on them. I heard some of those explosions and saw the smoke from a great distance. They made a very loud noise and a big smoke sign in the sky.

"Lt. Allan J. Cobb"

Lt. Allan J. Cobb was the co-pilot on my crew when we went overseas. He was trained to be a fighter pilot and graduated as a fighter pilot. There was a great need for bomber crews and crews had to have co-pilots. Cobb became a bomber co-pilot and a very good one.

When four members of my crew were killed on their first mission, the other six crew members were assigned to crews as they were needed. On November 11, 1943, Lt. Cobb was co-pilot on Lt. McCollum's crew. The mission was to bomb a target in southern France. The primary target was the Annecy Ball Bearing Factory in Annecy, France. The first alternate was the Villa Ball Bearing Works. The second alternate was the Turtin Fiat Engine Works, and the third alternate was the Anthear Viaduct which was used by rail and auto traffic.

We were flying out of Hergla, Tunisia, and we had to cross the Mediterranean Sea. I was a gunner on Lt. Keating's crew that day. We were flying in "Old Green I" and lost an engine on the way to the target. "Old Green I" had seen better days. There wasn't anything to do but abort the mission and return home. Our flight time was five hours, so we would have been 2.5 hours flying time on the way to the target. No combat credit was given.

Whenever we were returning to our home base alone, we were hoping not to meet any enemy planes. This target area was in the French Alps, and in the wintertime it was very cold at high altitudes. The outside temperature gauge would go down to 60 degrees below zero on the plane. I have seen it get there and stay. I don't know how we made it. It was extra cold for the waist gunners. The wind would be coming in the large open area adding to the 60 below zero temperature.

It got extra cold when our electric suits stopped working. That happened to me on two missions. A person would get so cold he couldn't control his water, and he wouldn't have any warning. It just happened. The first time my suit malfunctioned I felt a burning in my back, and the next time it was on my left elbow. There wasn't anything I could do about it. I would stay cold, but I would think about getting warm when we returned to the base.

That day Lt. Cobb's crew had to go to the third alternate target. Soon afterwards they became lost in some clouds. They were separated from the formation. When they got out of the clouds, they were attacked by two ME-109 planes and the plane's controls were shot out. They had to bail out in northern Italy. All of the crew in the front of the plane made it out, but some in the rear didn't.

Cobb had told me several times before that if he ever had to bail out, he hoped it would be near France. He could speak their language. Lt. Cobb told me he landed near the coast in northwest Italy. He wasn't injured. He hid his chute and started to look for someone to give him some help and information.

In the bomb group we had meetings on "do's and don'ts" when flying over different countries. One of the don'ts was to stay away from any house that had a telephone line going to it. Cobb found a little house and went to it. The people there were friendly and helped him. He found out he was about thirty miles from France. He traded his leather flying clothes for some old clothes, a piece of bread, and some cheese. Cobb was a heavy smoker, and he said they gave him two packs of Old Gold American cigarettes. He started walking toward France. About three o'clock on the second day he had walked about half of the thirty miles. He was whistling as he walked. We had been told in some of our meetings we should not whistle because the people of Europe do not whistle.

A group of Italian Freedom Fighters jumped him and took him up a mountain to their campsite. There were two groups of them located on two mountains with a guerrilla group on each one. The same group that got Cobb had also found Lt. Moran. Lt. Moran had injured his back when he landed in his chute. This group of partisans had dressed Moran in a German officer's uniform and taken him to a hospital where he was operated on. He was taken back to their hide-out after a few days.

The flight engineer on the crew was T/Sgt. Dale Johnson from Texas and I knew him. He had two pistols in leather holsters on a big belt on him at all times. He told me his grandpa had given them to him, and he knew how to use them. He was always proud of those guns. I told him I didn't know how he got through the bomb bays with those guns on him. He said, "Where I go, these guns go."

Lt. Cobb told me about his and Lt. Moran's time with the Italian guerrilla group. The guerrilla groups were very good to the Americans. When they got food they would serve it to the Americans first. The guerrilla fighters had a real hate and dislike for the Germans. Some of their family members had been mistreated and killed in the villages in the valley near the mountain. Lt. Cobb said he saw a hate for the Germans in the Freedom Fighters he had never seen before. It was a passionate hate - a killing hate.

The Germans had a garrison area and a supply warehouse down in the village. The guerrillas would raid the warehouse at night to get supplies. Lt. Cobb wanted to go with them, but at first they wouldn't let him. Finally, however, they agreed to let him go with them on a big raid. Cobb told me he didn't know what he was going to see but it was awful to witness. He said he had asked for it, and he got it.

Before they left camp they told him all he was to do was to watch and be quiet. Everyone put soot on their faces before they left camp. When they got to the warehouse the guerillas killed the guards on the outside of the building. They knew how many there were and where they were. The raiding party had done this before. They didn't have to tell anyone anything. Cobb went with the ones who went to the warehouse door. The guerrillas knew what to do, and when the guard opened the door, one guerrilla had a hand over the guard's mouth and a knife in his heart at the same time. The raiders backed up one of the German trucks to the loading door, and the raiding party went to work. They took food, guns, ammunition, blankets, and clothes. In a few minutes, they left and returned to their campsite. Before leaving the village they destroyed the telephone system.

Lt. Cobb told me this raid really made the Germans mad. Usually, after the small raids, the Germans would send a group of their soldiers up the mountain. The guerrillas would hide behind big stones. As the Germans moved up the mountain, the guerillas would kill them. This raid made the Germans more determined to get this group of freedom fighters off the mountain.

The Germans brought a number of small tanks into the village to use against the guerrillas. The two groups of guerrillas had runners each day to communicate with each other. A meeting was held to decide what the Americans wanted to do. Lt. Cobb and Lt. Moran wanted to try to get back to their old group, but Lt. McCullum and the others on the other mountain didn't want to leave. T/Sgt. Dale Johnson was running the group. I remember him as a slim, tall, red-haired fellow. He was known as "the two-gun man from Texas". He had done a lot of talking about his life in Texas and his shooting ability with his guns. They believed him because he had taken over as their leader and was calling all the shots for the group.

Cobb told me that there was great risk in trying to get back to the group, but he and Lt. Moran made it back okay. He visited me in my tent at Lecce on the afternoon of March 1, 1944, after his return. It was a wonderful surprise because we didn't know anything about the crew. We kept checking the Red Cross listings of POWs, but none of that crew's names were ever on them. I was wearing Cobb's dress shoes that afternoon, when he walked in my tent. He and I wore the same size - 9C. I told him I was saving them for him and keeping them warm for his return. I said I was going to polish them for him to wear back to the States. He said he would be back home soon and he would get a pair then. I thanked him as I was taking them off and started brushing them. I said, "No way. You wear them home."

He said, "I will."

He talked while I polished them and told me more about how he and Lt. Moran got to Corsica on their way back. They were put on a boat with an old engine and a sail mast on it. They left Italy one dark night headed to Corsica. The engine stopped running the first night, so they put the sail up. They got in a storm, and the sail mast broke. They had to row the boat then. There were three British soldiers and two American flyboys to row the boat. About four days and nights later they arrived at Corsica. They had made it on the first part of their journey home. Lt. Cobb was very happy to be going home and I enjoyed the time with him.

Lt. Cobb had another co-pilot friend who had been trained as a fighter pilot. He had red hair. I was told by a number of friends in the 344th squadron that when this co-pilot could get away for a few days, he would visit some of his friends in the fighter groups. He completed his 50 missions in the B-24 Bombers about the same time I did. As I was going around the 98th Group headquarters area, I would see him. I was told he wasn't going home. He had signed up for a tour with a fighter group. He wanted to fly fighter planes really bad.

"Colonel 'Killer' Kane, our 98th Commander"

This story was told to some of us about the time our Commander, Colonel "Killer" Kane, told his former crew chief, John R. Supko, to put wood platforms in a certain B-24 for him. Supko had been Colonel Kane's crew chief for his plane "Hail Columbia." The colonel informed Supko he wanted him to go to Cairo with him to get some American food for us. We were being fed by the British, and the food was bad. We got coffee once a week on Sundays at breakfast. The rest of the time it was a half-canteen cup of hot tea, some salty, dried mackerel fish or a piece of meat they called bully beef. It was a dark red, long-grained, stringy type of meat they said was Australian beef, but we called it horse meat. You could chew and chew on it for a long time, but you couldn't get it down.

Colonel Kane wanted Supko to be the flight engineer for the trip. The colonel had expectations of bringing a lot of food back to the group. Supko said they went to the supply center in Cairo and the general in charge wasn't there, so no one would let them get anything without the general's okay. Kane found out the general was in a bar somewhere in the city. Colonel Kane and Supko went from one bar to another until they found the general. Kane told the general his request for the food, but the general was drunk and replied, "You're not getting anything, because you 'fly boys' aren't doing anything."

Colonel Kane pleaded with him, but the general wouldn't change his mind. After a few moments, Colonel Kane took action. He did what he needed to do and what the general needed. He gave the general a few hits with those big fists of his, and Supko said they walked out of the bar and left the general lying on the floor. They left Cairo without any food and returned to the base. He didn't know if the colonel got in any trouble over that Cairo incident or not, but I would say Colonel Kane didn't lose any sleep over it.

Colonel Kane was a good commander for the group, and if he told Supko to have a plane ready for him the next morning, everyone would know we were going to have a big mission. The colonel didn't go on so-called easy missions. He was a leader and a very good man. He was awarded the Congressional Medal of Honor and he was a hero to all the men of the 98th group.

One time, as we were returning to our base in Tunisia flying over the southern part of Italy, a plane left our squadron formation. No one knew the reason. There wasn't any flak and there were no enemy attack planes around, so their leaving was a mystery to us. The Allies had control of a section of the southern part of Italy, but we didn't know where the bomb line was. We continued our trip to base.

Three or four days later, we found out the reason for the plane leaving us. We didn't have a mission on the day when the cause of the disappearance of the plane was revealed. About midday on that day we heard a plane coming. We went out of our tents to see what plane it was and we saw the B-24. We got a buzz job. The B-24 came back over our tent area again and it was flying fast and low. It almost blew our tents away. We hurried out to the landing area to meet it and see what the reason was for their leaving the formation three days prior.

The pilot spoke for the crew and told us why they had left. They had to have a break from the war. They had picked an area where they could land the plane close to a town. They must have done their homework well in selecting a safe place to stop off and enjoy themselves. They said they had a good time, and I'm not saying most of the crew was drunk, but they weren't feeling any pain. I don't know if they were punished for their escapade or not, but I'm sure they at least got a very strong reprimand by the squadron and group commanders.

"More about Colonel Kane"

A master sergeant from the 344th squadron of the 98th bomb group was given a promotion to officer and was moved up to the 47th wing of the 15th Air Force. He worked in the office where the missions were selected and planned. He had been in the 98th group for a very long time and had a lot of old-time friends in the 344th squadron. He would come by to visit with them whenever he could. He was a very good and smart man; he had been promoted to captain in September, 1943. All of his friends spoke well of him and he wouldn't let his officer's rank keep him from visiting with the sergeants.

He told his friends about Colonel Kane's behavior at some of the planning sessions. He told about some of the general's remarks and how Kane's suggestions were being ignored. He could see Colonel Kane getting mad and could tell the Colonel had about all he could take. Kane would get up and pound the table with one of his big fists and tell them off and leave. He would tell them they didn't know what they were talking about, and he wasn't staying any longer. He'd say, "When you have all the plans completed, let me know and the 98th will be there and we will do our part. We always have and we always will." He would leave and return to his group.

Such a story might explain why he never received a general's rank. He was a great leader and dedicated to his missions and to the men under his command. The Army Air Corps needed to get the B-29 bombers into the war in the Pacific, so Colonel Kane left the 98th bomb group on November 1, 1943, to return to the States to help in that project. He never went on the so-called "easy ones." He led the group on the "Big Ones." I heard him make his farewell speech to the group. We knew we would never have another commander like him. He was the only "Killer Kane."

Lieutenant Colonel Julian Bleyer (0-22423) took temporary command of the group until Colonel William Karnes arrived and took over as commander on November 18, 1943.

"The Tragedy of Colonel William Karnes and His Crew"

On January 13, 1944, plane # 782P, crashed on take-off, and our group commander, Col. William E. Karnes, the navigator, Lt. Dwire, the bombardier, Lt. Dewar, and the radio operator, Sgt. O'Keefe were killed. My friend, flight engineer Blackmon, got an arm and leg broken and his back injured when the top gun turret hit him.

We were never told what caused this plane accident. The runway at Manduria, Italy, had a high raised place on it. When a pilot would think his plane was air-borne, it would drop down on the runway for a time before it actually became air-borne. We thought the landing wheel lever had been moved too soon. Accidents will happen. This plane was from the 343rd squadron.

Those killed were buried the next day at the U.S. Cemetery at Bari. A flight of eighteen bombers flew over the cemetery in salute. Lt. Col. Marshall R. Gray, the group deputy commander, assumed control of the group.

Chapter 8

BRINDISI, ITALY

"Our Time at Brindisi"

One afternoon when I was at Brindisi, Burns, DiBenedetto (Dim-Dom) and I decided to go into the city and look it over. We had been told by some of the crew to go to the harbor area and get one of the rowboat men to take us across the harbor. They told us it would cost one dollar for each of us, but it would save a lot of walking. So, that is what we did.

We looked in a number of stores and came to a wine shop. The Italians call it "Vino". There wasn't any bottled soda drinks there then. They told us to stay away from drinking the water except at the base. They had grape juice and two kinds of fermented wine in the shop. Dim-Dom and I drank the plain wine, but Burns ordered the strong wine.

The wine shop was small. It was about mid-afternoon, but it became dark in the shop. We looked at the doorway, and we saw the reason it had become dark. There stood five large dark-skinned British soldiers with turbans on their heads and a waistband around their middles the same color as the turbans. Each one had a long, curved machete type knife in his waistband. The men must have been over six feet tall. I remembered the big man in "Little Orphan Annie" who carried the big knife in his waistband all the time. They reminded me of him.

After they ordered their drinks, one of them came over to us and introduced himself. He told us who they were. They were from India and were in the British Army. He told us the soldier with the purple turban and waistband was a maharajah and ruled a certain area in India. He told us not to pay for anything while the maharajah was in the shop. He said no one pays for anything but him. Then he told us more about the maharajah. He said he was an educated man who could speak seven languages. He said he could speak five languages himself. He told us he and the other three men were under the maharajah and ruled smaller areas. All of them came over to talk to us, and they were very friendly.

They asked us all kinds of questions about our missions and our flying at high altitudes all the time. We noticed they had diamonds and rubies on all their fingers. The maharajah wrote his name and address on a paper and gave it to each of us with an invitation to come and visit him if we survived the war. He told us he would take us on a tiger hunt using elephants to ride instead of walking. We all thanked him for the drinks and his invitation to carry us on a tiger hunt.

Burns asked one of them to let him see his big knife. The Indian soldier took the knife out of his waistband and handed it to Burns. Burns looked it over and gave it back to the man. The man took it and cut his finger a little bit. We asked him why he did that and he said, "That's what we believe. We draw blood every time we take the knife out."

We asked Burns if the knife was sharp, and he said it was.

After the Indians left, Dim-Dom and I were ready to leave, but Burns told us he wasn't ready. We told him to take care and not to drink too much wine. We left and returned to the base. We were sleeping on the third floor in the large administration building at the base. About 11:30 that night, Burns woke me up and told me he needed me to help him. I got up and got him to a light to see what his trouble was. His right eye was closed and his face was black and blue.

I asked what had happened to him, and he said he would tell me later. He wanted me to go to the mess sergeant and tell him he needed a large piece of red meat for his eye. I told Burns I didn't know where the mess sergeant's bunk was, and Burns said it was in the kitchen area. I went to the kitchen and returned with the meat. I helped Burns undress and get in his bunk. I told Burns he needed to lie on his back and stay there with the meat on his face. I told him he could tell me about the fight the next morning. He said there wasn't a fight.

The next morning Burns's face was something to see. I told him Dim-Dom and I had asked him to leave with us, but he wouldn't. He told me what had happened to him. He hadn't caused any trouble to anyone. He said about 5:00 that evening a British "Red Cap" (British Military Policeman) came in the wine shop and walked up to him and told him it was time for him to leave. Burns asked him why he had to leave. He didn't have to have a pass, and there wasn't a curfew.

There was no love between the British military and the Americans. The Red Caps were always six feet tall or taller. The Red Cap told Burns he didn't have to have a reason other than to tell him to leave. Burns said the Red Cap left and returned about ten minutes later with another Red Cap. Burns told me he looked at them and said, "I don't think I can fight both of you. I will leave now."

One of them told Burns he was arresting him. Burns said okay and started walking to the doorway. One of the Red Caps twisted Burns's arm hard, and Burns asked him to ease up. The Red Cap gave it a greater twist then. Burns was a muscular man with big arms and legs. He told the Red Cap again to ease up on his twist, and again he made it tighter. As he twisted it more, Burns told me he gave a quick move and broke free from the Red Cap's hold on him. At that moment Burns turned, jumped in front of him and at the same time, kicked the man hard in the private area of his body.

The man fell to the ground hollering. Burns walked to their small truck and sat down. The other Red Cap was trying to help his partner. After a few minutes, the man Burns had kicked got up and came to the back of the truck. The truck had no hard top on it, just a canvas cover for a top. The man wanted to get revenge, and Burns didn't know the man was going to hit him until he felt the blow. Burns told me that man sure knew how to hit a man in the face.

The Red Cap put Burns in the British jail and wouldn't let him call the squadron. About 10:00 that night, Burns got them to bring him to the squadron. They turned Burns over to the "Officer of the Day" who was a major and a flying man. The major knew Burns and asked him why the Red Caps had him. Burns told him the whole story. The major asked him if he could get to his bunk, and Burns said he could. The officer told Burns to go to his bunk.

The Red Cap asked the major why he didn't put Burns in the brig. The major got mad and told the Red Cap not to question his decision about Burns. He told him to leave, or he would put him in the brig.

Burns's face was a bad face to look at the next day. His right eye was completely closed, and it was black and blue for several days. A number of the men said the meat he put on his face was the best thing Burns could have done for it. My reply was the best thing Burns could have done was to leave with Dim-Dom and me and not to have stayed in the wine shop alone. After a few weeks Burns's face returned to normal.

"Staff Sgt. Dominic T. DeBennetto – 'Dim-Dom'"

S/Sgt. DiBenedetto and I became close friends in the service and continued that relationship after we came back to the States. His father and mother were born in Italy, and they spoke Italian in their home. Dim-Dom used the Italian language all the time off the base when we were in Italy. When he and I were in town, he was the spokesman for us. He got us an invitation for an evening meal with an elderly couple we had met in Brindisi.

I got to see how they baked their bread. They had a large fireplace in their kitchen with a flat stone in it. The mother prepared the bread dough and brushed off the stone. Then she put the bread on the hot stone and covered it with hot charcoals. The mother did everything for the meal except make the sauce for the macaroni and meatballs. Dim-Dom told me making the sauce was always the father's job. I saw some of the macaroni hanging across two lines drying. We had a good meal.

Before we left the home we gave them some money for our meal. They didn't want to take it, but we asked them to accept it with our thanks for a good meal and their hospitality. I'm sure they had gone out of their way to provide us with that meal.

Before we left Brindisi, Dim-Dom and I went into the city for a noon meal in the largest restaurant there. He had found out which one was the finest Italian eating place there. We arrived at the restaurant about 11:30 that morning and were seated at our table immediately. I could see and feel this was a very fine eating place. I asked Dim-Dom if we were out of our price range by having a meal at such a place as this. He said the ticket would not be too expensive for us, and it wasn't.

I told Dim-Dom I knew I was in the wrong place, because I couldn't read the menu. He said he could order for me, if I wanted him to. I asked him what he was ordering. He said he was going to get a small baked chicken. I told him that would be fine for me, too. We ate our meal, and Dim-Dom said to me, "Jeff, I'm going to tell you something, and I don't want you mad at me. Italians clean the outside of a chicken, bake it, and then take the insides out."

I had noticed the baked chicken was extra dark on the inside and that explained why. I told Dim-Dom I had always been told what you didn't know wouldn't hurt you, but I wondered why he waited to tell me about it until after I had eaten the chicken. I told him I was not mad at him, but I was disappointed in him for not telling me before he ordered my meal. I told him the Italians were certainly different in their cooking from where I came from. We paid for our meal and left the restaurant. I didn't get sick from that meal, and I was thankful for that.

We were outside the building and saw a large group of Italian P.O.W. troops marching by. Dim-Dom said to them in a loud voice, with his head tilted back and his right arm held upward, "Mussollini buono, Mussolini molto buono".

I asked Dim-Dom what it meant. He told me it meant, good and very good. I told him it was very bad to taunt those soldiers like he did. They had been defeated, and they were now marching to a P.O.W. prison. He told me they needed those words. Dim-Dom and I returned to the base.

"A Visit to an Italian Monastery"

While I was in Brindisi, Italy, I heard about an old monastery located near us. I was told it was a strange place to see. Little monks lived there among mummies hanging on the wall in one of the large buildings. One day we didn't have a mission, so two of my friends and I decided to visit it.

We arrived and picked out the building we thought was the one we wanted to see. It was an old, ivy-covered building with a large front door. There was a small bell hanging on a bracket by the door. One of us pulled the bell rope. We waited a long time before the door was opened. There was a small man wearing a long robe standing there. One of the GIs could speak their language well, so we let him do the talking for us. I didn't think they would ever stop talking and moving their arms and hands at each other. At last he turned to us and said the monk would allow only one of us at a time to go inside. He asked us who wanted to go first. I wasn't sure I wanted to go inside without my friends with me, so I told him to go first. The other friend said that would be okay with him, so we were left outside as the door was shut.

We talked about how strange the little monk looked, how he acted, and how he wouldn't let us go inside as a group. Time passed and our friend hadn't come out. We didn't know anything to do but wait, and so we did. We decided we didn't want to go inside that building. All we wanted was for our friend to return to us.

He came out about an hour later. We wanted to leave, so we returned to Brindisi. On our way back to base, our friend who had gone inside with the monk told us about his visit with him. It was a strange and frightening experience for him. He was glad to get out of that building. He told us it was dark inside. The only light was a small candle the monk held in his hand. All around the room on the walls were small skeletons with a white shroud on each one. He said the monk would stop at each skeleton and say something to it. At some of them, he would lift up the shroud and tap the bones with a small metal object he took out of his pocket. Our friend thought it was a small knife. It was so dark in there he couldn't see. At times, the monk would turn and look up at him and give him a big smile.

My friend thought he was a strange character. He was glad when they finished all four walls, and he could get out of that building.

We were satisfied to tell the others back at the base that only one of us who went to the monastery went inside. The other two, which included me, chickened out.

"A Sergeant Named Louie"

After I was assigned to the 344th Squadron, I noticed a buck sergeant doing odd jobs around the squadron area. He was always happy and smiling. I asked one of the old timers about the sergeant who everyone called Louie and what his job was. He said Louie didn't have a job assigned to him; he did what he wanted to do and no one bothered him. He said Louie's mind was not right.

Let me tell you about Louie. He was a gunner on a combat crew whose plane crashed on take-off. All the crew survived except the first pilot who was penned in his seat and couldn't get out. The plane was on fire, and the pilot wanted someone to shoot him. All the crew could do was watch and listen to the burning man's call for help.

The plane had a full load of gas. It was a terrible accident to witness and Louie couldn't take it. The squadron took one grade in rank from him and allowed Louie to go about doing what he wanted to do. Whenever anyone called for Louie, he would come.

I remember one of Louie's episodes and how he handled the men using him. There was a USO show that came to the 98th Group in the spring of 1944. It was early in the evening and I was there. Part of the show was an escape artist act. The escape artist called for someone in the audience to come up and tie him up. At once there was a call for Louie to come forward. Louie came and went to work tying the man up. Louie asked the men for suggestions on where to go next with the rope. They told him and Louie did as they told him to do. I thought Louie had done a good job, and I couldn't see how the escape artist could get out of all that rope. The men were really in this along with Louie.

When Louie finished, the man broke free in a few minutes. The men blamed Louie for not doing a good job and Louie blamed them for not telling him how to tie the man. They went at each other until the escape artist stopped them and told everyone there was only one way he could not have gotten free. He told the men to never forget it. He said the only way he could not have gotten free was for Louie to have tied both of his hands to his feet. Louie laughed at the men and told them they didn't tell him to do that. Everyone had a big laugh at Louie and we enjoyed the rest of the show.

It was sad to see Louie in his condition, but if we looked at it another way, the Lord had blessed Louie. He was happy and laughing all the time. No one was telling him what to do. He was alive and in good health and doing what he wanted to do when he wanted to do it.

"An Ancient Roman Arena"

When we were in Brindisi, Italy, a few of us decided to visit an old Roman arena we had heard about. All the time I was overseas, we didn't have to have a pass to go anywhere at any time, night or day, as long as we did our job in our crew. We arrived about 10:00 that morning. We were surprised to see it was in such good condition after so many years.

It was built in a low area between two hills with stone seats placed on the hillsides. At the front part of the arena was the seating area for the dignitaries. This area was high up and over cages where the wild animals and prisoners were kept. Out in the middle was a large stone post set in the ground. We went into the cages and out into the middle of the open area and looked up to the viewing sections and the stone seats. I touched the center post and imagined what it would have been like to see those wild animals coming out of those cages while I was tied to the post waiting to be eaten by them. That must have been some kind of entertainment.

I have read that the Roman emperors wanted only two things from the people. They wanted them to pay taxes and not cause any trouble of any kind. To help the emperors accomplish this, the people were given free bread and entertained. Have we changed? I don't think so. The people in this country need to change before it is too late.

"Our Little 'Pearl Harbor'"

In late afternoon on December 2, 1943, the air raid alarm went off, and we rushed to a walk-in underground shelter. The shelter was open at each end and was long in length. It was about the length of a football field. In a short time, we heard bombs exploding. Someone came and told us the German planes were bombing the harbor docks at Bari, Italy. They had come in low under the radar, before they were detected. The bomb explosions continued for a long time. Someone came and told us to go to our rooms and stay inside with windows and doors shut.

A U.S. ship loaded with mustard gas was at the docks at Bari. The gas was to be used by the Allies, if Hitler started using such gas. Approximately an hour later we received an all clear notice. The wind had carried the gas away from land. The gas was heavier than air, so it settled in the Adriatic Sea and didn't do any harm to anyone.

Bari was about 60 miles north of us at Brindisi. At that time, I was a gunner on Lt. Keating's crew. He was the operations officer for the 344th Squadron. On December 3rd we went on a mission to bomb an airfield at Rome. That was only about a five hour mission, so we were back at Brindisi about noon. Lt. Keating told us we were going on a sight-seeing trip that afternoon. We were going to check on the damage the bombing had done to Bari.

We flew to Bari, and the dock area was a sight to see. Sunken ships were everywhere. Seventeen ships - I counted them. The 343rd Squadron of our 98th group had just arrived that day. They lost four men and all of the ground men's barracks bags. We called Bari "The Little Pearl Harbor".

All of those ships were at the docks at the same time. That's war - killing people and destroying things.

There was a request made of the other squadrons (the 344th, 345th, and 415th) in the group to donate one piece of clothing to the 343rd until the supply department could get some clothes in for the men. Everyone was willing to help.

On our return flight from Bari we talked about what we had seen, and we all asked, "Why were all the ships lined up at the docks at the same time?" Someone had made a bad call.

"The Group's P-40 Plane"

The 98th Group had a P-40 plane Col. Kane used to help the group planes get in their positions when they were forming after take-offs. He would fly around and help them get assembled in their attack formations. A number of the co-pilots were fighter pilots who were put on crews as co-pilots, and they didn't want to be the co-pilots. They could fly in the P-40 plane and enjoy it, but old bomber pilots wanted to fly the P-40, also.

In the afternoon of December 9, 1943, one of the older pilots had the group's P-40 up and couldn't land it. After several times trying to land the plane, he wrecked it with almost everyone in the group watching him. I'm sure it was an embarrassing situation for him, and the group lost a P-40. The best thing that happened was the pilot walked away from the wreck without being hurt.

"The British Squadron"

When the bomb group was at Brindisi, there was a squadron of British Spitfire planes there. They were located across the runway from us. The

British were assigned the responsibility of protecting the east coast line of Italy, and the Americans had the west side. The base was too small for the group of bombers, but we had to stay there until another place was made ready for us. Each day about noon we could hear one or two planes come over the base.\We couldn't see them, but we were told they were German reconnaissance planes. Two of the Spitfires would take off and stay gone for a while. Sometimes while we were at the base, we would go over and get a report when they returned. A number of times they told us the Germans were gone by the time they had gotten up to their altitude, but one time they told us they had shot down two of the planes.

We were having trouble with the Spits ourselves. While we were getting into our proper positions in our formation after take-off, the Spitfire pilots would make simulated attacks on our planes for practice. It was dangerous for the bombers, and some of the gunners wanted to take care of the trouble the Spits were causing, but the group commander said he would stop it.

He told them to stop those practice attacks. They stopped for a few days but started doing the practice again. A day or two later when I wasn't on a mission, I was outside and saw a Spit with only one landing gear down coming in for a landing. I was close to the runway and saw what happened.

The pilot made a very good one-wheel landing until the plane was almost stopped. The wing touched the runway and spun the plane around. A few of us were close to where the plane stopped. We were at the plane while the pilot was still in it. We asked him if he needed help to get out, and he said no. As he was getting out, we asked him what happened. He said to us, "One of your bloody Lightings shot me!"

The P-38 Lighting plane has plenty of guns. It has a 20 mm cannon and four .50 caliber guns in the nose of it.

I knew the group commander had taught the British Spitfire Squadron a lesson. We told the Spitfire pilot he was lucky he wasn't killed, and we were sure his squadron would know not to do those simulated attacks again. They didn't.

" A Friend From Another Crew"

In the 344th Squadron there was a radioman from another crew who was a good friend to me. He told me the squadron commander had asked him to be the radio operator for him, especially when he had to go on some overnight trips from our base. He also wanted him to learn to do some flight engineer's jobs. He asked me if I would help him. I told him I would and I did.

He was a very good radio operator and he became a good engineer. He told me about two trips he went on that were bad experiences for him. The crew he was on left the base late one evening to fly to Naples, Italy, and arrived over the city about 8:00 that night. As they were directly over the city, there were German bombers above them who started bombing the city. The American guns on the ground were shooting up at the German planes and they were caught in the middle with nowhere to go. The B-24 plane wasn't damaged. He told me they were glad when they got on the ground that night.

The other episode happened at Lecce, Italy, when we were still stationed at Manduria. The squadron commander wanted to go to Lecce to check on some repairs being done on some of the buildings before we moved there. They had to stay over that night and my friend was told to pick out a bunk in one of the barracks, so he did.

The bunks were double with only mattresses on them. He said he checked one of them out and chose a top bunk in a row of bunks on the right side of the building. He was the only one in the barracks that night. Because there were no lights in the barracks, he got in his bunk when it got dark and went to sleep. He woke up when he heard a plane flying low over the base about 5:00 o'clock the next morning. He sat up on his bunk and saw and heard machine gun bullets making holes in the left side of the building. He knew then he had chosen the right bunk the evening before.

He said he thought it was an ME-109 giving them a wake-up call. I told him I thought he had better quit his job as the squadron radioman before he got killed. He did.

"The Bomb Bay Door Incident"

On one of my missions, I had to decide what to do when the left rear bomb bay door didn't open. We had a bomb bay door control lever in the flight deck that the engineer used to operate the doors as we turned on the bomb run. We had six 1,000 pound bombs on the plane. There were two bombs in each front bay and one bomb in each rear bay. They were the type bombs that had the new delayed action fuses on them. They would explode when fuses were being removed. We couldn't carry them back to the base, so I told the crew we needed to drop all the bombs on the target. I suggested we let the bomb carry that left door down with the bomb load. All agreed. In a few minutes, the bombardier said, "Bombs away". We dropped all the bombs on the target, but the door didn't leave the plane. It was flopping on the side of the plane, held only by the top part of the door. I told all on the intercom I would do something as soon as we could let down and come off oxygen. I did not know how I would fasten that door, but I knew I had to do it. I tried to come up with a plan but could not.

As we were coming down, I came up with the idea of using a gun cleaning rod and some safety wire. With a lot of luck I might be able to hook one end of the door. Success depended on the strength of the wire and my patience in trying to pull the door up after it was hooked. After we were off oxygen, I went to the back part of the plane and told them about my plan. I told them I needed their help in getting the door tied up soon. It was flopping bad and fast. I got the cleaning rod and the wire ready and talked with the crew about what I wanted them to do. I had to get out of the back section of the plane, kneel down on the catwalk, and try to hook the lower back corner of the door. I had my chute harness on but no chute. I wanted one of the crew to reach out of the back section of the plane and hold onto my harness. I wanted another man to hold onto the man who was holding onto me.

We were ready to go to work. I had one of the crew call the pilot and tell him to try to keep the plane as level as possible. We started the plan, and I was surprised how well it worked. I hooked the rear corner on the first try. I passed the rod and wire to one of the crew in the back and told him to just hold it. I told him not to try to pull the door up. I said I wanted to get off the catwalk and get back into the rear section of the plane. I was glad to get off my knees and to stand up for a little while before I tried to pull the rod and wire up. I told all of them to do as I had told them, and that now we were going to finish it.

I stayed inside the back and reached through the doorway with one of the crew holding onto me. I pulled easy on the wire and in a little while I had the wire tied to the catwalk and one of the bomb rack support posts. Then I took the roll of safety wire and pliers to the front end of the door. I put one of my legs around the center support post, and I tied the front end of the door to the center post. Next, I went to the front and told the pilots the door was up and tied.

I was glad to get the door tied. I went to the rear and thanked all the men for their help. We returned to the base, and I showed the crew chief what we did to his plane. After a bad mission, it was good to be back at the base and to get another mission credit.

Chapter 9

MANDURIA, ITALY

"Episodes at Manduria"

We left Brindisi and arrived in Manduria, Italy, on December 20, 1943. We left Manduria on January 18, 1944. During our stay, there was rain, rain, rain, and more rain. This created mud everywhere. The 344th Squadron was put in tents in a large olive grove. Olive trees were everywhere. The mud would stick on our shoes and keep building up until we would have to stop and get it off. We had a combat mission on December 25, 1943, and missed our Christmas meal. We had our K-ration and enjoyed it.

As we were walking from the flight line one afternoon we were caught up in a fireworks display. As we entered the tent area, we saw red, yellow, and green flares going everywhere. We were told to help keep them off the tents. Someone had let a fire start in the tent where the flares were stored. That was a sight to see. A few tents were damaged, but it was soon over.

Around the 30th of December 1943, we were told that all January 1944 flights would be pilot formation flying and bombardiers' practicing bombing missions. There would be no combat missions in January. We heard they were waiting for new groups to arrive.

On January 5, 1943, Lt. Col. Marshall R. Gray was appointed Deputy Group Commander.

There had been some German guns left behind at Benghazi, and a lot of them had been around our area at Hergla, Tunisia, too. Our base area at Hergla was close to the Mediterranean Sea, which was where some of the German forces left North Africa. We called the confiscated guns, "The German Zip Guns". Each gun had a steel rod and a curved steel strap welded on it instead of a wood stock. It was the German's carbine and it could spit ammo out fast. Some of the men had brought these guns with them to Manduria. They also brought plenty of ammo because there were plenty of boxes of guns and ammo left in the sand dunes there in Hergla. In Manduria there was a crew that had one man who would get a kick out of shooting his gun inside the tent. A number of times at night he would drink Italian wine and shoot a number of holes in the tent. I do not know how many tent holes he had to patch or how many tents he had to buy. We had a wood floor in our tent, and when he started shooting, we would roll off our cots and hit the floor. We would lie on the floor until he stopped shooting.

The squadron had an executive officer, Captain Fred S. Lear, whose actions weren't enjoyed by all of the enlisted men. A day or two before

December 31st, Captain Lear had a notice posted on the bulletin board that said there would be no shooting anymore, especially on New Year's Eve. To make matters worse, he said he was going to enforce the "no-shooting order" himself. That notice shouldn't have been put up. He should have called a meeting and asked the men to stop shooting. The captain was asking for trouble, and he got it.

At once the plans were made to welcome Captain Lear to the real world. The men had a trap set and ready. I knew about it, but in the Army you didn't tell on anyone. About 8:00 p.m. on New Year's Eve, Captain Lear started on his first patrol. Each tent had someone watching for the Captain all the time. When he was at the right spot – by a big watery mud hole - a gun started shooting, and the captain fell to the ground. The GI shooting the gun was shooting the ammo up into the sky, but the noise was something to hear; there were two or three blasts and it was over. It was a good lesson for all. We know the captain got off the ground and rushed back to his tent. I'm sure his patrol duty was over for the night, and it was the last time we had the "zip gun" shooting up the tents.

"General 'Hap' Arnold's Letter to Combat Crews"

Near the end of December, 1943, there was a copy of a letter sent to all the crews in Europe, telling us what we had to do. This was the message General "Hap" Arnold wanted us to hear. A copy of the letter was put on the squadron bulletin board for all to see as follows:

> Before an invasion of Europe can begin, the German Luftwaffe has to be destroyed. Effective immediately, weather permitting, the primary target each day will be an aircraft factory. The Army Air Corps is in a position to lose a four engine bomber with a crew of ten for each plane that Germany has.

Someone wrote at the bottom of the letter the following words: "You Are Expendable". The words someone wrote were appropriate for ending the general's message, which, as far as messages go, certainly wasn't a morale booster.

"A Bad Gunner"

One afternoon I was told the squadron operations officer wanted to see me. I went to see him and he asked me if I would go on a mission the next day with a crew that needed a flight engineer. The crew's engineer was sick, so I told him I would go. I was trying to finish my combat tour and the operations office had been helping me. I had heard about that crew's left waist gunner's reputation – that his gun was "out of service" on a number of missions. I left the operations office and went to that gunner's tent to have a talk with him. I told him I was going to be their engineer the next day and I wanted all guns operating.

"Is your gun ready to go?" I asked. "If not, get out to the plane and clean it now. I know your reputation. I mean what I say. If your gun goes out tomorrow, you'll be in trouble. I will toss you out of the plane. I mean it! You're a no-good man for your crew and I'm giving you good warning."

He assured me his gun was clean and ready to go. There were two or three of his crew who were in the tent and heard me talking to him. I told them they should have kicked him off the crew a long time ago.

We took off on the mission the next day and were hit with fighters approximately thirty minutes before we got to the target. We were flying left wing to the lead plane of the group, and the fighters were hitting us from the left of the formation. The left waist gunner got off one short burst of shots from his gun and it stopped. He called out on the intercom that his gun was out and for the top or ball gunner to take care of the left side. That was impossible because the fighters were attacking us at the same altitude we were flying. Some of the gunners on the plane came on the intercom to me and said they would help me throw him out, if I was ready. I told them I had changed my plans. I was going to make a gunner out of him and teach him how to clean his gun. I don't remember his name, but I do remember his hometown. He was from Cleveland, Ohio.

After we got back to base, there were a number of things the flight engineer had to do. I didn't go to the briefing with the crews, but I had to fill out the log records and talk with the crew chief about things on the plane.

I had told the waist gunner not to leave the plane with the others, but to start cleaning his gun and I would get with him in a little while. He informed me I was not his boss. I told him a few things, and then I sat him down and gave him some good advice. I told him if we would have had to come back alone with his gun out, we might not have made it back. He not only let his crew down, but also himself. It takes a crew working together to be a good combat crew. Then I told him to clean and oil his gun, and call me when he finished with it and I would look it over. He said he would and he did. He did a good job on the gun, and I told him to do that kind of cleaning and oiling job after every mission. We shook hands and he thanked me for helping him. I never flew with that crew again.

"Goering's 'Yellow Belly' Squadron"

Herman Goering was a German Air Ace in the German Army and was Hitler's close associate and advisor during World War II. He had his personal group of pilots and planes which we called Goering's "Yellow Belly Squadron". You had to be an "Ace of Aces" to become a pilot in this group. We heard that a German pilot had to have 100 credits to join this elite group of pilots. A credit was earned by the number of engines on any plane a pilot shot down. I don't know if that was true or not. I do know the "Yellow Belly" pilots were excellent pilots. That's not just what I heard – that's what I saw. They had new planes (ME-109's) with the underside of the fuselages and prop spinners painted yellow. That was their trademark.

I admired them when we met up with them on a mission to a target in Romania or Bulgaria.

It was about 8:30 one morning and we were being escorted by the P-38's. They saw us part of the way to the target and about nine o'clock they left us. They met back with us about three o'clock that afternoon to escort us back home. Our P-38 escort planes were close to us on our left. The ME-109's could have waited until our escorts left us and then attacked them or us, but they didn't. They took on our P-38 escorts and the bombers at the same time. That is why I said I admired them.

They took on every P-38, man-to-man, and the ME-109's that didn't have a P-38, attacked the bombers. They made frontal attacks on the lead planes of each attack formation. This was before we had planes with front gun turrets. I was a right waist gunner on the lead plane of the 98th Group that day, and the only time I could shoot at them was when they were diving down between our plane and our right wing plane. They attacked us at a place where the top turret or the ball turret guns couldn't shoot at them. On one of their passes at us, I saw the pilot throw his hand up as he went by. We were in a close formation and they would tilt their wings to get through. That day I saw one of them fly head-on into a B-24 creating a big ball of fire.

I couldn't keep from looking at the dog fights going on at our left. There were planes falling and parachutes in the air everywhere. I don't know how the P-38's did against Goering's Yellow Belly pilots, but from what I saw, I would call it a draw. Both sides had all they wanted and knew they had been in a good fight.

"A Waist Gunner on Another Crew"

I had a friend on another crew who was a waist gunner; his last name was Brown. He and I became close friends, but I have forgotten his first name. When I was in the Army we didn't use first names. Brown and I were together at Manduria, Italy, in December, 1943. Not far from the dirt strip with steel matting on each end that we used for a runway, crews were camped in large tents.

Late one afternoon, one of Brown's crew members came to our tent and asked me to come outside. He had something to talk about with me and he didn't want my crew members to hear it. We went outside and he told me about Brown needing to quit combat missions. The crew knew it, but Brown wouldn't do it. The crew knew I was a friend of Brown's and they wanted me to talk to him about quitting. I told him the crew was in a better position to get Brown to quit than I was, but if they thought I could help Brown, I would try.

I went to Brown's tent and got him out of the crew's tent and had a long talk with him. I explained to him that God didn't make all of us alike. "We all are unique individuals. Some can take combat where others can't. It's just that simple. I'll go with you to operations, if you want me to, and explain you want to call it quits. Brown, no one will say anything to you about it. They'll find you a job in the squadron. You won't be the first or the last to quit combat missions. Your crew wants you to quit."

Brown told me he appreciated me talking to him and he would make up his mind in a few days. I told him not to wait a few days, but to do it right then. I checked with him a day or two after that, and he told me he hadn't made up his mind yet. I tried to get him to go with me to the operations office, and I would tell them he wanted to quit, but he said he didn't know yet. I told some of the crew I had failed. I told them I was sorry.

A few days later, one of Brown's crew came to my tent and told me Brown had sent him to tell me to come to their tent. He was going to tell them something and he wanted me there. I was sure he wanted me to go with him to operations and quit. I was wrong. His crew and I were in a group outside their tent, with Brown in the center talking to us, when he made this statement. "I'm going on the mission tomorrow and that's my last one."

I think I was the next one to speak and I said, "No, Brown, don't go tomorrow. Come on, let's go to operations and you can call it quits today."

He answered, "No, I'm going tomorrow and that will be my last mission. My mind is made up." He thanked us for trying to help him and told us again the next day would be his last mission.

I wasn't on the mission that day, and Brown's crew was the first plane in for landing that afternoon. They had shot a red flare when the group arrived at the base. That was the signal to let them land first because there was a wounded or dead crew member on the plane. When I wasn't on a mission, I would always check with the operations clerk to find out how many planes the squadron sent off that day. Most of the time, I would go out to the landing strip and count the planes as they returned. When I would see a red signal, I would run to where the ambulance was to see who was hurt or dead.

That day the ambulance men went into the plane and in a few minutes, they had the stretcher with Brown on it coming out the right waist window. That was the reddest blood I have ever seen. He had a hole right over his heart. The left waist gunner told me the planes had hit them before they got to the target and Brown was hit on the first pass. The cannon shot went through Brown's body and out the left waist window. No other crew member was injured that day. Brown was killed instantly. I was glad he didn't have to suffer a long time with a lot of pain. I did a bad job of getting Brown to stop combat missions. I told his crew I didn't do a good job. They told me I shouldn't feel that way. They had tried and failed. They said to me, "You tried." Did Brown know that mission was to be his last? Only God knows. There is a time to be born and a time to die. That I believe.

"Almost Going to Switzerland"

On one of the missions to a target in Germany, the squadron operations officer asked me to go with a crew as the flight engineer. I had been with this crew on missions before, so I said okay. I never went to briefings when I was going as the engineer, but I went to the plane to talk with the crew chief and to do the pre-flight checks. There were no two planes alike. They had their different characteristics, just as humans do - no two alike. They may have looked alike, but they were different.

The crew arrived about the time I finished the pre-flight checks. The pilot came to me and told me he needed to speak to me in private. We got away from the plane and he informed me we wouldn't be coming back to the base that evening. Before he could tell me anything else, I asked why.

He said we would be landing in Switzerland that day. He told me they had been planning to do this for some time and today was the day. We would be close to Switzerland on the way to the target and we would pretend to blow an engine to have an excuse to go there. He told me he had told the crew they owed it to me to tell me their plan. Many things went through my mind all at the same time. I was in a bad situation and I had to come up with something fast. He said the crew was tired of the war and they wanted out and this would be the day. I told him this was not the thing to do and they would get in trouble with the group and the 15th Air Force. He told me I had time to tell operations I didn't want to go on the mission that day. I asked him what time take-off was and he looked at his watch and said, "Ten minutes."

My answer was, "There's not time enough to do anything, but for me to go on as planned."

I had many thoughts about my decision. I didn't make or accept the plan, and if I hadn't gone on the mission, the crew might have been courtmartialed. I told the pilot I was thankful he told me about the plan, but he didn't give me much time. It turned out okay in the end. The Lord took control of things, as He always does.

About ten o'clock that morning, the radioman on the crew got the bends and told me he was sick. I told him to lie on the flight floor and relax. We had been on oxygen about two and a half hours and he was in a bad condition. His knees were drawn up to his stomach and he told me he thought he was going to die. I talked to the pilot and co-pilot about him and they told me to do something to help him. I told them I had been doing all I knew to do, but I would try again. I tried to straighten him out and put him on his back, but I couldn't help him. He said again he was going to die. I told both pilots I had heard about the bends and all I knew to do was to let down and let him come off the oxygen.

That's when the co-pilot made me mad by telling me I was messing up their plan. I told him to get off my back and tend to the radioman himself. I told both pilots I had nothing to do with their plan and I pointed to the radioman in a balled up position on the floor of the flight deck and said,

"You two tend to him. I've done everything I know to do and I don't want anyone to talk to me about it anymore."

The co-pilot got out of his seat and tried to help the man to lie flat on the floor and be quiet. The co-pilot couldn't do any more than I had done. He spoke to the pilot and they decided to leave the formation and drop down and return to base. All of this talking on the intercom didn't bring forth any comments from any of the other crew members. They didn't say anything about it while it was going on or after we turned back and let down. I didn't tell anyone about that day and I didn't make any notes about it. I don't remember any names of the crew and that's a good thing, but it did happen. The radioman was taken off flying status and I didn't fly with the pilot or co-pilot again. I was glad to be back at base.

"A Friend Who Spent Time with Tito"

I had a friend who had to bailout over Yugoslavia and was picked up by Marshal Tito's Patriots. He was carried to Tito's hideout place and lived with them for two months. He told me they treated him well while he was with them. Tito's Patriots had found several more American airmen and had contacted the 15th Air Force regarding plans to pick them up. There were about twelve airmen in all ready to be picked up. My friend told me they had a landing strip cleared and buckets ready to light to mark the landing strip on a set time and night. There was a heavy fog that night, and they could hear the plane, but the pilot couldn't see the strip markers to land. There wasn't anything to do but abort that night and try the next night. They were in radio contact with the pilot and plans were made for the next night. There was some fog, but the plane was able to land. He said all were happy to see that plane on the ground.

The first thing taken off the plane was a new jeep for Tito. Tito and his German shepherd dog left in the jeep after the other supplies were unloaded and the airmen got on the plane. My friend said they were all happy when the plane took off that night. He told me Tito had requested a new jeep and had been anxiously waiting for it. It had been a very good night for all of them, especially good for the airmen who were being returned to Italy, for Tito's Patriots who got their supplies, and for Tito, who got his new jeep.

"At the Right Place at the Right Time"

One evening after we had returned from a mission, I was checking the rear section of the bomber to see if the gunners had left it as they were told to. They were to clean out all the 50-caliber shells, remove all the trash from the floor, take all their flying gear with them, and leave the plane ready for the next crew to use. The right waist gunner was at his gun getting ready to clean it. He was the only gunner in the plane. The others were outside with one standing about eight or ten feet from the plane. The gunner had the ammo belt of cartridges disconnected, but he had not pulled the handle to get the last cartridge out of the gun. As I got near him, he pointed the machine gun toward his crew mate and yelled at him, "I will just shoot you."

I hit the gun barrel down at the same time he pulled the trigger. The 50-caliber bullet went into the ground in front of his crew mate and the noise of the gun got everyone's attention. The gunner had thought the gun was empty, but it wasn't. It was not intended to happen, but it did, and I know the Lord put me at the right spot at the right time to save that young man's life. There wasn't time to think about what to do.

I always told everyone guns were not to play with, but to kill someone or something. The gunner was really upset with himself. I knew he received a good lesson and the crew mate on the ground was scared to death. It wasn't long before there was a crowd there. The squadron and group men wanted to find out all the facts and I told them. "It was just a playful prank that went bad. No harm done. It could have been real bad with at least one death. I happened to be at the right place at the right time and hit the gun barrel down at the time he pulled the trigger."

I was a little late that afternoon in going to the rear of the plane to check things and I don't remember why. I do know the Lord does work in mysterious ways and "His Wonders to Behold." I also know the gunner never pulled that prank again.

"The Path Finder Plane"

On a number of our missions, we arrived at our primary target and found it completely covered with clouds. We would have to go to a second or third selected target. We had heard the 15th Air Force was going to get a new Mother Plane that would locate the target for us. One day we were told it was there, and a crew had been selected from the 344th squadron to take it on the mission the next day. A sergeant from operations came and told me they had made up a crew for it and I was down to be the flight engineer. "Can you go?"

I answered, "Yes."

He told me we would be leading the 15th Air Force and it should be a good mission for me. I was at the plane early the next morning to pre-flight check the plane. I was surprised to find the plane had a guard standing by it. Someone from operations was there to verify that I was who I said I was. Soon after, a major came to the plane and introduced himself to me. He said he was the radar man on the plane and wanted to show me his room inside the plane. That B-24 was a new model plane and had been modified for the radar "mother" job. All bomb racks had been removed and a room full of equipment was in it. A passageway was on one side to walk to the rear of the plane.

He told me when we were in the air that I should come to the room, and he would explain some of his work. I was amazed at what he explained to me. He was going to guide the pilot of the plane we were on to our target with all the other bombers following us, and he would signal with a flare the exact time to drop the bombs. The only thing I remember saying was, "That's amazing!"

He showed me the first absolute true altimeter and I saw it showing every little thing as we flew over it. He said the radar was sending signals toward the ground and receiving them back all the time. I thanked him for showing and explaining the new tech things to me. I left him and went back to the flight deck. We were told when we got to the target, but we couldn't see it. Clouds completely covered the area. I'm sure we got plenty of ack-ack; we always did. I didn't know when the Mother Plane was leaving the squadron or whether we dropped bombs on the intended target or not. There was one thing I did know - that B-24 was a beautiful plane.

We returned to our base. I completed my paperwork and went to my tent. I sat on my cot and suddenly remembered my A-2 jacket. I had left it on the plane. I returned, but the guard wouldn't let me near it. I asked him to go and get it for me. He wouldn't go. He told me I would have to get an officer to go and get my jacket for me. I went back to the squadron, and asked the first officer I saw to go with me. He went with me, and I introduced him to the guard; he went into the plane and got my jacket. I thanked him for helping me with the guard and getting my jacket back.

Chapter 10

LECCE, ITALY

"Lt. Colonel Marshall R. Gray"

Lt. Col. Marshall R. Gray was Deputy Commander of the 98th group when our commander, Col. Karnes, was killed in a plane accident on January 13, 1944. Lt. Col. Gray took over as our commander. Very few of the group knew him.

On one occasion at a restaurant in Lecce, a GI from the 376th group and his friend from the 98th were having a meal, and they didn't know Col. Gray was at the next table. The man from the 376th group asked his friend how he liked the new commander. The 98th man's reply was, "No one has seen the rascal. I don't know him. He doesn't go on the tough missions."

Col. Gray heard the conversation but didn't tell them who he was.

On the afternoon of January 28, 1944, our group commander, Lt. Col. Gray, had the entire group out in a formation. He was on a little platform so all could see him. The first thing he did was to give us a talk on our upcoming missions and what the 15th Air Force expected from us. Then he introduced himself to us and told us about the episode at the restaurant in Lecce. That was something he should have done a couple of weeks earlier.

He didn't go on a tough mission until the February 22nd mission to Regensburg, Germany. I was a gunner on the commander's crew that day, and I think that combat mission changed him. He said after he got back to the base he wanted to spend some time with us and thank each one of us for getting him back home. He gave each one of us a big "thank you" and handshake. There were some in the group who still didn't accept him as a good commander. I told them to just grow up and accept things as they were. I said, "Do your job well and make it a good day."

Later, all the enlisted men had to help with guard duty on the planes. They assigned a man to each plane for a six hour shift. The assignment was for all enlisted men, ground and combat men, all ranks. Anyone who was to be flying the next day would be put on the first shift, and would hit the sack at 12:30 p.m. and get only about four hours of sleep.

Word got out that Col. Gray was going to be the "Officer of the Day" and check on the planes' guards to see if they were doing their guard duty job and not sleeping. There was one old sergeant who asked for the front entrance position to the planes' parking area. He said he wanted to teach the colonel a lesson. I wasn't at the first plane, but I was at the second one, and this is what happened.

At the entrance was a large mud hole with about a foot of water in it. At approximately ten o'clock that night, Col. Gray's jeep arrived, and the guard stopped it in the middle of the entrance's mud hole. The guard told Col. Gray to come forth and be recognized. The colonel tried to talk the sergeant into letting the driver drive the jeep out of the mud and water but had no luck. The colonel and driver had to do what the guard ordered them to do. I don't know and I didn't ask the sergeant what the colonel had done to him to make him do what he did.

"Dropping Warning Leaflets on Sofia, Bulgaria"

On one of our trips to a target in Romania we were told we would come back to our base by a different route. We had a number of boxes of warning leaflets in the plane to drop over Sofia, Bulgaria. The railroad had a large rail center in the middle of Sofia. Close to it were schools, churches, and homes. It had to be bombed, and this was a warning for the people to leave.

While we were over the city tossing out the leaflets, we were really getting the ack-ack. I was there helping toss the papers out. At the time we were getting the heavy ack-ack all around us, we didn't think it was such a good idea to warn the people to leave. We did get in trouble a few days later when we came back to bomb the Marshalling Yard.

The enemy fighters were ready and waiting for us. We had asked for it, and they let us have it. The fighters hit us first but left us while we dropped our bombs. They had time to go down, refuel, get more ammo, and climb back up to attack us again when the ack-ack guns stopped shooting at us. They had a large number of gun towers built in and around the large cities and industrial centers and a large number of mobile anti-craft gun units they could move as needed. They had their spies everywhere, even near or on our base. They had radar to aim their guns on us, and if they could get our altitude to set the shells' explosion time, they could get us. They had some B-24s with German crews who would fly close to us and call our altitude to the gunners.

The 15th Air Force was getting a large number of new groups in from the States, and we didn't know whether they were friends or enemies. We would know they were the enemy when they would drop down fast and leave us. I don't care how high we were, there was always some ack-ack above us. Right after the anti-aircraft guns stopped shooting at us, they would send the fighters a signal to indicate they were stopping. The signal was a colored shell explosion of orange or red. After the signal, the fighters would hit us again.

I was fortunate to be in the 98th Bomb Group. The group had a reputation for having good gunners, and it was the older group in the 15th Air Force. When we were in the 12th Air Force in North Africa, the 98th and 376th groups had B-24s and the 12th Air Force had one group of B-17s. I read a book written by a former B-17 pilot who had been in North Africa, and he made this statement about the 98th group: "The 98th group would pass us on the way to the target. We always thanked God for the 98th because they got the fighters. That was planned that way."

We knew the enemy would be ready for us and they were. Our target, the Marshalling Yard, was used to get supplies to the Russian front, and they wanted to protect it.

"The Colt .32 Caliber Automatic Pistol"

Back when I was stationed at Pueblo I had a friend on another crew who had a pearl handle Colt .32 automatic pistol his grandfather had given to him. He had taken it apart and couldn't put it back together. He had taken every screw out and had all the parts in a cloth bag. He had tried and tried to get it back together but couldn't get anywhere with it.

One day he came by my bunk and asked me if I wanted it. I told him I would help him and maybe we could fix it. He said, "No way. I have given up, and if you don't want it, I'm throwing it away."

I told him to give it to me, and he did.

After a few days I found I wasn't getting anywhere with it either. I thought it would be like the Army Colt .45, but I was wrong. I carried it with me when I went overseas. That gun was a challenge for me. I was hoping to find someone who could help me with it, but I had no such luck.

I didn't give up on it. I consoled myself by using the old "try and try another method" way, hoping I might find a way that worked. I worked on it at odd times and made some progress. Then, I would get upset and frustrated with myself and put it back in the sack for a while. It was a big challenge for me. It taught me to not give up when I face failure. I would just have to try and try again.

My father had told me "Can't" could never do anything, so I had to keep on trying. I tried for almost a year. About two weeks before I left the squadron to come back to the States, I succeeded in getting the gun back in one piece. My friend was still in the squadron. I went to his tent and handed the gun to him. It was in the cloth bag. He opened the bag and a big smile came on his face as he said, "That's your gun. I gave it to you. Don't you remember?"

My answer was, "That gun means so much to you. It's yours. You keep it."

He was one happy friend. I told him, "Don't take all the screws out again."

He got up and said to me, "Shiver, you are my friend." He gave me a big handshake and another smile.

As I left his tent I said, "Remember, don't take the screws out of your gun again."

"Bombing Foggia Harbor"

I lost some of my mission notes, but I know of one recall mission that turned out okay for our crew. This mission started out good and ended good for us. It was what happened from about 9:00 a.m. until 3:00 p.m. that was really bad and I mean bad, bad. We left our base at Lecce, Italy, for a target in Austria about six o'clock that morning. The pilot, Lt. Keating, told me the group weather officer had told them that on the way to the target about mid-morning we would run through about 200 feet of ice as we were climbing. "Don't worry. You won't be in it very long," he had said.

I was the flight engineer on the crew that day. I told Lt. Keating we couldn't stay in ice very long. We had no anti-ice equipment or de-ice boots on the wings or the rear stabilizers. Those are the first things removed when a new plane gets to the group.

We got in the ice and fog. It was bad. About that time, Burns in the tail turret came on the intercom and told us a P-38 escort was about to ram us. We were in a mess. B-24's were everywhere. The group leader called the mission off and said everyone was on their own. "Find your way home," he told us.

A B-24 came over us on our right and the next moment one came under us from the left side. That was a bad situation to be in and there was not a thing we could do about it. That was a time in my life I know the Lord had mercy on all of us and let us get through that day. It was the second time in my combat missions when we were caught in a situation like that. Planes were flying everywhere.

We got into a warm layer of air in between two layers of ice. We tried to climb up to get out of it and we tried to drop down. Ice would form on the leading edges of the wings and stabilizers. The plane would begin to shake and stall. Lieutenant Keating would bring the plane back into the warm area and the ice would melt off. He asked me to go to the rear and see how bad the stabilizers were when we started to stall. I told him when I was ready. He tried to let down and the stabilizers were about to shake off. I told him to come up and let the ice melt, and then we would try to go up. We did, and then we had to come down to the warm area. We were trapped in that warm area, and we couldn't get out of it. It was a thin layer, about a sixty or seventy-five foot layer of warm air. We stayed there. We would try and try again. Same story.

I have heard you will not find an atheist in a foxhole. That's a true statement about flying combat missions, too. You will pray and ask God to get you out of a bad situation. I had no idea where we were.

About three o'clock that afternoon, we saw a hole in the clouds off to our right at a two o'clock position. Everyone was happy and we headed there. We still had our bomb load on the plane - ten 500-pound demolition bombs and they were armed.

The plane's IFF switches were off. On the wall at the rear of the flight deck on the B-24 were two switches. We called them the IFF switches - short for "Identification Friend or Foe". If these two switches were on, then there was a signal being sent from the plane. We wanted to turn them off when we crossed over what we called "the bomb line," where the enemy was. The flight engineer would turn them off when the navigator came on the intercom and told us that we had crossed the line. He also gave the signal when we were returning to the base and re-crossed the line and the switches were turned on.

We didn't know where we were. We headed for the hole and went down through it. All hell broke loose on us. Ack-ack was everywhere. We were not on oxygen yet, and I think we were about 12,000 feet high. They had us on target and I was leaning between the pilot and co-pilot seats. Lieutenant Keating pushed the controls to go down as quick as he could, and we went down fast. We hit about 375 mph, as he started to pull the controls back to come out of the dive.

Lieutenant Goucher, the co-pilot, reached for the bomb release lever and released the bombs at the right moment. I didn't think about the bomb load, but Lieutenant Goucher did. He pulled the release lever at the right time. The crew thanked him for his action. The bomb load could have broken the plane in two if it had still been in the bomb bays.

Lieutenant Goucher had nothing to do after the plane was in the air, unless Lieutenant Keating told him to take over. He was a good co-pilot and always had his camera with him. He would take a picture of a plane when it was shooting at us. He was always getting as close to the enemy plane attacking us as he could. He would tell us he didn't have a gun and for us crew members to just do our job and he'd do his. As we pulled out of the steep and fast dive, we saw our bomb load hit the water. Lieutenant Dever, the navigator, told us we let down over the harbor at Foggia, Italy, and for me to flip the IFF switches on as quickly as I could. I did, and we didn't get anymore ack-ack. Our bombs fell in the middle of the harbor. We couldn't have picked a better place to unload them.

There were ships at all the docks. There was a strip of stones about a mile long that protected the docks from the Adriatic Sea with a passageway at the north end of the strip. The bombs hit the water in the middle of the harbor. We were glad we didn't do damage to anything or anyone. We didn't get any more ack-ack. The plane got a lot of holes in it, but no one on the crew was hit by any of the small pieces of shells, although two crew members got close to being hurt. Lieutenant Keating's seat chute, on which he was sitting, was damaged and Burns, the tail gunner, had a part of his heavy flying jacket collar taken off. Those two incidents were close.

We returned to Lecce that afternoon and found out we were the last plane to return. No other crew had it as bad as our crew did. The plane was out of service for a few days and none of the crew members received credit for that day's mission.

"Landing on a Wing, Prayers, and Fumes"

The B-24 didn't have accurate gauges. On the plane's flight deck left wall were two glass tubes with a valve on each tube at the tube's lower end. One tube and valve was for #1 and #2 fuel tanks and the other tube and valve were for #3 and #4 tanks. We called them sight tubes. We called them sight tubes. They were marked so the fuel would rise and fall in proportion to how much fuel was in the tanks. The plane had the fuel tanks in the wings. Each engine had three fuel cells connected together for a total of twelve cells. Sometimes there could be one or two large fuel tanks mounted in the forward bomb bays with a fuel transfer pump. On the B-24, there were two large selector valves mounted up in the top forward corner of the front bomb bays. All fuel tanks were manifolded together through these selector valves. It was possible to use any combination of fuel usage or transfers wanted, if the valves were turned to the correct positions. For example, #1 engine could run off the #4 fuel tank or any one selected.

The two most important gauges in the instrument panel to watch were the engine temperature and oil pressure. To me those were the most important. To conserve fuel, the fuel mixture levers for all engines would be moved to the lean side as much as possible. Rich mixtures would keep the engine's temperature down, but would use more fuel.

On one of the missions when I was flight engineer, the plane engines were using an extra amount of fuel. I had talked this over with the pilot and co-pilot and we had done everything we could to conserve fuel. To make matters worse, the gas gauges were not accurate. They told us we had more or less gas than what the sight tubes indicated. They read - "as much as fifty gallons, more or less." I told the pilot we needed to find an airfield closer than our base at Lecce to stop and get some gas. He said he didn't know of one.

We were now about an hour from the base. I told the pilot what I thought we should do. "Tell all of the crew about our fuel shortage and radio our flight leader that we're leaving the formation and dropping down closer to the ground."

The pilot said, "I understand everything except the last part. Why closer to the ground?"

"So we don't have far to fall! As we get close to our base, call the tower and tell them about our situation and ask them to clear us to come straight in. No landing pattern for us," I said.

I had all the tanks the same on the sight tubes - empty! We got everybody's attention at the base. They were waiting and what a wonderful sight to see the base come into view. We came straight in and when we were eight to ten feet off the ground, the two outboard engines cut off, but we made it. As we continued on our landing roll, both of the inboard engines stopped. The pilot let the plane roll to a stop off the runway. There is an old saying, "coming in on a wing and a prayer." Well, we came in on "fumes and prayers"! It was great to be back at the base and all in one piece.

"Stormy Weather"

When we were on missions, we never knew what weather conditions we would run into. The weather information was received from the P-38 reconnaissance planes in the early hours of the morning. Sometimes we would come into a weather front we were not expecting. The old saying is true, "You can't fool Mother Nature".

There were some things we knew not to do. One big "no-no" was to go under the thunderstorm. We had to go over or around it. Fuel, oxygen supplies, where we were going, and where in the mission we were had to be considered in making the decision of what to do. If we were going to a target and came to a storm, the mission would be canceled and we would return to base. If we were returning after a mission, we had to check on our fuel and oxygen supplies.

On a number of return trips, when the oxygen was running low, we would let the pilot and co-pilot stay on oxygen while the rest of the crew would try not to move about. We would turn the oxygen on only when needed.

We heard about one crew in another group that decided to go under a thunderstorm and they didn't make it. The plane was lost and only one gunner survived. He had been sitting on the floor in the rear of the plane with his chest chute on when the plane was destroyed. He said large pieces of the plane were all around him when he came to lying on the ground. He didn't remember pulling the chute handle, but his chute saved him.

"The British 40 Millimeter Gun Crew"

At the rear of my tent at Lecce was a British 40mm anti-aircraft gun crew. The crew lived in tents, and part of that crew was at the gun all the time. They had a tent for their kitchen and tents to sleep in.

There was a sergeant major in charge of the crew. He and I became close friends. He told me about himself and his family. Before he was called up for British Army duty, he was the manager of the Chase Manhattan Bank's London office. In 1939 he sent his wife, who was expecting their first child, to the United States to live. He had good connections with the right people in England and the States. He told me they went out of their way to help him and his wife. Their daughter was born in the United States in 1940, and he had not even seen a picture of her. The British wouldn't let any photos go out or come in by mail. He asked me if I would carry a charcoal drawing of his face to the States and mail it to his wife. I told him I would and I did. He gave me her address in Long Island, New York. She sent me a long letter thanking me for what I did for them. She asked me about him in a way I couldn't answer - such as, "Has he changed a lot?" Then she would say, "But you don't know how he looked then, do you?"

I still have her letter. She and the sergeant major appreciated my sending the drawing to her, and I received a blessing for doing it.

The sergeant major had fifteen men in his gun crew. It was impossible for them to know when one or more German planes would come over. The ME-109s would come by in the early mornings or in the late afternoons.

The gunners would get a few shots at them as they were leaving the base. They strafed us a number of times.

We were always amazed at the British and their tea times. They would have to take time off to get their spot of tea in mid-mornings and mid-afternoons. We would joke with them about that and they would say, "We have to have our tea."

"The 344th Squadron's Armament Officer"

The gunners were taught and always told to hold our fire until an attacking plane was 600 yards from us. If our fingers were on the gun's trigger, and we could see those little yellow dots coming from the enemy's plane, we were going to pull the triggers as long as the plane was coming at us. We couldn't fire short bursts and let the gun barrel cool off; we had to continue shooting. After a few days of combat we would need a new barrel. The armament officer would lecture us when we requested a new barrel, but in the end he would usually okay one. Eventually, though, it got harder and harder to get a new barrel from him. We hated to try to get a new one because he always gave the same lecture.

One day he gave a long lecture to two other gunners and myself and then turned down our request for a new barrel. I told the officer this was the straw that broke the camel's back with me, and we would be back later. I told the two other gunners to follow me, and I would do the talking for all of us. We went to the squadron operations office, and I told Captain Keating our trouble with the armament officer. He said, "Follow me."

We returned to the armament officer's office, and Captain Keating asked him if he had gun barrels in stock. The officer said he did. We got our barrels with no lecture.

"Sgt. Underwood's Coffee Drinking"

Edward Underwood was a ball turret gunner in the 344th Squadron and a very good one. He was a friend of mine, and I was on a number of missions when he was in the ball turret. He was my tent mate in Lecce, and I was as close as anyone to Edward. He really was a lonely man, but I got to know him. He didn't drink any alcoholic drink, but he never got enough coffee. He and the squadron mess sergeant were good friends, and Edward always had plenty of coffee.

Early each night Edward would fix his coffee for the night. Every plane that came to the squadron would have a small Coleman gas stove in it. Edward always had one in the tent and a gallon can. He would fix up a can as full as possible and boil it before we hit the sack. By the time the clerk woke us in the early hours of the morning, Edward's coffee can would be empty. I would tell him he was drinking too much coffee, and it was not wise to drink so much. He wouldn't slow down. He was nearing the end of his missions, and it was taking its toll on him. Some of the men didn't make it on those last one or two missions. Their planes were shot down. The old saying is true, "It's not over until it's over."

I had to help him. I went to operations and told the officer I needed a closed door talk with him. He told me to close the door and sit down. I explained Edward's problem to him. I told him Edward didn't know what I was doing, and I wasn't sure that he would go along with it.

I told the officer my plan. I would be going on a mission the next morning and Edward wouldn't be going. I wanted to get the officer's permission to add Edward's name to the manifest instead of mine, so if I made it back he would get the credit for the mission. Edward's nerves were not good enough for a final mission. I asked the officer if he would help me. The operations officer told me as he smiled at me, "I cannot give you permission to do that, but as for me, I will not be telling anyone about your visit."

I thanked him and left. I didn't tell anyone else.

The next afternoon I added Edward's name to the manifest. I listed him as an extra gunner. I signed it and turned it in. I didn't hear anymore about it. I did what I thought I had to do and I had no bad feelings about it.

I told Edward about it and explained my actions to him. I didn't tell him about my visit with the operation's officer. He just looked at me as I was talking and didn't say anything - nothing - no comment - not even a thank you.

I did tell him the records would show him completing 50 missions. If he wanted to, he could make another one. I certainly wasn't going to stop him. Still he made no comment.

He didn't make another mission and he did accept my help. He left the squadron after a few days. I didn't do what I did for myself but to help him. I was disappointed in his reaction.

"The Black Guard Company"

We had an Black Guard Army Company that guarded the area around our planes at night. We were having planes exploding during take-off or when they were climbing up at take-offs. The enlisted men were guarding each plane every night, and I was pulling some of the first shifts. Some of my planes were close to the area where the Black Guards were walking. They would stop and talk to us which was good for us. It made the time pass fast. I got to know one of the guards and he enjoyed telling me about his Army life overseas.

He said his guard company was all black except their commander, a major who was white. The major was a fair man but very strict on them. He was "all Army". The guard told me they had a tent inspection every morning at eight o'clock, and the major would be in front of the others. He said the major didn't miss much, but if he did the others in the inspection team would catch it. Each of the black guards had to cover his bases, and then get the 1st Sergeant to see what he had done, and he would mark it off. The guard told me they got ice cream every Sunday. I told him they were treated better than us. That was a true statement. I never tasted ice cream while overseas.

The guard told me about their trip from the United States. The major gave them talks on what they would be doing when they got to North Africa. Their ship was in dock at Casablanca. The major got them on deck and gave them a final talk before they left the ship. He pointed to a small mountain, where a number of trucks were coming down and told them this: "Men, for a number of days before we got here, I have been telling you we are going to be in the war soon. Now we are here. Do you see those trucks coming down that mountain? They are bringing the dead soldiers from the other side of the mountain. That's where the fighting is."

The guard said they believed what the major told them until, a few days later, they were talking to some of the truck drivers. The truck drivers said the major had wanted to scare them. They said there wasn't any war on the other side of the mountain. In fact, there was no war in Africa at that time. The driver told the guard they were bringing truckloads of rocks down the mountain.

The guard told me they hadn't done anything but guard duty since they had been overseas. I told him he was living the good life and to just keep on doing it.

There were things happening at our base we couldn't believe a GI would do. One example was something that happened before we started guarding the planes at night. At every station on the plane was a medical kit attached to the plane. On one mission, someone needed the morphine to use on one of the crew who had been injured, but the morphine was missing. The kits had a zipper opening, and all were checked. But, there was no morphine on the plane. When they returned to the base and reported it, they discovered every plane's kit was missing the morphine. That was when all medical kits had to be checked out and returned after every mission. Later, we were told they found the guilty one. A GI in the service group who worked on radio equipment on the planes was a drug addict. We were never told what they did to him. There was another GI in that service group I read about in a book written after the war by a pilot in the group whom I knew. The GI he wrote about had been caught putting altitude bombs on some of the planes and bombs in the main landing wheel-well openings on others.

Searching for bombs that may have been placed on a plane was an extra job given to those of us who were engineers. I had to climb up onto a plane's tires and, using a flashlight, satisfy myself that no bomb had been placed on the plane. The GI who placed the bombs was being paid by Germany; he was court-martialed and found guilty. He was shot by a U.S. firing squad.

I know we had spies on our base. Sometimes the radio operator would hear our mission target being sent to our enemy while we were getting into our attack formations. It was by the grace of the Lord that I made it through the war without being killed. I am a believer that there is a time to be born and a time to die. I thank the Lord for another day of life each morning when I wake up.

"A Troubled Gunner"

I had one friend when I was in the 98th Group who wouldn't accept my help or advice about a problem he had. I remember his name, but I'm not going to tell it. He was from Chicago, Illinois, and his problem was that his father was in a federal prison for life.

His mother had to raise him and a younger brother alone. She owned some bowling alleys in Chicago. My friend was mad at the world because he didn't have a father at home when he was growing up. His father was one of Al Capone's men and was in charge of getting whiskey from Canada into Chicago. That's what he told me and I believed it to be true. I do know he was not a happy person, and I tried to help him. I told him what his father did was his own choice, and his father was paying for what he had done. I also said if he got through the war and got home, he should visit him as soon as possible. I told him he should learn to accept things as they are and show his love to his father. I also told him to remember who his father was and that he would always be his father. He couldn't change the past. He was living now, and he had his future life ahead of him. I suggested he pick up the pieces and enjoy life.

"Jack McKenna's Plane"

When the 98th Group moved to Lecce, the Italians were allowed to keep some of their planes and some of their hangars and personnel. The base at Lecce was one of their main air bases. In one of their hangars was a new fighter plane they had never gotten in production. They had a few old transport planes with three engines. The Allies let the Italians use them to fly loads of supplies across the Adriatic Sea to Tito in Yugoslavia. They had a few fighter type planes they would fly around some days and show off flying the planes at high altitude. Some of the Italians on the ground would get in a group and point up to the planes in the air doing stunts. They wanted to impress us, and they wanted us to recognize what they could do.

About once a week our group commander would have one of our fighter groups send one or two of their planes over to our base to put on a show for the Italians so they could see some real flying close to the ground. We all enjoyed these good shows. The Italians got a view of all types of stunts and maneuvers the American pilots could do. The last act would always be a corkscrew flight down the runway with the wing tips almost touching the ground. It was something to see.

The Italians were short on food after they surrendered. One day I saw two Italian officers cutting some green grass and putting it between two pieces of bread and eating it. We didn't have much to eat, but we didn't have to do that.

One of the GIs at Lecce was Jack McKenna. He was a top turret gunner on another crew and a very good one. I was the flight engineer on his crew sometimes, and I could count on Jack to do his job. He and I were good friends. He was from Michigan. He told me about racing his motorcycle back home at night. Later in the war Jack was injured when a piece of flak hit his head and he received the Purple Heart Medal.

Jack had noticed an old Italian training plane in a hangar and he wanted it. Jack made a deal to trade the Italians something to eat in exchange for the plane. He went to our mess sergeant and the only food item he could get was a gallon can of apricots. Jack took that can of apricots to the Italians and traded it for the plane. None of the brass knew about that deal.

Jack got some of his friends to help him, and one night they moved the plane from the hangar to a spot behind a row of tents. Jack worked on the plane and after a few weeks, he was ready to start the engine. To everyone's surprise it began running. He would taxi it around in a large area behind the tents. We knew Jack wanted to get it up into the air. I can't remember if he ever got it up or not, but he ran the plane at a fast speed on the ground while he was playing with it.

One day he went farther than he had been going before. He ran the plane into a wire clothesline and did a lot of damage to it. Jack had to take his damaged plane to the plane junk area. Every base had one. The only thing Jack had left was his story about swapping a can of apricots for a plane. Not everyone can claim that.

"A P-38 on Fire"

One afternoon, when we were over the Adriatic Sea on our return home, one of our escort P-38 plane's engines was on fire. We were about halfway across the sea, and the plane was close to us on our right. Our radio operator told us he had the fighter group's flight leader talking to the burning plane's pilot and for us to turn on our control to hear it. It was something to hear while we were watching what was happening. The plane's radioman made a call to the Air-Sea Rescue to pick up the pilot. One of the bombers was to stay and fly around the pilot when he was in the sea. The B-24 had better radio sets to direct the rescue plans to the man. Two of the P-38s were to stay and fly over the operation. The other planes were to continue back to base.

There was one thing wrong. The burning plane's pilot was still in the plane. The flight leader was telling him to leave, but the pilot wouldn't jump. He was making all kinds of excuses: "The water's cold. There are sharks down there. You are going to leave me. I don't want to leave now."

His flight leader's patience had been tested to its limits by the burning plane's pilot. The fire was really burning now, and he told the pilot, "Leave! That's a direct order, and I mean now!"

The pilot answered him, "Yes, sir, but if you all leave me and I die, I'm going to haunt you to your dying day!"

He left the plane, and we saw his chute open. We arrived at the base, and I found out later the rescue went as planned. That was an exciting trip home.

"A Forgotten Episode"

In the records of the 344th Squadron on sheet number 19 of the *War Diary* for February 1944, there is an entry of an episode which I do not remember. The record says that on February 28, 1944, T/Sgt. Rector Long, S/Sgt. Robert Burns, S/Sgt. John Shiver, and T/Sgt. Donald Stoll, bet S/Sgt. Edward Underwood he couldn't run three lengths of the runway without stopping. The record states all four men followed S/Sgt. Underwood up and down the runway, expecting and hoping that S/Sgt. Underwood would not make it. The article continued to say, although Underwood was hard pressed, he finished strong and collected between $25 and $40.

Even though I do not remember this, I know it is correct. I know all of us were in good physical condition, but I am amazed we were able to run that far. I have said that when I was overseas, I could fight a wildcat and win that fight. We had to be in good condition to survive. I'm not bragging but just telling it like it was.

"An R&R Week at Naples and Capri"

After waiting for months, my R&R trip came up. Some said that R&R was a code for "Rest and Recreation" and others said it was for "Rest and Return". For me it was a way of getting away from combat flying and rough living conditions. I wanted to sleep late in the mornings and get up when I wanted to, sleep on a bed with sheets and a pillow, see some things I'd never seen before, eat good food for a change, and just have a vacation from war.

There were several from the 344th Squadron going on R&R at this time and some from the other squadrons. We were flown to Naples on a B-24 from another squadron (#41-11815-Red J), and we heard that Mount Vesuvius, a volcano north of Naples, had erupted during the nights of March 20th and 21st. The volcano was still active, and we would get to fly around it.

We arrived at the volcano around 1:30 that afternoon, and old Vesuvius was still active. We had only a small amount of oxygen on the plane, so we let the pilots use it. The others on the plane stayed still, and we got up to 15,000 feet. We didn't see anything but billows of ash and smoke shooting up.Everything was dark, and we didn't stay up at that altitude but a few minutes. We landed at one of the airstrips near the city and were carried by a truck to the transit hotel in the center of Naples. While in Naples, we had planned to visit Pompeii, but Mount Vesuvius's eruption prevented us from going there.

We were assigned to a room on the 5th floor. There were three cots to a room, and I was with Darrell George and Dominic DiBenedetto. A GI at the main desk told us the hotel next to ours had been destroyed by German bombs the night before. That hotel had been the transit mess hotel, so he told us to pick up a K-ration from his desk for each meal. He told us we were to get to the cellar immediately whenever we heard the anti-aircraft guns shooting. He said there could be no lights on except our flashlights. We couldn't use them much.

We were told the US Navy had a ferryboat that would take us to Capri the next morning. We saw a notice that a famous opera was to be at a large opera house in the city that evening. We had nothing to do, and someone said, "Why don't we go?"

We went, but we all left at the first intermission. It was a large, world famous opera house. The building was beautiful inside and outside, but the opera wasn't for us.

We got back to the hotel, picked up our K-ration and went to our assigned rooms. We lay on our cots and discussed our plans for the night. We would sleep with our clothes on and our shoes off. If the guns started shooting, the first one up would wake up the other two while he was putting on his shoes.

I woke up when I heard the first gun fired, shook the other two, and called out loud, "It's time to get to the basement. Let's go!"

DiBenedetto was up and we were ready to leave the room, but George was still asleep. I started to leave the room just as the anti-aircraft guns were really going at it. I kicked George's cot again. I told DiBenedetto to try to get George awake. I left the room. We were on the 5th floor. There were ten flights of stairs to get down into the basement. "Dim-Dom" was right behind me. About half way down the stairs George passed us, and he was really giving "Dim-Dom" and me some choice words as he went by. I thought we were coming down fast, but George passed us as if we had stopped. He was yelling at us as he passed us, "Some friends you two are - leaving me to get killed."

Our building wasn't damaged. We returned to our room after about thirty minutes in the basement. We ate our K-ration for our morning meal and went to the ferry at the Capri docking place. The Isle of Capri was about twenty miles out in the Bay of Naples. The ferry made a trip to Capri and back to Naples each day. It was operated by the U.S. Navy.

We got on the boat about mid-morning of March 25th and arrived at the Isle of Capri for a week of vacation. There was a cable car we could get on to take us up the steep road to the top of Capri. The cable car or funicular of Mount Vesuvius is referred to as the "Funiculi Funicula" because it inspired the song with that title. The ride was something. There was a large cable winch at the top of the mountain. It was turned by an old gas engine, and it was a very steep angle to the top. I had my doubts we would make it, but we did. That was the first and the last time I got in the cable car. I did walk the winding road down to the harbor area several times while I was at Capri.

Dominic and I were assigned to a villa with a balcony and a wonderful view of Naples Bay. We really enjoyed our vacation there. I was fortunate to have Dominic with me. He made friends with the Italians everywhere we went.

We visited the harbor area a few times. On one of the visits, we talked to a number of U.S. sailors from a Navy destroyer that was there. We met a sergeant from a B-25 base where planes were destroyed when Mount Vesuvius erupted. He said the area around Mount Vesuvius was hit with burning rocks falling from the sky. The wings of the planes were broken off. The ash dust was in the air when we first arrived at Capri, but after a few days it was gone. I have read that after eleven days of eruptions, "Old Vesuvius" stopped erupting on March 29, 1944. It was over.

A few of us took an old bus from Capri to Anacapri. For a fee, the bus driver took us on a tour of Anacapri and explained things to us. Anacapri was the summer resort area for the Roman emperor, Claudius Tiberius (42 BC-AD 37). He was the emperor of the Romans from AD 14 to AD 37. Vesuvius was a friend of Tiberius, and they would use smoke signals to communicate with each other. I was at the place where the fire had been and sat on the stone seat where the Roman Emperor sat. All of this is what our guide told us. Tiberius was a no-good ruler. The guide took us down to the bottom floor of the emperor's home, where the large water reservoir was. It was the second level floor down. The first floor down was the dungeon and it was something to see. The walls had arm and leg shackles, chains on three sides and a walkway on one side. There was an iron-bar wall, with an iron-bar door and lock that, according to the guide, still worked. There wasn't a roof on the home, and only the lower parts of the walls were left.

The guide told us a prisoner was thrown over the cliffs every morning for the emperor and his guests' entertainment. Tiberius was known to be a glutton, and his room was next to the place where he ate. The queen's living area was at the opposite end from his. The guide said the emperor would sit at his table and eat until he couldn't eat anymore, then turn to his left and vomit the food up into a large stone bowl on a stand. While the bowl was being cleaned, the emperor would be eating again. He had troubles. I sat down at his table turned to my left, as the guide said Tiberius did, and touched the bowl.

We left after viewing the area around Anacapri. One of the old ruins had a floor and parts of the walls. The floor had a painting of three animals on it. I found it amazing as it was still a beautiful thing to see. We enjoyed the trip up to Anacapri.

One afternoon Dominic and I went to see the Blue Grotto. It is the famous cave of Capri. The cave had to be seen by boat, and the visit had to be made at low tide because the entrance hole into the cave was almost at the level of the water. The Italian who rowed the boat knew the time to go in the cave and the time to get out. When we got to the entrance hole, we had to get low in the boat. He told us we had to get out in thirty minutes, but we had time to see its beautiful water, rock walls, and overhead rocks. When we were inside the cave, we felt as if someone had turned on the lights. The boatman said the light inside is a mystery. How could sunshine be inside a cave? Anyone who visits the cave will know why it is named "The Blue Grotto".

The villa where Dominic and I stayed in Capri was located in a place that gave us a good view of Naples Bay. I would wake up each morning, look out a window, and see the three large peaks located in the bay close to Capri. It was a beautiful view.

We went into several of the gift shops while we were in Capri. We enjoyed watching the old men making cameo pins and necklaces. They had a small hammer and a variety of very small chisels. Some of the chisels were as small as toothpicks. We were amazed to see them work. They had such patience and skill. We were seeing real craftsmen at work.

We got to meet one shop owner and his wife one afternoon. Dominic and I stopped by their shop two or three times a day after that. I wouldn't know what Dominic and they were saying to each other, but I would enjoy seeing them talking and moving their arms and hands as they spoke. I have said that if you tied an Italian's hands and arms, he couldn't say a word to you.

On one of our visits to their shop they introduced their young daughter to us. She was a beautiful, young teenager and a very polite young lady. After a little while we left and were returning to our villa when we heard someone screaming behind us. We turned and saw the teenager running and two British soldiers chasing her. They were on a little street to our right. The girl ran to an apartment close by and went in. We ran as fast as we could and found two drunk British soldiers knocking on the door. We pulled them away from the door and gave those two a good talking to and warned them not to do that again. We got them away. Then the girl opened the door and thanked us for helping her.

The next morning we went to the shop, and the girl's father thanked us and told us the family wanted us to come to their apartment that night for a meal with them. We accepted and we had a good Italian meal together.

We had to leave Capri in a day or two. Before we went to the ferry docking area, we stopped by the gift shop and thanked them again for the meal and their friendship. We had a wonderful time at the Isle of Capri.

On our ferry trip back to Naples we had to stop in the bay and let a Navy convoy pass on their way to Corsica. That was something to see. There were a large number of landing craft with several destroyers and a heavy cruiser. The Navy men on the ferry told us what ships they were and where they were going. It was about thirty minutes before we could continue our trip to Naples.

We got to the transit hotel and were told about a USO show in Naples that night. We went to see it and really enjoyed it. The main person in the show was Irving Berlin. He was in the Army in World War I, and he was dressed in his old uniform when he sang some of his songs. He was great when he sang "This is the Army", and everyone wanted him to sing some more. I appreciated his closing song, "God Bless America". He was great. We returned to the hotel and got a good night's sleep. A truck carried us to our plane. The group had sent a B-24, named "The Black Joe", from another squadron to get us back to the base.

When we arrived at the base, everything looked like it had when we left. I enjoyed the vacation, but I knew it had to end. I had to get my missions finished, so I could return to the States. So after all was said and done, I was glad to get back.

"Sweating A Mission Because I Didn't Go"

One day in April 1944 the operations officer asked me if I would go with a crew as the engineer on the mission the next day. I told him I would, and they assigned me to it. Later that day I told a friend that operations had asked me to go with a crew, and I had accepted. He told me he would go if I didn't want to. I thought about it, and I said okay, if it would be all right with the office. We asked, and they agreed to the change.

I thought I would enjoy another day of rest, but I was wrong. I didn't get much sleep that night. I had never done that before, and all I could think about was that I was supposed to be on that mission.

The day went by slowly for me. I was a miserable person all day. I told myself I wouldn't do that again. I was really sweating the mission out. I had always accepted things as they happened; I wanted to see that plane on the ground and the crew not hurt.

I went to the flight line about thirty minutes before they were to return. When the plane landed, I was a happy person. Again I told myself this would never happen again, and it did not.

"A Radio Operator Named Sleepy"

In my squadron there was a crew that had a radioman who was known as "Sleepy Hall". I never heard anyone call him by any other name. He and his crew were friendly to all. They had trouble with Hall staying awake. We said "Sleepy Hall" certainly lived up to his name because he tried to sleep all the time.

I saw this happen. I was with a small group after a mission, standing near the planes talking about the mission. Hall was in the group, and someone asked him a question. He was standing up but didn't answer. One of his crew said, "Hall is asleep. I will wake him up, and you can ask him again."

On one of our missions Hall's crew happened to be the lead plane for the 15th Air Force. The lead plane's radioman had to send the target report to the Air Force Operations as soon as the bombs were dropped. "Sleepy Hall" was asleep and his crew member in the top turret kicked him to wake him up. Hall didn't check with anyone on the crew about the bomb drop. He assumed it had gone as planned, so he sent the usual report - "Primary target hit - Mission successful". But that report was wrong, and the #2 radioman on another plane corrected it. That evening when we returned to the base, there was a staff car waiting to take Hall to wing headquarters. That radio report should have been "Primary target was covered and the secondary target hit".

I never asked anyone how "Sleepy Hall" made out at wing headquarters. I think that they got him awake, and he stayed awake while he was up there. They needed to know which targets were hit and those that still needed to be bombed.

Honorable Discharge

This is to certify that

JOHN J SHIVER JR 34 335 079 Technical Sergeant

239th Army Air Forces Base Unit

Army of the United States

is hereby Honorably Discharged from the military service of the United States of America.

This certificate is awarded as a testimonial of Honest and Faithful Service to this country.

Given at SEPARATION CENTER
              Fort Mc Pherson Georgia

Date   9 September 1945

CONWAY BORUFF
Major AUS

ENLISTED RECORD AND REPORT OF SEPARATION
HONORABLE DISCHARGE

1. LAST NAME - FIRST NAME - MIDDLE INITIAL	2. ARMY SERIAL NO.	3. GRADE	4. ARM OR SERVICE	5. COMPONENT
Shiver John J Jr	34 335 079	T Sgt	AC	AUS

6. ORGANIZATION	7. DATE OF SEPARATION	8. PLACE OF SEPARATION
239th Army Air Forces Base Unit	9 Sep 45	Separation Center Fort Mc Pherson Ga

9. PERMANENT ADDRESS FOR MAILING PURPOSES	10. DATE OF BIRTH	11. PLACE OF BIRTH
211 3rd Avenue Atmore Ala	28 Aug 20	Perdido Ala

12. ADDRESS FROM WHICH EMPLOYMENT WILL BE SOUGHT	13. COLOR EYES	14. COLOR HAIR	15. HEIGHT	16. WEIGHT	17. NO. DEPEND.
See 9	Grey	Brown	5'8"	171½	0

18. RACE	19. MARITAL STATUS	20. U.S. CITIZEN	21. CIVILIAN OCCUPATION AND NO.
WHITE X NEGRO OTHER (specify)	SINGLE X MARRIED OTHER (specify)	YES X NO	Automobile Mechanic 5-81.010

MILITARY HISTORY

22. DATE OF INDUCTION	23. DATE OF ENLISTMENT	24. DATE OF ENTRY INTO ACTIVE SERVICE	25. PLACE OF ENTRY INTO SERVICE
21 Jul 42	None	3 Aug 42	Fort Mc Clellan Ala

26. SELECTIVE SERVICE DATA	26. REGISTERED	27. LOCAL S. S. BOARD NO.	28. COUNTY AND STATE	29. HOME ADDRESS AT TIME OF ENTRY INTO SERVICE
	YES X NO	2	Escambia Co Ala	Atmore Ala

30. MILITARY OCCUPATIONAL SPECIALTY AND NO.	31. MILITARY QUALIFICATION AND DATE
Airplane Mechanic Gunner 748	Expert Carbine Aerial Badge (Crew Member)

32. BATTLES AND CAMPAIGNS
Rome-Arno GO 40 WD 45
Naples-Foggia Air Offensive Europe GO 33 WD 45 Air Combat GO 46 WD 45

33. DECORATIONS AND CITATIONS Good Conduct Medal AR 600-68 Leaf Clusters GO 605 44
Air Medal GO 17 Hq 15 AF 43 with 1 Silver Oak Leaf Cluster AR 600-40 and 2 Bronze Oak/
European African Middle Eastern Service Medal with 4 Bronze Stars *

34. WOUNDS RECEIVED IN ACTION
None

35. LATEST IMMUNIZATION DATES
SMALLPOX 5 Aug 42 TYPHOID 25 Aug 42 TETANUS 5 Oct 42 OTHER (specify) YF 22 Apr 43
23 Apr 44 23 Apr 43 5 May 43 Typh 25 Jan 44

36. SERVICE OUTSIDE CONTINENTAL U S AND RETURN
DATE OF DEPARTURE	DESTINATION	DATE OF ARRIVAL
31 Jul 43	European Theater	19 Aug 43
31 May 44	US	14 Jun 44

37. TOTAL LENGTH OF SERVICE
CONTINENTAL SERVICE		FOREIGN SERVICE	
YEARS MONTHS DAYS		YEARS MONTHS DAYS	
2 3 6		0 10 13	

38. HIGHEST GRADE HELD T Sgt

39. PRIOR SERVICE
None

40. REASON AND AUTHORITY FOR SEPARATION
Convenience of the Government AR

41. SERVICE SCHOOLS ATTENDED
None

FOR CONVENIENCE, A CERTIFICATE OF ELIGIBILITY NO 40275-Ala
HAS BEEN ISSUED BY THE VETERANS ADMINISTRATION TO
USED FOR THE FUTURE REQUEST OF ANY GUARANTY OR INSUR-
MENT ACT OF 1944, AS AMENDED, THAT MAY BE AVAIL-
THE PERSON TO WHOM THIS SEPARATION PAPER WAS ISSUED

42. EDUCATION (Years) High School 4 College 0

PAY DATA

43. LONGEVITY FOR PAY PURPOSES	44. MUSTERING OUT PAY	45. SOLDIER DEPOSIT	46. TRAVEL PAY	47. TOTAL AMOUNT NAME
YEARS 3 MONTHS 1 DAYS 19	TOTAL 300 THIS PAYMENT 100		1540	150.31 Capt FD

INSURANCE NOTICE
IMPORTANT IF PREMIUM IS NOT PAID WHEN DUE OR WITHIN THIRTY-ONE DAYS THEREAFTER, INSURANCE WILL LAPSE. MAKE CHECKS OR MONEY ORDERS PAYABLE TO THE TREASURER OF THE U. S. AND FORWARD TO COLLECTIONS SUBDIVISION, VETERANS ADMINISTRATION, WASHINGTON 25, D. C.

48. KIND OF INSURANCE	49. HOW PAID	50. Effective Date of Allot-ment Discontinuance	51. Date of Next Premium Due (One month after 50)	52. PREMIUM DUE EACH MONTH	53. INTENTION OF VETERAN TO
Nat. Serv. X U.S. Gov't None	Allotment X Direct to V.A.	31 Aug 45	30 Sep 45	6 60	Continue Continue Only Discontinue X

54. REMARKS (This space for completion of above items or entry of other items specified in W. D. Directives)
Lapel Button Issued
ASR Score (2 Sep 1945) 99
Inactive Service ERC 21 Jul 42 to 2 Aug 42
*Distinguished Unit Badge GO 78 WD 43

55. SIGNATURE OF PERSON BEING SEPARATED
John J. Shiver, Jr.

57. PERSONNEL OFFICER (Type name, grade and organization - signature)
DAVID GOLDBERG
1st Lt AUS
David Goldberg

WD AGO FORM 53-55
1 November 1944

This form supersedes all previous editions of WD AGO Forms 53 and 55 for enlisted persons entitled to an Honorable Discharge, which will not be used after receipt of this revision.

41-19.2 Atmore Ala.

2nd Lt. Denver, 2nd Lt. Goucher, 1st Lt. Keating, 2nd Lt. Chain;
1st Lt. Totter, T/Sgt. Teetz, S/Sgt. Di Benedette, S/Sgt. Underwood,
S/Sgt. Easterday, S/Sgt. Burns, S/Sgt. Shiver, & S/Sgt. Harry Flannagan.

"Combat Crew"
S/Sgt. Burns, T/Sgt. Easterday, 1st Lt. Keating, S/Sgt Underwood,
Major Heneel, 1st Lt. Supiano, Col. Karnes, S/Sgt. Shiver,
Gen. Ridenour, S/Sgt. Di Benedette

1stLt. Charles Dever, Capt. Clifford White, Lt. Col. Gray, 1st. Lt. Shappell, T/Sgt. Shiver, T/Sgt. Teetz, S/Sgt. Burns, T/Sgt. Easterday, S/Sgt. Stokes, S/Sgt. Underwood, S/Sgt. Di Benedette

B-24 Bomber taking off from Tunisia, Africa

S/Sgt. John Shiver, enjoying a cigar in front of Jack McKenna's plane in Leece, Italy.

Jack McKeena with the Italian training plane he got in exchange for a gallon of apricots. He wrecked the plane by driving it into a clothesline and never got to fly it.

Sovereign Hotel, Miami, Florida. John Shiver stayed here for two weeks post combat duty before receiving his new stateside orders. While here he was given physical and mental exams

☆

John Shiver, Jr.

John Shiver's tentmate, S/Sgt. Max W. Roach in Benghazi, Libya

✯

B-24 Bomber with an unidentified group of men. The picture was taken in Manduria, Itlay. Mud was everywhere

Myrtle and John Shiver, Jr. The portrait was made after John returned from the war overseas

Myrtle Dean Shiver. The portrait was made when John had an eight-day leave before going to war overseas. John carried this picture in his pocket over his heart on combat duty. He said that Myrtle went with him on all his missions.

Chapter 11

COMBAT MISSIONS

"My Combat Missions"

The dictionary says combat can mean a number of things. Here are some of them: "a struggle, a battle, a conflict, to fight, to duel, or a contest. Combat can be between two or more individuals, groups, or armies".

In the war I learned what combat meant to me. It meant getting there first with the most ammunition and using it. In plain words, it meant killing people and destroying things. There is nothing beautiful or glamorous in war. My war was trying to keep Germany from conquering the world with the help of its allies, Italy and Japan. They had a good start in accomplishing that goal. The United States wasn't prepared for war when the Japanese bombed Pearl Harbor. It is amazing what we were able to do in such a short time. All Americans went to work with one goal in mind - to win the war. The military and civilians did almost the impossible in battles and in the production of things for the war. War was a personal thing to me. It was either live or die on every mission made.

There were accidents on take-offs and landings, mechanical problems, weather conditions, enemy planes, ack-ack, and always the possibility of having to leave the formation and trying to return to the base alone. That happened to me a number of times - over thirty times. I have been on the ground when we were strafed by ME-109's and bombs were falling close by. I was on missions when the ack-ack was really thick, and then it would get thicker. We would say you could get out and walk on it. The blasts would be loud and then extra loud. The noise would sound as if we were in a metal building and someone was throwing stones at it.

When we reached the IP, the Initial Point for the bombing run, the formation would begin the run, and then the bombardier would take over the control of the plane. The plane had to be on a straight and level flight for about ten to fifteen minutes. That always seemed like an eternity to all of us. Time passed slowly for everyone on the plane and we would take no evasive action, just stay flying straight and level. We thought those two words - "bombs away" – never came soon enough from the bombardier.

When I was the flight engineer on a mission, I would be leaning on the backs of the seats of the pilot and co-pilot. I would look up and see a formation of bombers directly above us with their bomb bay doors open. That wasn't supposed to happen, but it did a number of times. We didn't ever get bombed from above, but I have heard about some accidents that happened to other planes.

Some of the men on active combat duty couldn't get a good night's sleep. They would be re-living the day's mission over again. They would wake up all of us whether we were in tents or in barracks. Sometimes after one of the men had a night of bad nightmares, someone would tell him to go to operations and tell them to mark another mission for him. The Lord sure blessed me. I had asked Him to take care of me each day, and I still do. I have peace with my Lord, peace with my fellow man, and peace within my own heart. That is a great feeling.

Through most of my combat flying, I didn't have the comradeship that most of the men had. My pilot, Mills, and three other crew members were killed on their first mission on September 2, 1943, while flying to a target at the R.R. Marshalling Yards at Sulmona, Italy. The remaining crew members who were left were used when needed on different crews. I had a desire to do my duty to my country and to get back to the United States and my wife as quickly as I could.

I went to the operations office and asked them to help me. I told them I would go as a flight engineer or either top turret or waist gunner, but to give me an option to go or not. The crew's reputation would determine my decision. They agreed to help me when they could and they did. All the time I was in the 344th squadron, I enjoyed my associations, operations, all pilots, crew members, and crew chiefs. If ever a problem came up, we would settle it then. I always tried, and I still do, to let my "yes" mean "yes" and my "no" mean "no". I am not a yes-man to anyone. I can live with myself and for that I thank my Lord. I also thank my grandpa for lessons he taught me which served me well in combat.

My Grandpa Shiver would spend time with me when I was a small boy and was always giving me some good talks. I have always remembered some of them:

> "Always tell the truth and you will always know what you said."
> "Pick yourself up by the seat of your pants when you are down."
> "Don't wait for someone else to do it for you."
> "Life is always full of surprises for you."
> "The best thing to do to a person who has done something bad to you is to be extra good to him. He won't be expecting that, and that will hurt him really bad."
> "You are never out until you count yourself out. Get up and try again."
> "Be honest to others and to yourself."
> "Always admit your mistakes and remember them. Let that be a lesson for you."
> "Hard work will not kill you; you will always stop and rest before you pass out."

As I was growing up, he was always telling me things. He had been a businessman during the 1910's, 20's and 30's, but the depression in 1929 hit him hard. I was visiting him when I was about twelve or thirteen years old. I was looking through one of his store accounts receivable books. It was a thick book - about four or five inches - and had papers and notes on most of the homesteads in north Baldwin County. I asked him why he didn't take ownership of those places, and he answered me, "Son, I don't think the Lord would smile on me for taking a homestead away from a man who had cleared it up, lived there and raised his family there. That man would have no hope for tomorrow. The next reason is the man might have killed me."

I was proud of his answer to my question. Another talk he gave me was about worry. "Don't worry about the past - it's gone. You cannot change what's already happened. You have the moment now, and you don't know all that is going to happen to you tomorrow. You can make plans for tomorrow, but you don't know if your plans will work out as planned. Life is full of surprises."

98th BOMBARDMENT GROUP (H) AAF
344th BOMBARDMENT SQUADRON (H) AAF

T/Sgt. John J. Shiver, Jr. ASN #34335079

COMBAT MISSIONS CREDIT

September	17	1943	11:30	Prescara
	18		11:45	Prescara
	22		8:10	Rhodes
October	4		7:30	Menidi
	5		8:05	Eleusis
	8		6:30	Crete
	9		7:10	Crete
	20		7:10	Crosseto

November	15		10:15	Eleusis
	19		6:40	Aviano
	25		3:30	Klagenfurt
	30		6:45	Klagenfurt
December	3		4:50	Roma Casale
	6		5:20	Eleusis
	15		7:25	Avisio
	16		6:40	Dogna
	19		4:10	Augsburg
	20		5:25	Sofia*
	25		6:40	Udine
February	4	1944	5:45	Toulon
	10		5:45	Anzio*
	15		5:35	Arezzo
	16		6:50	Arezzo
	17		7:15	Anzio*
	22		9:05	Regensburg*(2)
March	7		9:00	Poggibonsi
	17		8:00	Schwechat*
	18		6:50	Gorizia
April	12		7:30	Weiner-Neustadt*(2)
	15		7:45	Bucharest*(2)
	17		6:00	Sofia
	20		7:00	Mestre
	24		8:15	Ploesti***(2)
	25		8:00	Parma
	30		8:30	Alessandria
May	2		7:30	Bologna
	6		7:55	Brasov*(2)
	7		8:00	Bucharest*(2)
	13		9:30	Fidenza
	14		7:50	Vicenza
	17		6:30	San Stefano****

COMBAT MISSION DETAILS OF PREVIOUS CHART

September 1943 Flight Record   T/Sgt. John J. Shiver, Jr. 34335079

Air Corps APO #68   Ninth Air Force (IX bomber command)
           98th BG   344th Bomb Squad (Engineer- Gunner)

16	B-24D	6.5	#42-41006	(Flying Jinny)	Lt. Atwood
17	B-24D	11.5	#42-41006	(Flying Jinny)	Lt. Atwood
18	B-24D	11.8	#42-41006	(Flying Jinny)	Lt. Atwood
22	B-24D	8.2		(Coral Princess)	Lt. Kale
26	B-24D	4.8			
	Hours	42.8			

1st Lt. Joseph H. Campbell - Operation Officer

Combat Missions - September 1943

<u>9/16</u>   Mission - Potenza - Railroad Jct. - 7-500 # Bombs

One prop. gov. out - #3 engine. We turned back and returned to base. We dropped bombs in water - 6.5 hours. This was my first mission. No mission credit. We were about one hour from target when we turned back and returned to base. Twenty planes from group left on this mission on the 16th.

<u>9/17</u>   Pescara, Italy   11.30 Hrs.

The 98th sent out 22 planes. Railroad M/Y and bridge. Hit target 2:40 500# bombs.

Plane name - "Flying Jinny" #42-41006. Lt. Atwood - engineer - no gun

<u>9/18</u>   Pescara, Italy   11:45 Hrs.

Railroad M/Y and bridge. 500 # bombs - "Flying Jinny" #42-41006

Lt. Atwood – engineer – no gun. The group had 17 planes on this mission.

376th bomb group bombed above us - no damage to us.

9/22   Rhodes Island - Martiza Aerodrome   8:10 Hrs.
        500# bombs - "Coral Princess"
        1st ack-ack. (anti-aircraft fire) Low. Not our altitude. Lt. Kale
Flew right wing to Col. Kane's lead plane "Skipper." The group had 23 planes on this mission. Col. Kane circled back over target to see bomb hits. I fired right waist gun.

9/26   4:80 Hrs.
I was placed on Lt. Keating's crew as an assistant engineer and right waist gunner. The group was being moved to Hergla, Tunisia. The planes and crews with crew chiefs and assistants left Benghazi desert to go to Tunisia. The group and equipment would leave by trucks the next day. We arrived in Tunisia about mid-afternoon and set up our tents not far from the Mediterranean Sea - about 150 yards from the water. It looked so good after being in the desert. We had a supply of K-rations to eat. We had no way of knowing what was in the near future for us. The Germans took Crete back from the British soon after we left Benghazi. We got orders to return back to our old base where the British would feed us and help us by supplying gas and oil. Our group was en route to Tunisia. So, on October 3, 1943, we returned to our old base. We did bring our crew chiefs and assistants with us. The trip back was made in 4.1 hours.

October 1943 Flight Record   T/Sgt. John J. Shiver, Jr. 34335079

Air Corps	APO #683 98th BG(H)	Twelfth Air Force (XII bomber command) 344th Bomb Squad (Engineer – Gunner)		
3	B-24D	4.1	#795-I	Lt. Keating
4	B-24D	7.5	#795-I	Lt. Keating
5	B-24D	8.1	#795-I	Lt. Keating
7	B-24D	5.0	#733-J	Lt. Keating
8	B-24D	6.3	#890-H	Lt. Keating
9	B-24D	7.2	#799-C	Lt. Keating
10	B-24D	5.3	#795-I	Lt. Keating

12	B-24D	4.7	#795-I		Lt. Keating
17	B-24D	2.3	#795-I		Lt. Keating
18	B-24D	1.7	#795-I		Lt. Keating
20	B-24D	7.2	#795-I		Lt. Keating
24	B-24D	<u>7.1</u>	#795-I		Lt. Keating
	Hours	66			

Sept. 42.8
Oct. <u>66.5</u>
Total 109.3

Combat Missions - October 1943

<u>10/3</u>	Returned back to Benghazi from Tunisia Lt. Keating - #795-1	4:10 Hrs.
<u>10/4</u>	Menidi - Aerodrome (Greece) Lt. Keating - #795-1 - 28 planes. Fired right waist gun. Moderate ack-ack. Accurate.	7:30 Hrs.
<u>10/5</u>	Eleusis - Aerodrome (Greece) Lt. Keating - #795-1 - 26 planes Fired right waist gun Moderate ack-ack. Accurate.	8:05 Hrs.
<u>10/7</u>	Kastelli - Pediedo Aerodrome Lt. Keating - #733-1 - 24 planes Had to return to base - engine out (no credit).	5:00 Hrs.
<u>10/8</u>	Crete - Heraklion Aerodrome Lt. Keating - #890-H - 22 planes Fired right waist gun. Moderate ack-ack. Accurate.	6:30 Hrs.

10/9 Crete - Heraklion Aerodrome   7:10 Hrs.
    Lt. Keating - #799-C - 21 planes
    Fired right waist gun.
    Moderate ack-ack. Accurate.

10/10 Crete - Heraklion Aerodrome
    Lt. Keating - #795-1 - 21 planes
    Had to return to base - engine trouble. No mission credit.

10/12 Returned to Tunisia from Benghazi   4.70 Hrs.
    Lt. Keating - #795-I

10/17 We left base on a mission and were called back to base. I lost some of my notes. My flying record had me on #795-1 with Lt. Keating and flying time was 2.3 hrs.

10/18 No Group record for the mission but my flying record had me on #795-1 with Lt. Keating with flying time of 1.7 hrs. Group records do not show any missions for October 17th or 18th.

10/20 Grosseto, Italy - Railroad Bridge   7.10 Hrs.
    Lt. Keating - #795-1 - 26 planes
  Lt. Campbell led a four-plane formation. Element pass target. Mistake - Lt. Huckleberry turned off and left us. We left target like a bat out of hell! About 210 miles indicated and caught up with formation. We had 1000# bombs on the plane that day and one of them didn't drop. The bombardier checked the bomb rack and he thought we could bring it back to base. It was the old type in which the fuses could be removed, so he put the pins in the front and rear fuse blades. I was the assistant engineer on the crew and Teetes was on the flight deck calling the landing speed to the pilot, so we needed to get the auxiliary power engine going as soon as we were on the ground. I had told Teetes I would get the put-put engine started and for him to have the radioman turn off the plane's generator, because we had low-charged batteries. I was standing on the catwalk close to the flight deck before the plane's wheels touched the ground. The bomb was in the

top rack on the right front of the plane and I was looking at it when the wheels touched down; the bomb fell and tore the bomb door off. What a noise that was and what a scare for me! No damage, except the bomb bay door was off.

<u>10/24</u>   Weiner-Neustadt Air Frame Works   7:10 Hrs.
           Lt Keating - #795-l - 21 planes

We had "Old Green I" (Ickie) that Lt. Keating was flying when I joined the crew. It was one of the planes the group had when they left the States in 1942. It didn't have a ball turret. It was a plane that wanted to fly, was easy to fly, and used half the fuel the other planes did. The group tried to use it for a lead plane, but that didn't work. "Old Green I" would run off and leave the others. But "Old Green I" got old and worn out, and the group needed to keep it flying because we couldn't get any new planes. Before we got to the target, we lost an engine; we had to turn back and come back alone. We couldn't go over a target with one engine already out. It was a very bad feeling to not get credit for a mission and it was hard to get home safely. But, we made it back to base.

<u>November 1943 Flight Record</u>   T/Sgt. John J. Shiver, Jr. 34335079
Air Corps   APO #683   Fifteenth Air Force (15 AF)
             98th BG(H)   47th Bomb Wing
                             344th Bomb Wing (Engineer – Gunner)

11	B-24D	5.0	#795-I	Lt. Keating
15	B-24D	10.3	#795-I	Lt. Keating
18	B-24D	4.3	#795-I	Lt. Keating
				(Trip to Brindisi, Italy)
19	B-24D	6.7	#795-I	Lt. Keating
24	B-24D	2.5		
25	B-24D	3.5		
30	B-24D	<u>6.8</u>		
	Hours	37.1		

1st Lt. Philip J. Keating, Operations Officer
Nov.   37.1
Previous 109.3
Total   146.4

Combat Missions – November 1943

11/11   Anthear Viaduct   5.00 Hrs
        B-24-D – Lt. Keating - #795 I– 16 planes.
        Had to turn back. Engine out. No credit.

11/15   Eleusis Aerodrome (Greece)   10:15 Hrs.
        Lt. Keating – 795-I – 22 planes

Plenty of ack-ack. Big stuff – 88 and 128-millimeter guns. Some fighters. We were the last plane in our group. The 376th group was supposed to follow us over the target, but they didn't. They cut in front of us and we had to follow them. That made us in "Old Green I" the "tail-end Charlie" that day. The 376th didn't get any ack-ack, but fighters shot down one of their planes. I guess they were saving the ack-ack for us. After we left the target, three FW190s hit us. One came at us on the right side and I shot about 20 rounds at it, but Seitz, the pilot of another B-24, got in my way. I couldn't shoot anymore. Things went well after that. Our P-38 escorts came to our rescue. They shot down two of the FW190s and the other one left.

We flew over Athens and got no ack-ack. Then we flew back over the airfield at a lower altitude and got some more ack-ack. I still don't know what the reason was. When you're in formation you just follow. We saw a big four-engine transport plane at the end of the runway ready for take-off. After that we left Athens and headed home with the P-38 escorts with us.

After a few minutes our radio operator told us to turn our station box switch off intercom to the command position and enjoy the P-38 pilots talking to each other. In a short while the Fighter Group C.O., a colonel, told his wing man to follow him down and keep his tail clean, that he saw a train below and he was going after the locomotive. The wingman's name was "Red."

Red answered the colonel, "I can't. I'm low on gas and I have no ammo left."

The colonel replied, "Red, you don't need gas or ammo. Follow me down!"

Red said, "I can't. I have to head home."

"Red, you're yellow!" The colonel answered. "You go on home and I'll tend to you when I get home."

He went on down and he got the engine on his first pass at it. We saw it when it blew up, because we had a front row seat. The P-38 had a lot of guns in a small space: four .50 caliber guns and one 20 mm cannon - all in the nose of the plane. Luftwaffe pilots called the "Lightin", the "fork-tailed devil." It was great to have them around. We said we hoped the men on the train engine jumped off before the engine exploded. But, it has been said, everything's fair in war. War is hell here on earth. It means to kill or be killed and it means destroying things.

11/18   Left Tunisia for Brindisi, Italy   4:30 Hrs.
       Planes left with the crews, crew chiefs, and assistant crew chiefs.
       Lt. Keating - #795-1 - B-24D

The group was to follow by ships later. The plane was really loaded, so I made the flight in the nose section. I always wanted to see the view from the nose section while taking off and landing. I enjoyed the flight, but I didn't tell anyone about it until later. Lt. Keating told me if he had known about it before, he wouldn't have let me do it. I told him that was the reason I didn't tell anyone what I was going to do.

We were going to live in a large administration building close to the runway. It was a large building - three or four stories. We had come up from tents, mud and sand and we were going to be living uptown. We had indoor plumbing and showers. We were told late that evening we had a mission the next day. There was no one to load the bombs, so we had to do that with a small hand-crank type winch that was in each plane. We also had to help service the plane, but we did what we had to do. We got to our bunks about ten o'clock that night knowing we would be eating K-rations for the next few days, but we were happy to be at Brindisi.

11/19   Aviano - Aerodrome (Venice)   6.70 Hrs
        Lt. Keating - #795-1 - 16 planes

We went over the target area, but it was covered a hundred percent with clouds, so we didn't drop the bombs. We brought the bombs back, but we got credit for the mission. They must have had mercy on us and given us credit for the effort. We sure tried and we were happy for the credit.

11/24   Sofia (in Bulgaria)
        Lt. Keating - B-24 #795-1 - 15 planes   2:50 Hrs
        Mission recalled after a short time. No credit.

11/25   Klagenfurt (Austria) Aircraft Factory   3:30 Hrs
        Lt. Keating - B-24 - #006-B - 23 planes

This was a very bad morning for all of us. Formation went into "soupy" clouds. We had a "scatter" formation plan to be used for such an occasion. But, the plan didn't work for us because our instruments went crazy. The flight indicator showed bank left and our needle and ball showed bank right. We were in the soup for about forty-five minutes. One B-24 flew under us - very close - from left to right. It had to be close to us to be seen. After a little while we got in the open and couldn't see anyone else. We dropped our bombs in succession into the sea and returned to base. Got credit for the mission.

11/30   Fiume - Klagenfurt   6:45 Hrs.
        Lt. Keating B24-D - #795-1 - 20 planes.

December 1943 Flight Record   S/Sgt. John J. Shiver, Jr. 34335079
Air Corps   APO #683   Fifteenth Air Force
             98th BG(H) 47th Bomb Wing
                         344th Bomb Squad (Engineer – Gunner)

1	B-24D	4.2	#795-I
3	B-24D	4.9	#136-K
4	B-24D	1.5	#029-A
6	B-24D	5.4	#029-A

14	B-24D	3.1	#799-C
15	B-24D	7.5	
19	B-24D	4.1	
20	B-24D	5.5	#890-H
22	B-24D	1.9	
25	B-24D	6.7	#890-H
28	B-24D	3.5	
31	B-24D	<u>2.5</u>	
	Hours	50.7	

1st Lt. Philip J. Keating, Operations Officer

Dec.	50.7
Previous	<u>146.4</u>
Total	197.1

(*12/16/43 Flight to Dogna <u>6:40 Hrs</u>. Left off flight record, but it was on my combat missions record. Plane #890-H)

<u>Combat Missions - December 1943</u>

<u>12/1</u>   Bolzano (Northern Italy close to Switzerland) M/Yard   4:20 Hrs
Lt. Keating - B-24D #795-1 - 18 planes

We had a recall on this mission - <u>no credit.</u> Everything was fine until we were landing. I was on the catwalk ready to start the put-put and the wheels hadn't touched down yet. I saw through a small opening at the bomb bay door the large building as we went by. We were always on the runway as we went by that building. I looked at Keating in the pilot's seat and he was fighting the controls. I heard him yelling "Get down! Get down!"

I got on the flight deck as fast as I could. I knew we still hadn't touched down yet. We had a short runway and "Old Green I" was still in the air with the throttles pulled all the way back. "Old Green I" wanted to fly. I thought about the seawall coming up on us fast. I didn't think about the empty 55-gallon gas drums left there. In short order, we were on the ground and off the runway. It had rained some and we were slowed down in the muddy grassy area off the runway. We stopped short of the seawall and the drums. "Old Green I" had been stopped.

<u>12/3</u>   Roma Casale "Aero" (Rome) - 13 planes   4:50 Hrs.
         Lt. Keating - B-24H - #136-K

"Spratt's" was a new plane in the squadron. It was the maiden trip for the plane and Lt. Spratt went as co-pilot on his first mission. Only two planes from the 344th made the target - Lt. Shappell's plane and us. The P-38s flew "escort" duty for us that day and it was great. They flew all over the place while we were there, looking for trouble, but they didn't find any. I went as a cameraman on this mission. The group operations officer asked me if I would be the cameraman for this trip, and I told him I would try. The group photo shop men were to set the big camera in the plane and show me what to do. The plane had a camera door over a 5' by 5' opening in the rear floor between the waist windows and the tail turret. They installed the big camera on a plate made for the opening with one hinged side and outfitted with ropes and pulleys. Before we got to the target area, I would pull the door to the opening and tie it, then let the camera plate down in place and call the bombardier and tell him it was ready. The camera was wired to start when bombs were dropped. It was very big. I was instructed to hold a hand camera out the left waist window. It was a very heavy camera and I was told not to drop it. It was a bad job, with my hands and head out of the window in the wind. One of the cameras had this on the plate:

F-5 .0 306 M.M. 12"
Lens Cone Aircraft
Minus Blue Filter
(Fairchild Aviation Corp.)

After a certain time when we left the target, I pulled the big camera up, tied it up, and then dropped the door down over the opening. I was glad when it was over. There is always danger of a mishap when the door is open, but I didn't have any trouble. The photo men came and got the cameras out of the plane after we landed.

12/4 Menidi – AD   1:50 Hrs.
      Lt. Keating B-24 - #029-A
We had a recall on this mission. No credit.

12/6 Eleusis - AID - (Greece) - 24 planes   5:40 Hrs.
      Lt. Barker - B-24 - #029-A

It was cold that day and some of the bombs were slow on their release, so we dropped some bombs on the city of Athens. It was not intentional. It was an accident.

12/10 Sofia-M/Y- 16 planes   No Time
      Lt. Barker - B-24 - #029-A - 16 planes
      No take-off. Engine trouble.

12/14 Tatoi - AD - #799-C - 23 planes   3:10 Hrs.

12/15 Avisio Viaduct (Brenner Pass) - #890-H - 25 planes   7:50 Hrs
      47th Bomb Wing - Commander – General Ridenous
      Pilot - Colonel Karnes - #890-H
      Co-pilot - Lt. Keating
      Navigator - Group Navigator
      Bombardier - Group Bombardier
      Observer - General Ridenous
      Flight Engineer - John Shiver
      Radio and Top Gunner- Easterday
      Tail Gunner - Burns
      Ball Turret - Underwood
      Waist Gunner - DiBenedetto

This crew was picked for the 98th commander to take the wing commander, General Ridenous, on a bombing mission. We had an 8:00 a.m. take-off. The crew was all at the plane before 8:00 and we were ready. Colonel Karnes had already run the engines and had them warmed up and had cut them off, but he remained seated in the pilot's seat. We were still waiting for General Ridenous to arrive. All the others were standing outside. I was told the general would be co-pilot on the plane. I had left the co-pilot line blank on the manifest I had filled out for the record of who's who on the plane. I didn't know his ID number. We waited for the general.

At about 8:15 I saw his car coming - the flags on the front bumper indicating his rank. When the general's car stopped, Colonel Karnes was still in the pilot's seat and all of the crew got in the plane, leaving only me to greet the general. The sergeant, his driver, opened the back door and the general got out. The sergeant got the general's chute, armor vest, and oxygen mask and gave them to me. I welcomed the general and asked him for his service ID card. He asked, "What do you want with my card?"

I told him I had to add his name to the manifest in case we didn't come back. Then he said to me, "Where do you want me?"

"I was told you would be the co-pilot today."

He replied, "I have never flown a B-24 before. I'm a B-17 man, but I'll go as co-pilot. I can fly anything. Sergeant, what's your hurry this morning?"

I answered, "General, we were supposed to take-off at eight o'clock this morning. The engines have already been warmed up. We don't want to waste gas by having to warm up the engines again. We might need that gas to get back home."

I thought to myself - *Somebody has dropped the ball and I have got to come up with something fast.*

"General, you need to go as an observer today and not work," I said. "I will find a stool for you to sit on in back of the Colonel's, so you can talk to him today."

I got up on the flight deck and explained the situation to Colonel Karnes. I rushed out and found Lt. Keating who was on the sidelines to see us off. I asked him if he would go with us and he said he would. I told him while he was getting his stuff together, I would get the manifest filled in and get the general aboard.

I went back and finished the manifest and gave it to the crew chief. Lt. Keating arrived and we were ready to leave on the mission. After we were in the air, I made it a point to tell all except Colonel Karnes how happy I was about them leaving me to welcome General Ridenous. "You all scattered like a covey of quail when the general's car drove up to the plane."

When I got back to the flight deck, the general and I started talking. We were going to destroy the Avisio Viaduct in Northern Italy, known as the Brenner Pass. We wanted to stop the Germans from using it.

The general said, "We are going to destroy that bridge today."

I didn't say anything. He asked me if I agreed with him. I said, "I hope you're right, but the way the bombardiers have been doing lately, I would say 'no'."

The general told me to just wait and see. Then he asked me where my flak jacket was. "It's there in the corner of the flight deck. I can't wear it."

He answered, "I will have you know I sent out orders for all to use them, and if you're not going to put it on, why did you bring it with you?"

"General, look out at the bomb bays and the narrow catwalk I have to use to get to and from the rear of the plane. I can't even wear my Mae West and I have trouble wearing my chute harness. When we get flak or when we go over the target, I will put my flak jacket on the floor and stand on it."

He said, "You've made your point."

We were coming near the target and he asked me what I did when we were dropping the bombs. I said, "I lie on my stomach on the floor with the trap door up and my head out in the bomb bay and watch the bombs leave the bomb bay. If I don't take my eyes off the bombs, I can see them hit. I will lose sight of them just before they get to the ground, but if I keep my eyes fixed where they were when I lost them, I will see where they hit."

The general asked me if I had a pair of binoculars on the plane. I told him there was supposed to be a pair in a box over the bomb bay. The general had his hanging from his neck. He asked me if I would let him use my spot on the deck floor and told me to go to the back and get the binoculars to watch the bombs drop. I fixed a spot for him by putting my flak jacket on the floor for him and went to the rear, found the binoculars and got ready.

We got a lot of flak, but we got the bombs away. I was on the intercom and watching the bombs. We came close, but the bridge was still standing after we left. The general said over the intercom, "It's a direct hit. That's right, isn't it, Sergeant?"

"No sir," I answered. "We were close, but the bridge was still standing after the group left it."

He said, "Your eyes are playing tricks on you. You need to have them checked."

I told him I wanted him to be right, but I was thinking the bridge was still standing. I said, "We will know when the films are developed."

One of the gunners came on and had some fun over my conversation with the general. He told me I should know better than to disagree with a general and I would find this to be true later.

I answered, "The general doesn't want a yes-man. He wants an honest one. I called it like I saw it. Nothing more, nothing less."

We didn't have any trouble getting back to the base and when we landed, the general asked me if I would make him a copy of the manifest. I told him I would and I did. After we returned, we were met with a large number of officers from the wing headquarters who were there to welcome General Ridenous back and to present him a Silver Star medal for the raid. All the rest of the crew got a "thank you" from the general and Colonel Karnes. That was appreciated and it was nice to be back. It had been a good day.

That was the end of the bombing mission, but that night I wanted to find out if I was right or wrong about the bridge still standing. About eight o'clock I went to the group photo room and saw the picture. The bridge was still standing. The bombardiers had had to use information taken by a P-38 reconnaissance plane at an earlier hour that morning. Things can change in a number of hours at a target.

<u>12/16</u>   Dogna - Viaduct- Railroad Junction - 20 planes   6:40 Hrs
Colonel William K. Karnes - #890-H

The Group Commander was to lead the group on this mission. I was asked to be the flight engineer. The group navigator and bombardier came for the mission. It was a good day with some ack-ack but not too bad.

As we were getting ready to land, one of the officers told me he had never seen a pilot who could land a B-24 as smoothly as Colonel Karnes. He told me I wouldn't believe it. He picked up a .50 caliber shell off the floor and stood it up on the radio sergeant's table. Then he said the spent shell would not fall until the colonel applied the brakes.

I said, "I will believe it when I see it."

He said, "Just wait and you'll see."

In a short time we landed and the shell was still standing. We were then on the roll and I told the officer it was the best landing I had ever seen. I told him, "Now, I believe it!"

I then gave the colonel a handshake and thanked him for a good mission and a good landing. He said, "I thank you for the compliments and for your help."

12/19	Augsburg, Germany (Aircraft Factory) - 20 planes	4:10 Hrs.
12/20	Sofia- M/Y (Bulgaria) - 20 planes - #890-H	5:50 Hrs.
12/22	(Mission not recorded or detailed)	1:90 Hrs.
12/25	Udine – M/Y (Northern Italy) - 15 planes Lt. Col. Marshall Gray - #890-H	6:70 Hrs
12/28	Vicenza (Northern Italy) - 20 planes - B-24D	3:50 Hrs.
12/31	B-24D	2:50 Hrs.

January 1944 Flight Record   T/Sgt. John J. Shiver, Jr. 34335079
Air Corps   APO #520   Fifteenth Air Force
            98th BG(H)   47th Bomb Wing
                          344th Bomb Squad (Engineer – Gunner)

4	B-24D	3.0	
8	B-24D	3.2	
9	B-24D	3.2	All January '44 flights were bombardier
11	B-24D	2.8	practice missions at an area bombing site
13	B-24D	3.8	and we were waiting for new groups to
14	B-24D	2.7	arrive from the U.S.
26	B-24D	4.0	
30	B-24D	<u>3.0</u>	
	Hours	25.7	

1st Lt. Philip J. Keating, Operations Officer
Jan.   25.7
Previous 197.1
Total   222.8

February 1944 Flight Record   T/Sgt. John J. Shiver, Jr. 34335079

Air Corps   APO #520   Fifteenth Air Force
             98th BG(H)   47th Bomb Wing
                            344th Bomb Squad (Engineer – Gunner)

4	B-24D	5.8	#023-D	Lt. Keating
8	B-24D	5.5		
10	B-24D	5.8	#023-D	Lt. Barker
12	B-24D	3.3		
14	B-24D	4.9	#779-C	Lt. Keating
15	B-24D	5.6	#795-I	Lt. Keating
16	B-24D	6.5	#795-1	Lt. Keating
17	B-24D	7.3	#136-K	Lt. Keating
22	B-24D	9.1	#854-M	Lt. Col. Gray
	Hours	50.7		

1st Lt. Philip L. Keating, Operations Officer
Feb.   63.8
Previous 222.8
Total   286.6

<u>Combat Missions - February 1943</u>

2/4   Toulon - Harbor - 20 planes   5.80Hrs.
       Lt. Keating- 023-D

About thirty minutes before we got to the target, I saw a B-24 join a formation of B-24s off to our right. I was at the right waist gun and I didn't recognize the marking on the rear of the plane. The 15th Air Force was getting new groups in, and I thought maybe it was someone who had gotten separated from his unit. After a few minutes, they opened fire on the plane next to them, peeled off and left. The B-24 they shot went down in a spin, and I did not see any chutes or anyone leave the plane. I'm sure it was a German crew in a B-24 they had got their hands on.

We were bombing the Toulon Harbor in southeast France and we always called it "Sub Pens" because it was used for a naval base. We didn't see fighters, but we had plenty of ack-ack. We always said we could get out and walk on the flak sometimes when it was that thick. They sure could put it up fast. I have read they could fire the 88-millimeter anti-aircraft guns at the rate of forty rounds a minute. They could really throw it up and with some bigger stuff, too.

<u>2/8</u>   5:50 Hrs.

No mission on record for the group for this day, but it must have been a recall because I had a record for the time of 5.5 hours. Some of my notes have been lost. No mission credit.

<u>2/10</u>   Campoleone - 39 planes   5:80 Hrs.
         Lt. Barker - #023-D

Some of my notes have been lost for this mission. I have some record of it and I received mission credit for it.

<u>2/12</u>   Anzio Beachhead - 19 planes   3:30 Hrs.

Some of the records/notes lost for this mission. I am sure our plane had a turn-back on this mission, because I received no credit and the group did drop bombs on the target. My flying time was not long enough for the complete trip to target and back to base.

<u>2/14</u>   Ferrara M/Y - Northern Italy - 19 planes
         Lt. Keating - #799-C   4:90 Hrs.

This was a turn-back - engine trouble. Coming back alone was bad. It could be very bad if we met up with a fighter plane or a group of them. No credit for this day. I was on the right waist gun.

<u>2/15</u>   Arezzo – M/Y - 32 planes   5:60 Hrs.
         Lt. Keating - #795-K

I have no record of anything unusual happening on this flight. It was the usual ack-ack, and never knowing when the ME-I09s or the FW -190s would show up. I was on right waist gun. Credit for mission.

2/16   Arezzo - MIY - 18 planes   6:50 Hrs.
      Lt. Keating - #795-K

Everything the same as it was for the previous day's mission. Credit for mission.

2/17   Invasion Beachhead - 25 planes   7:30 Hrs.
      Lt. Keating - #136-K

This mission was to bomb the German troop concentration. I was on the right waist gun. The mission plan called for us to fly up the east side of Italy, turn left and fly the bomb line to the west coast of Italy in order to boost the morale of the Allies on the ground. The ack-ack was bad for us.

2/20   Invasion Beachhead - Anzio - 30 planes   7:00 Hrs.
      Lt. Barker - #023-D

<u>This mission was not on my records.</u>

This mission was the same as the mission on the 17th, except we didn't fly along the bomb line. That was not a good thing for us in the planes. They wanted us to fly low enough so the Allies could see us, but we were being shot at by the Germans at the same time. On this mission, we went west to the water and then went north to the target area. We had anti-personnel bombs; those were to kill the Germans who had stopped the Allied invasion on the ground. It was a hard thing to do at high altitude. On one of our trips, we tore up an Army general's trailer. His letter was posted on the bomb group's bulletin board for all to see.

We had to make our bomb run off the coast toward the beach. While we were making the bomb run, our U.S. ships were shooting at us. We didn't like that at all. Later on, while I was on R&R in Capri, I noticed some sailors there. I was talking to some of them about them shooting at us and they said, "We were told you would be over at twelve o'clock. You were over at ten minutes to twelve!"

I told them they were crazy - they scared us because we were not expecting that!

2/22   Regensburg (Germany) - 14 planes - #854-M   9:10 Hrs

Obertrawbling A/C Factory
G5 Prifenig A/C Factory
Colonel Marshall R. Gray - Pilot
Lt. Shappell – Co-pilot
Lt. Dever - Navigator
Lt. White - Bombardier
Sgt. Teetes - Engineer
Sgt. Easterday - Radio
Sgt. Stokes - Top Turret Gunner
Sgt. Underwood - Ball Turret Gunner
Sgt. DiBenedetto - Left Waist Gunner
Sgt. Shiver - Right Waist Gunner
Sgt. Burns - Tail Turret Gunner

<u>Double Credit - Two Missions</u>

The crew above is the crew picked to go with Col. Gray on the Regensburg raid. On four previous days in February the raid had been scheduled, but was cancelled because of bad weather. We knew they would be ready for us. On the evening before the raid, I saw a plane having an engine change parked next to the one we were to use the next day. There was no way it would be flying on the planned mission. I checked to see if there was any ammo on board. I found plenty of boxes in the plane. I went and told Burns and no one else.

About eight o'clock that evening, Burns and I went out to the plane and told the guards we were going to borrow a few boxes for the next day's raid. "If we don't use it, we'll return it when we get back, and if we don't get back, forget it."

The bombs and ammo had already been loaded for the next day's raid and this was extra ammo. We carried five or six boxes and put them in a place above the rear bomb bay. The boxes were heavy, but we got the job done and kept it to ourselves.

The extra ammo sure was put to good use the next day. We were the first to take off on that morning and on the take-off, Col. Gray remarked over the intercom the plane was really loaded. I had not told the other crew members about our extra ammo on board - that was Burn's and my secret until later. Now it was time to tell the other gunners about the extra ammo and to get some of the boxes down and opened.

I went up front and told Stokes to come and get some extra ammo and to help get some for the nose guns. I had Underwood put a box at a place close to the ball turret so when he needed some, I could help get it to him. Burns and DiBenedetto, nicknamed "Dim-Dom", helped place some boxes close to the tail turret and the waist guns. Meanwhile, we had gotten into formation and were climbing to our altitude. We usually bombed at twenty-six or twenty-seven thousand feet. The higher up we were, the better, but we would use fuel at a higher rate. It didn't make any difference how high we were; there was always some ack-ack above us. It certainly felt better to be higher.

We were crossing over the Alps and what a sight to see! I had seen the Alps from above a number of times, but each time it was a beautiful sight. They had a pleasing appearance, to say the least. I couldn't help but admire the landscape, but I always thought about how bad it would be to have to bailout over the Alps.

After we crossed the Alps going to the target, the fighters started coming up to us. A fighter group couldn't stay with us very long, but they had them placed at the right places so we would have the planes on us all the time - going to target and coming home. We were supposed to be the third group from the rear of the 15th Air Force. We crossed over into Germany and it wasn't long before we saw trouble coming. We could see the planes as they were coming up to our altitude a ways in front of us. To make matters extra bad for us, our planes were loaded with Napalm bombs that contained a highly incendiary, jelly-like substance. We called it "liquid rubber and aviation gasoline". The German planes started to work on our bombers. They concentrated on the last group first. That group was the next to the last group to our rear and was off to our left. Some of the last group was shot down, while some dropped out and turned back. There was one plane left of the last group which joined up with us. The German fighters left and the ack-ack started – and it was bad – very heavy ack-ack. We had noticed we would usually get an ack-ack burst and then there would be three more at the same altitude, getting closer to us all the time. Burns, the tail gunner, called the colonel and told him he needed to go faster; they had us on target. When flying in formation, a plane can't change speed like that. Burns thought the next burst of flak would get us. The flak came and got the plane to our rear, which was slightly below us. That plane was the lead of another three-plane formation. I was looking at it when it got hit. It was a big ball of fire. One moment it was there and the next moment – gone.

We were getting close to the target, but there were two rings of ack-ack around the target. We were inside the ring of ack-ack and getting ready to turn on the bomb run with the bomb bay doors open. As we started to turn on the bomb run, the #2 group cut in front of us. They were supposed to follow us over the target. That put us in a bad place. If we chose to make another bomb run over the target, we would have to take the bomb load out of the ack-ack rings and bring it back through again. The colonel made the decision. He told the crew, "War is hell here on earth, and we are not carrying this load of bombs through two rings of ack-ack anymore."

He told the bombardier to drop them on the city and we would try to get home. The other planes dropped their bombs on our bomb drop. We were going to try to get home, but the Germans had other plans for us. They weren't going to let us go without more fighting. They had used the ME-109s and the FW-190s. Now they were going to shoot rockets at us. They would stay a long way off from us and lob the rockets in our direction. They had twin-engine planes and they looked like they would slow down and shoot their rockets and leave, then another would take their place.

At the time of the rocket attack, the guns on our plane were shooting. The tail, ball, and top turrets were busy returning fire. All the time this was going on, Colonel Gray, who was on his first tough mission (he had been criticized for not going on a tough one), was saying, "Save the ammo! You've got to get us home!"

At one time during the rocket attack, I saw one coming directly toward our plane. I told Dim-Dom we were going to get hit. It came by the left waist window between the tail section and the left wing, barely missing our plane. Dim-Dom commented very calmly over the intercom, "Jeff (my nickname), that was a pretty one, just like an Easter egg; I could have reached out and caught that one."

"Dim-Dom," I said, "you are the only one who would say that at a time like this!" The Lord was with us on that mission.

The turret guns were still busy and I was helping get ammo to them. When I first started getting ammo to Burns at the tail turret, I used a small oxygen bottle, but later I would get a big shot of pure oxygen, get the ammo to Burns and get back to my station. The used .50 caliber shells were about six inches deep in the back of the plane. Dim-Dom and I had trouble standing at the waist guns. We were under attack (fighters, ack-ack and rockets) for a total of 93 minutes. After the twin-engine planes had left us, I noticed an ME-109 off to our right. I thought it was out of range for me to hit it. Lt. White called me and asked me if I knew it was there. I answered, "Yes, I'm looking at it now and I know he is telling them our altitude."

Lt. White told me to get him. I replied, "I think he's too far off, but I'll try."

I gave him three long shots and I was surprised to see black smoke coming from the plane as it was falling.

Lt. White said, "You got him! You file a claim for him and I can verify it for you." I told the lieutenant I wouldn't claim it because there would be 19 other gunners claiming that kill. I did not claim it, but I should have. That night Lt. White came to my tent and told me no one had claimed it. A gunner's mission was not to shoot down planes, but to help deliver bombs to targets. Certainly, that does help to destroy the enemy.

The mission to Regensburg was a bad one. We were on our way home and we didn't need any more that afternoon. On our right, a little higher, there was a formation of planes coming. I saw them and reported it. The colonel asked if I had any binoculars back there in the plane. I told him there was one in a box and I would get it and see if I could tell what planes they were. I said for us to pray for them to be our escorts—not more German planes! I got the binoculars and saw they were P-38s and told the crew the good news. They had come to bring us home. It wasn't long before we re-crossed the Alps.

As we got close to our base, the radioman got us Axis Sally's broadcast. She was really giving the 98th Group hell for bombing the city with napalm bombs and killing innocent women and children. I was glad to get rid of those bombs, but I didn't make that call. No one here on earth knows if we could have gotten that bomb load through two rings of ack-ack or not. No one except someone who has been on a bombing mission knows the great feeling of relief when the bombardier comes on the intercom and says, "Bombs away!" There is someone who will always say – "up to now we have been working for 'Uncle Sam'. Now, we're working to live another day."

When we arrived at base there were a number of group personnel to welcome Colonel Gray home. I will always remember what his remarks were: "I appreciate the welcome but you'll have to wait. I'll have time with you people later. I have to spend time with the crew now. They got us home."

And he spent a lot of time with us. First, he gave us a thank-you speech and a handshake. But he never asked where we got all the ammo and there wasn't much brought back. We had a busy day and we were glad to get back.

<u>March 1944 Flight Record</u>   T/Sgt. John J. Shiver, Jr. 34335079

Air Corps   APO #520   Fifteenth Air Force
              98th BG(H)   47th Bomb Wing
                              344th Bomb Squad (Engineer – Gunner)

4	B-24J	3.3		
7	B-24J	9.0	#439-A	Lt. Keating
11	B-24J	6.8	#006-B	Lt. Atwood
15	B-24J	4.3	#006-B	Lt. Atwood
17	B-24J	8.0	#646-H	Lt. Repp
18	B-24J	6.8	#006-B	Lt. Atwood
24	B-24J	<u>1.5</u>		
	Hours	39.7		

Captain Charles D. Huckleberry, Operations Officer

March	39.7
Previous	<u>286.6</u>
Total	326.3

Combat Missions – March 1944

<u>3/4</u> Breslau, Germany   <u>3:30 Hrs.</u>
B-24J – No Credit - 15th Air Force called mission off.

I remember the morning this mission was scheduled. I don't remember the crew, but I was to go as flight engineer; some of my records have been lost. I had been at the plane waiting for the crew to arrive from a mission briefing and the plane was ready to go. The crew arrived and no one had to tell me anything. I knew by their looks and actions that it was going to be a bad mission. The pilot told me he needed to talk to me away from the rest of the crew. He and I got away from the plane and he gave me the bad news. We were going to Breslau, Germany. I told him we didn't have enough gas to get there and back. He said, "Are you sure?"

I told him, "Yes, I'm sure! These new planes with the nose turrets are bad on gas. They're not like the old planes."

I told him some of the brass in the wing or the 15th AF must be crazy. I told him we would have to go with the group and see what happens. We took off and formed up in our proper places and started for Breslau. (The next day we found out why this raid was planned. Berlin had been bombed and Hitler had the German headquarters moved about 180 miles east of Berlin). We were approximately one and half-hours into our trip. The radioman was in the top turret and I was sitting at the radio table, looking out a small window at #3 engine when a cylinder of #3 came out and the engine cowling stopped it. I was looking at it as it was happening! The propeller button was pushed and the prop was feathered and the engine was stopped. The intercom was busy with talk about what to do. We couldn't make the trip with an engine out, and if we pulled out of formation and headed back home, we'd be accused of blowing the engine deliberately and not going on to the target. We were in a bad situation. While we were thinking about it, the pilot got this message: the mission was called off. We were happy and someone came on the intercom and said, "The brass have come to their senses."

That was one aborted mission that came at the right time. We returned to base. The 8th Air Force in England was closer to that target than we were. I don't know if Breslau was ever bombed.

3/7   Poggibonsi – M/Y   27 Planes   9:00 Hrs.
      Lt. Keating - #439A
      Records lost. Mission Credit.

3/11 Toulon (S.E. France)   Sub Pens   28 Planes   6.80 Hrs.
      Lt. Atwood - #006B
      This was a bad day – engine trouble. Had to come back to base alone.
      No mission credit.

3/15 Cassino, Italy – 26 Planes   4.30 Hrs.
      Lt. Atwood - #006B
      Turned back – engine trouble. Had to come back to base alone.
      No mission credit.

3/17 Schwechat, Austria – A/C Factory – 31 Planes   8:00 Hrs.
      Double credit: 2 missions
      Lt. Repp - #656H
   No records on this target. It must have been a good day. Bombs were dropped on the target and we got credit for the mission.

3/18 Gorizia (N.E. Italy) – A/D – 37 Planes   6:80 Hrs.
      Lt. Atwood - #006B
   This target was north of Trieste on the Isonzo River. This was a bad day for us; there was ack-ack and more ack-ack and then more. We turned on the bomb run and the #3 engine lost power; we had to push the prop red button and cut the engine off. Lt. Atwood told me that we couldn't go over the target with three engines. My reply was, "We have no choice!"
   He said he knew what had happened. The plane had the Honeywell electronic-controlled supercharger system on it and there was a box on the plane that had four control units in it (one for each engine). We always tried to have one replacement on the plane. Lt. Atwood said that was the trouble. I told him I thought we had blown a supercharger duct off. He was all excited and I tried to calm him down. I told him we had the bomb bay doors open and we were on the bomb run. I said I would check it after we dropped the bombs, but that didn't satisfy him. I saw what I had to do. I

got my small oxygen bottle and put it in my pocket and motioned to the radioman to get the extra control unit, and I got out on the catwalk. I held on with my left arm and hand, then pulled the #3 unit out and handed it to the radioman; he gave me the new unit and I put it in place.

All this time the flak was bad around us. We were still on the bomb run when I got up on the flight deck and told Lt. Atwood and the co-pilot to try the #3 now. No luck—same as before. The control cabinet was in the upper right corner of the bomb bay and I had no chute on. Lt. Atwood was a very good pilot, but he was not a combat pilot. He wanted everything to be perfect and with old planes that would never be. I decided right then what I had to do. I had been with Lt. Atwood a number of times, but we had too many returns by ourselves. That's too dangerous and too many no credits. I had to talk with the squadron operations officer, but I knew I wouldn't go on a mission with him again. When a plane has a bomb load on a bomb run, it's no time or place for a pilot to lose his cool. He didn't think I knew what I was talking about, but I had seen the ducts blown off before.

We made it back to base okay and that afternoon I had a talk with the operations officer. I told him not to put me with Lt. Atwood again. He was a good pilot, but not a combat pilot. The officer told me he would find someplace for him. He said the bomb wing might need an ex-combat pilot to help the wing in planning missions. After a few days the operations officer told me he had placed Lt. Atwood at the bomb wing. Everything worked out okay.

<u>April 1944 Flight Record</u>   T/Sgt. John J. Shiver, Jr. 34335079

Air Corps   APO #520   Fifteenth Air Force
              98th BG(H)   47th Bomb Wing
                              344th Bomb Squad (Engineer – Gunner)

11	B-24J	2.4
12	B-24J	7.5
15	B-24J	7.8
17	B-24J	6.0

20	B-24J	7.0
21	B-24J	3.0
24	B-24J	8.3
25	B-24J	8.0
29	B-24J	4.5
30	B-24J	<u>8.5</u>
	Hours	61.0

Captain Philip J. Keating, Operations Officer

April	61.0
Previous	<u>326.3</u>
Total	387.3

Combat Missions – April 1944

(Most of April's mission records lost.)

<u>4/11</u>   B-24J   <u>2:40 Hrs.</u>

This was a recall because there is no record of a mission for the 98th on this day.

No mission credit.

<u>4/12</u>   Weiner-Neustadt (Austria) – 34 Planes   <u>7:50 Hrs.</u>
B-24J - This target in. Double credit – 2 missions.

<u>4/15</u>   Bucharest (Rumania) – 36 Planes   <u>7:80 Hrs.</u>
B-24J - S.A. Leonardini, Pilot
Double credit – 2 missions.
     Bucharest, Romania Mission

The Lt. Leonardini Story

The squadron operations officer asked me if I thought Lt. Leonardini was ready to move up to a pilot position now and take on a crew. I had flown with him as co-pilot and he was very good at that position. My answer was, "I think so."

He told me we were in need of first pilots, and he asked me to help make Leonardini one. I told him I would try. I didn't know what I was getting into. The following story is the only time I went with Lt. Leonardini. It was my first and last mission with him as first pilot. What a trip I had! When he and the other crew members arrived at the plane, I got him off away from the others, so they couldn't hear us. I knew he was excited and nervous and in need of some help. I welcomed him on his first mission as the crew commander and told him we were going to have a good day. He was nervous and excited as he was telling me about our position in the formation for the mission. "We're the last plane in the 15th Air Force today and we're not coming back."

I laughed and told him we were going to have a good mission and for him to look forward to his first mission as the crew commander, and that there always has to be a "Tail-end Charlie." We had a good take-off, and as we were getting into our position in the formation, I was talking to him about our position for the day. We were the last plane in the 15th, but we were in the low slot or the fourth plane in the last echelon of the 98th Group.

I told him it was the best spot and for him to stay in formation. "Look straight ahead, don't pull in too close, and relax."

But he wouldn't listen to me. He would pull in too close and I was afraid we were going to run into some of the planes. I told him we were coming in too fast. But he wouldn't slow down enough and we would have to go off to the left by ourselves. Sometimes we would be about a half-mile from the rest of the planes. I could not get him to do what I told him to do. Sweat was pouring off him. Time after time after time—the same thing happened, over and over again. There was only one good thing about his flying that day! I didn't have to synchronize the props. The throttles weren't in a fixed position long enough to worry about. But I *was* thinking about the extra gas being used all day long.

The lieutenant gave me so much trouble not doing what I told him to do that I didn't have time to worry about the target, and before I knew it, we were there. We were expecting fighters to be waiting for us and the target area was full of our new long-range P-51s. We had been told they were coming, but we didn't know when. The sky was filled with them. No enemy planes!

What a beautiful thing to see. The P-51s had hit all the area air bases around and had taken over the target. We had been waiting for this for a long time.

After we dropped our bombs, they accompanied us back home. Lt. Leonardini did a better job coming back to base than he did going to the target, but our troubles weren't over for that day. We were the last plane to take-off that morning and we were the last one to land that evening.

After we got into the landing pattern, Lt. Leonardini told me he couldn't land the plane. I told him he was going to land the plane and I was going to help him. The flight engineer always called the speed of the plane to the pilot on take-offs and landings. We were coming in on the final approach about twenty feet from the ground and he told me he couldn't bring it on down. I told him he had done a nice job so far, so just bring it on down. He told me he couldn't do it, so I told him to give it more power and we would go around and try again. I told him he had done a good job on the approach before and he was going to land this B-24 now! His approach was good on his second try, but like the first attempt, he couldn't bring it on down. I told him to go around again. I asked the co-pilot if he would bring it in and he told me he had never landed a B-24 before. That was it for me. I told him he shouldn't be a co-pilot on a bombing mission. I said there were ten men and one B-24 in the air that needed to be on the ground now, all in good shape! I think Lt. Leonardini tried three times, but I don't remember. I knew we couldn't stay up in the air forever. I had to try something else, so I came down hard on him. I think I could have landed the plane all in one piece. He was a lieutenant and I was a sergeant, but I really let him have it. I thought I could make him so mad at me he would land the plane just to show me he could do it. I told him to get out of that seat, to let me have the plane and I would land it. I gave him some plain talk. I told him he was a better pilot than he thought he was, but he sure showed himself not to be a commander of a crew. I told him he was going to become the talk of the group for not landing the plane and I couldn't see how he could live with himself after that.

I asked him to bring it onto the runway this time and he said he would and he did. He made a good landing and I told him so. He never thanked me for my guidance, and that was all right with me. I never met up with him face-to-face again and I told operations not to put me with him again. That was the end of that episode with him. I hope he got a good lesson in life from that day with me. I sure got a good lesson on being patient with a man that day.

I know sometimes in life I have to do and say things without thinking. I don't have time to think about the consequences of my words and actions. This was one of those times in my life and I was glad when it was over that day. I never heard any more about it from anyone. It was good to be on the ground in one piece and to get another mission credit.

4/17	Sofia (Bulgaria) – B-24J – 37 Planes	6:00 Hrs.
4/20	Mestre (Northern Italy, Venice) – B-24J – 39 Planes	7:00 Hrs.
4/21	Breslau, Germany (Southeast of Berlin) – B-24J	8:00 Hrs.
4/24	Ploesti (Romania) – B-24J – 37 Planes Double credit – 2 missions.	8:30 Hrs.
4/25	Varese (Parma) – B-24J – 15 Planes	8:00 Hrs.
4/29	Toulon (Southeast France) – B-24J – 33 Planes	4:50 Hrs.
4/30	Alessandria (Northern Italy) – B-24J - 37 Planes	8:50 Hrs.

May 1944 Flight Record   T/Sgt. John J. Shiver, Jr. 34335079
Air Corps APO #520   Fifteenth Air Force
               98th BG(H)   47th Bomb Wing
                                  344th Bomb Squad (Engineer – Gunner)

2	B-24G	7.7
5	B-24H	5.6
6	B-24D	7.9
7	B-24J	8.0
10	B-24J	3.0
13	B-24J	9.5
14	B-24D	7.9
16	B-24D	7.3
17	B-24D	6.5
	Hours	62.6

(Correct total hours – 63.4)
Captain Philip J. Keating, Operations Officer

May	62.6
Previous	387.3
Total	449.9

Combat Missions – May 1944

5/2	Castel Maggiore (Bologna) – 37 Planes	7:70 Hrs.
5/5	B-24H – No credit	5:60 Hrs.
5/6	Brasov (Romania) – B-24D – 38 Planes Double credit – 2 missions.	7:90 Hrs.
5/7	Bucharest (Romania) – B-24J – 41 Planes Double credit – 2 missions.	8:00 Hrs.
5/10	No credit – called back – B-24J	3:00 Hrs.
5/13	Fidenza (Italy) – B-24J – 37 Planes	9:50 Hrs.
5/14	Vicenza (Italy) – B-24D – 34 Planes	7:90 Hrs.
5/16	No mission credit.	7:30 Hrs.
5/17	Porto San Stefano (Italy) – Harbor Installations Lt. J.C. DeWitt – B-24D – 36 Planes	6:50 Hrs.

"My Last Combat Mission"

This was the mission I had been looking for—my last combat mission. I went out to the plane I had been assigned to as the flight engineer for that day. I met and talked with the crew chief about the plan and I didn't put my flight bag on the plane. I thought the weather was too bad for the mission that morning. I finished the pre-flight check on the plane and the crew had not arrived yet. Someone told me that the mission was on hold, so I went where my flight bag was and lay down on the grass and used the bag for a headrest. At about seven o'clock, the crew came from briefing and told me there was a fifty percent chance that we would be going and we would wait on a signal flare from the tower: yellow was hold, red was cancelled, and green was go.

Lt. DeWitt told me the target that day was a harbor on the west coast of Italy north of Rome and it was a good mission for us. We would only be over land for a short time and we would be in the first flight of the group - flying left wing to the lead plane. We would come into the target from the water and drop the bombs, then fly on over land for the other planes in our flight to drop their bombs. Next, we would make a slow turn to our left and head back to the water. There was nothing to do but wait.

At about eight o'clock a green flare was in the air. Forgetting about my flight bag, I jumped up, got in the plane and went about my duties. As we taxied into our position for the runway, I suddenly remembered my bag. I didn't have anything - no chute, oxygen mask, Mae West, headset, or flak jacket. Actually, I didn't use the flak jacket anyway, and I thought I could find some extra things on board to replace what was in my flight bag. I told the pilot about my dilemma, and he said he was not losing our take-off position by returning to our parking area to get my bag. I told him that was fine with me.

There's usually an extra chute and oxygen mask in the back of the plane and I thought I would check after we were in the air. I checked later and didn't find anything but a headset. I had my throat mike in my pocket. It was unusual not to have a chute and an oxygen mask in a box over the bomb bay - but there was none that day! I put the headset on that I had found and with the throat mike, I could talk to and hear from all the crew.

There was a lot of talk about me leaving my bag, and on my last mission at that! I told the crew I wanted all of them to do a good job that day and help me get back safely. I had been with most of them on missions before and they told me not to worry; they wanted to get back, too. One of the waist gunners told me he would share his chute with me and we could come down together. I thanked him.

At about eleven o'clock we arrived at the target area and turned right to bomb the harbor. We were told that we were after the sub pens. There was flak, but it was not too bad, because we were bombing on the lead plane's bomb drop. We were on the left side of the lead plane, and the lead plane's pilot made a sharp left turn coming off the target, instead of making a gradual left turn. We were caught in a bad place. I thought we were going to run into the side of that plane, but our pilot was quick and we made a dive and missed the lead plane and the right wing plane. We were out of the formation about a mile away - all by ourselves and still being shot at. I know we had a lot of help from God to come out of a situation like that.

It didn't take us very long to catch up with the group and we were on our way home. We arrived back at the base and after we parked, I saw my bag, just where I had left it. I was asked what I did for an oxygen mask and I told them I didn't need a mask. I just put the oxygen hose in my mouth and used the oxygen regulator valve to turn it on and off as I needed it. It was a lot of trouble, but I made do. I always said "you make do with what you have when you have to do it". With that oxygen valve, I had to watch myself and turn it on before I felt like I was passing out. I had used the hose and valve off and on a number of times before, when the old oxygen mask would stop up with ice, but that was the first time I had used it for a complete mission. It was a wonderful feeling to have that last combat mission completed. I did get a good night's sleep that night and it was good to know the operations clerk wasn't going to be waking me up early shining a flashlight in my face. Of course, that was his job, but we always fussed at him when he gave us a big shake and told us, "It's time to get up."

<u>The 98th Bomb Group was never turned back from its target due to enemy opposition.</u>

"A Forgotten Mission"

After I finished my writing, I awoke one morning with a combat mission on my mind. It was one I had forgotten about. To me it was a bad mission. I remember the plane was a B24-J, and it was called the "Blue-F-Freddie".

I went on the mission as the flight engineer with a crew I hadn't flown with before.

The co-pilot was a Lt. Colonel (a West Point man), and he wanted everyone to know that he was the 98th Group Operations Officer. This was his first combat mission, and he had some things to learn in life. He was always barking orders, but on a combat mission crew the first pilot is the commander, not the co-pilot. I respected his rank, but I knew my job and I did it. It was a good mission. There was plenty of ack-ack. We left the target and headed home. We let down and when we were about 12,000 feet over a mountain in Yugoslavia, we got in trouble. The lead plane led the group over the 6,000-foot mountain that had a German mining operation on the top of it. They had a lot of guns, and they knew how to use them. The F-Freddie was hit with one or two hits on the right side. The right waist gunner, whose name was Conrad, called in and said he had been hit and blood was everywhere. At the same time the Lt. Colonel told me that hydraulic fluid was shooting out on his feet and for me to get it stopped immediately.

I told him I would check it later after I checked on the gunner who was hit. He informed me that was an order he gave me and he meant now. I gave him a look and turned to the pilot and asked him if he had the plane in control. He said he did. As I turned to leave the flight compartment, the co-pilot asked if I had heard his orders. I gave him a quick look and left to go to the rear of the plane.

When I saw the gunner, he still had his heavy flying jacket on. I asked the other gunner to help me get his jacket off and put him on it so we could check his arm. We used the medic's bag that all gun stations have and cleaned his arm. We put sulfur powder on the wound before we bandaged it. After the arm was fixed, I asked the other gunner if he thought we should give him morphine to ease the pain. Conrad told us he wanted us to. I had never done that before, but there has to be a first time for everything, so I did it. After a few moments, Conrad told us it was already feeling better.

I checked with the tail and ball gunners, and they said they were okay. I looked at the right wing damage. We had two places that were damaged. One area was large. I could see some of the cables but not all of them. I asked the top gunner if he could see them and he said he couldn't. There was hydraulic fluid everywhere. On the B-24 everything is operated by hydraulics (bomb bay doors, brakes, flaps, and landing gear). The assistant engineer and myself had our work waiting for us. Each plane had a kit with some hoses of different sizes and clamps. We had two cans of fluid on the plane.

We checked the reservoir in the bomb bays and it was empty. I went to check the bad leak at the co-pilot's feet. I told the assistant engineer to put some oil in the tank and I would try to see where the trouble was. I had to take my jacket and shirt off because of the tight places I had to work in. We had leaks everywhere. It wasn't long before we had to accept the truth that we didn't have brakes, flaps, or landing gear operating on the plane.

We talked it over and decided to wait until we got back to the base and try to crank the main landing wheels down. We could throw the nose wheel out and get it in a locked position. I told everyone that was all we could do. I suggested we call the base tower and tell them our troubles and ask them to put us last to land, so if we crashed on landing we wouldn't keep others from landing. I told the pilot that was all we could do to save the crew and plane. The shell blasts that hit the plane were close to the body on the right, and we didn't know the condition of the tire. We wouldn't know that until we landed. We wouldn't have flaps or brakes, and we would be landing at a higher speed. We would try to touch down at the end of the runway and we needed to ask the Lord to help us.

The pilot made a very good landing and I told him so. It was good to be back on base. The West Point Lt. Colonel didn't speak to me. That was fine with me. Colonel Gray was at our parking place, and he thanked me for helping to get the crew and plane back to base. The Blue-F-Freddie plane had to go to the service group to be repaired. Conrad received the Purple Heart the following day. When I left to come home in May, the "Blue-F-Freddie" was still in the service group being repaired.

Chapter 12

FINALLY HEADING HOME

"From Lecce to Naples, Italy"

I made my final combat mission on May 17, 1944, to San Stefano (Submarine Pens) on the west coast of Italy, north of Rome. That was a great day for me. I would be on my way home soon. The next day, I went to 98th Group Headquarters to start my paperwork to leave for the USA. My first stop was to the office of the 98th Commander, Colonel Gray, to get my DFC (Distinguished Flying Cross) medal. He knew me because I was a member of the crew that went to Regensburg, Germany, with him. He told me the group didn't have any of the medals now, and if I would wait until they came in I would get it. I asked how long.

He answered, "I don't know—it may be weeks. If you want to wait, you can."

"I am not waiting on a medal. I want to go home."

Colonel Gray said it would be given to me later. I have never received my DFC medal. I tried to contact the 98th group later, but they were en route back to the States. I think the office clerk didn't follow through with it. So be it.

When I left there, I went to the group flight surgeon's office. I went in and told him my mission to see him. That's when a heated conversation got under way. He told me the war was still going on and asked if I had forgotten that. I told him I knew that because I had made my 50th mission the day before, and that was a stupid thing to tell me. I asked him why he had made just one mission himself, instead of the three missions the Army Air Corps required flight surgeons to make, so they would be in a better position to help the boys who had troubles with combat.

He answered, "Oh, I have a wife and three kids at home."

I told him *I* had a wife at home and I *wanted* three kids!

"You can't talk to me like that!" he answered.

I told him he had started this and I wouldn't take anything back. I came to see him because I had to get his recommendation to go home.

This trouble began when I first walked into his office and he made this statement to me, "Well, you're like all the others. You don't sleep at night."

"No, sir, I don't have trouble sleeping."

"I will just mark you down for another 50 missions."

"I will when my time comes around but not now. When I first started, it was 25 missions in the 8th Air Force. I was transferred to the 9th and they upped it to 30, then to 300 combat hours in the 12th AF, and then to 50 missions in the 15th. I have had it! I want to go home!"

I got the ball rolling to go home. Flight Surgeon Captain Frederick A. Dickerman and Flight Surgeon Major Charles W. Longwell signed the paper. That was on May 18, 1944. Then, I had to go through the squadron, group, wing and 15th Air Force to get to go home. Papers were signed by the squadron commander on May 20, 1944, and group on May 21st, and sent to wing headquarters 15th Air Force on the 21st. Then, I had to wait for a plane that would get me to Naples. I was told it wouldn't be but a few days before a plane came, then the group would leave for Naples.

The next day I was told the group's public relations sergeant wanted to see me. I went to find him. His office was in an old building that had a porch on the front of it. There was a group on the porch. The sergeant was taking pictures and writing up an article on Thomas Kincaid from the 344th. His real name was Thomas Fletcher. He had gone into the Army when he was fourteen years old and had completed thirty-eight missions as a gunner. His mother had been trying to find him. After the sergeant finished with Kincaid, he came to me. He said he was told about me making my last mission without a chute and oxygen mask. He asked me if I would let him write up an article on my last mission. I told him no. He asked me why not. I told him I didn't want everyone to know about my mistake. He said it would make a great story and would be in all the papers and service magazines.

"Forget it." I said. He did.

After a day or two I was told a plane was going to take a few of us to Naples the next day. We were told to be at a certain plane with our bags at ten o'clock in the morning. I was there with some others – about six of us. It was a plane from another squadron. I didn't know the crew. We were all in the rear of the plane on take-off. As soon as we were in the air, I checked for any fuel leaks at filler caps on the right and left wings. The #3 cap was leaking badly, so I went to the front and told the engineer we had to return to base to fix it. We returned and landed. I asked him if I could help him and he said no. I didn't say anything more to him, because he was the engineer. He should have checked all the cap seals before we left.

We took off again. I checked after we were in the air. There was a #3 cap leak; gas was leaking badly, coming out and running off the back of the wing. I went up to the front of the plane and reported to the engineer and pilot. We had to land again. We landed and I told the engineer I would go with him and show him how to put the cap and seals on. He told me, "NO!" He said it was his job and he would do it. I told him I wanted to get to Naples and he had failed two times. Gas cap seals are one of the first things an engineer checks on pre-flight. I told the pilot I would show him how and I went up the hatch opening following him. That I did. We took off for the third time and everything was okay.

We arrived in Naples and a truck was waiting to take us to an old car and horse race track 26 miles from Naples. We arrived at the area and that was something to see. There were two-man tents everywhere. There was a tall fence around the outside of a huge area and a very large tent at one end. One of the men who worked there told us what to expect and what to do for the next few weeks: eat and sleep. The last group had stayed for a month.

"A convoy of about a hundred ships left Naples a week ago. Too bad you missed it," he said.

He told us to expect some bombing at night by the Germans, but there were no bomb shelters. The bomb line was about sixty miles north of Naples. He told us if we had a gun with us, just leave it on our cot and someone would pick it up. I had turned in my 45 to the squadron before I left. I even had to turn in my leather A-2 flying jacket. The squadron adjutant said we had to, because the ground personnel in the squadron wanted them. He wasn't a flying officer, so he didn't know how we felt about our jackets. He used this phrase, "If you want to go home, leave your jacket." So we had no choice. He was a major and not a very well-liked man. I don't know how many men there were at the Naples camp, but we were told approximately 10,000. Most of them were Army GIs who had been overseas a long time. Some had made three invasions and some had made four: Africa, Sicily, Italy, and Anzio. He warned us not to go to the fences. There were Italians trying to sell things, especially some type of drink. Some had died from drinking it. Each morning we would hear about two or three who had died.

They had good meals for us. We ate about seven o'clock in the morning, went back to our tent for an hour, and then went back to the mess line to get ready for the noon meal. They would feed four lines at each meal and we would carry a gallon can to sit on. We would carry the cans with us all the time. We would get back in line for supper about two o'clock. We used our mess kit all the time. The big tent was a mess tent. Those who cooked and served had to work night and day.

Almost every night we would hear the big anti-aircraft guns shooting at the planes. There were some men who had little radios in their tents. One evening I heard Axis Sally's broadcast in which she said, "You men in the race track area at Naples are going to have some visitors tonight."

Sure enough, about ten o'clock, all hell broke loose. The guns were shooting and bombs were bursting close by. We couldn't stay still. We had to move. We always slept with our clothes on. Men ran around with nowhere to go - myself included. We were falling over tent stakes and ropes. After about 30 minutes, all was quiet. Axis Sally's prediction was correct, and we were glad to be alive. She had known how many boys were there. She said about 10,000. We were all glad they missed their target.

We were told on May 30th some of us would be leaving the next day. That morning I found out I was leaving. I was happy. There were about two hundred in the group and we were told we had no transportation to Naples. We had to walk to get there by six o'clock that evening. We would have to carry our bags. We never did find out why there was no transportation for us. They gave us a GI for a guide. We started walking with our bags. I had my flight bag and barracks bag. They were heavy. If I hadn't been going home, I don't think I could have made it. The GI guide did not tell us the plans. When we started out that morning, he said we had to walk all the way.

About one-thirty we came to a small train station, and he told us we could take a rest. Then he told us a little train was due to take us to Naples. We had walked about halfway. About three o'clock the little train came by and it stopped. That was something to see and, we were happy to see it. It had narrow gauge rails, some flat-bed cars with wood bleachers on them and nothing to hold on to. We had to sit with our bags, but it was better than walking. After a little while, off we went to Naples. It was a rough trip, but we made it, though not all the way to the dock. We had to walk about two miles and we arrived at the dock about five o'clock. We sat down with our bags and waited to go on the ship. At six o'clock we walked up the gangplank onto the deck of the *Fred Lykes*—a small troop transport of the Lykes Line from New Orleans. It was one of the liberty ships. *I am on the ship that's going home*! I said to myself. It was May 31, 1944.

———

"On the Ship *The Fred Lykes*"

We went up the gangplank about six o'clock on the evening of May 31, 1944. We were told to go down the stairs to a certain compartment or hole and find a bunk and claim it, then leave a handbag or something on the bunk and carry our big bags to the front hold of the ship and leave them there. There would be someone to show us where to leave them. I picked a top bunk – sixth from the floor. Someone told me that was the best place to be, because I wouldn't have others climbing up bunks to get to the top. We were given a meal card and told to put our name on it and it would be punched every time we used it. There would be no meal that night, but the ship's store was open. They told us where the mess kitchen was and that they used meal trays.

About eight o'clock, the captain came on the speakers and welcomed us on board. Then he told us what to expect. We were leaving the dock then. We were part of a five-ship convoy including one large hospital ship, one small hospital ship, another small troop transport ship like we were on, and a tanker ship. The Navy had two gun crews and signalmen on board. We had seen two anti-aircraft 40 mm guns when we were at the dock. The ship had merchant seamen on board to do the work. We were going to go on a straight line to Norfolk, Virginia. The British would take care of German subs for us and when we got to Gibraltar, the Navy destroyers would join up and escort us all the way to the USA. We would arrive in Norfolk in fourteen days. He told us we could go anywhere on the ship we wanted to go but couldn't smoke on deck after dark. No matches or any kind of light were allowed. He told us the British would fly cover for us in the Mediterranean Sea and they may have, but as long as we were on the Mediterranean, I didn't see or hear a plane.

We passed through the Strait of Gibraltar at eight o'clock Sunday evening. What a rock and what a sight to see what was coming to join our convoy - eight destroyers! They soon had our convoy in the middle and they were all around us: two out front, two at the rear, two on the left side, and two on the right side. We were going from 350 to 400 miles a day. The weather had been nice so far. We were enjoying the showers we had, although I never got used to the hard water. I went to the mess about two times a day. I got breakfast early and a noon meal at twelve or one o'clock. I got boxes of chocolate candy and ate it all day long. Some of the men stayed seasick all the time. Some would see me eating the candy and they would head to the deck and lean over the rail bars. They stayed in trouble all the time. I have never been airsick or seasick. The Lord has blessed me all my life. I still have my ship mess card and it has twenty-seven holes punched for the trip.

We were two or three days from the Big Rock at about two o'clock in the afternoon, when the Navy boys got busy with the big signal light on the upper level deck of the ship. About the same time, the captain came on the speaker and told us we were crossing over a German sub, but not to worry, the Navy would take care of the sub. Two of the destroyers came inside the circle and the other destroyers brought the convoy into a smaller area. The two destroyers inside the area began shooting and rolling off drums of explosives. They were working a certain small area and we were amazed at their speed and how they could turn in such a small area. We left them and it was about thirty minutes before they joined back up with us, and everything was like it was before we crossed over the sub. I thought at the time and later on how bad that could have been - coming home from a tour of combat and getting sunk at sea.

There were always things to see on deck. The smaller ships and the destroyers would have to fuel up. The ship to be fueled up would come alongside the tanker, and then the tanker would shoot a rope to the ship to be fueled. Then, they would tie on the fuel hose and pull the fuel line over to the ship. After the ship was fueled, the fuel hose would have to be returned to the tanker. There were times when we could talk to the Navy men. There was no love between the Navy men and the merchant seamen. The merchant seamen were better paid than the servicemen. They got a $500 bonus for going into the Mediterranean Sea. They were always asking the Navy men to help them out, but they wouldn't help.

About halfway across the Atlantic, the captain told us we would soon be coming into a big storm. We would go straight into it. It was going to be rough but not to worry. We would be in it two or three days and nights. I don't remember if it was three days and two nights or two days and three nights. He told us to be careful when we went to mess. As we would come out of our compartment to the deck there would be a large rope next to the guardrails on the deck to keep us from being washed overboard by a big wave. We were to put our right arm over the rope and hold it with our other hand and when we returned from mess, to hook our left arm over the rope. The walkway was about three feet wide and about fifty or sixty feet long to the mess area. Those waves were big and very high.

On the second morning of the storm, we were told the front compartment where our bags were was getting water in it and our bags had to be moved. We had to help move them. Everyone helped. We formed a long line and passed bags to one another. We could see the trouble. One large plate had come loose about six or eight feet long in the bow, and when the ship went down in a big wave, the water would come in. I am glad the plate didn't come all the way off. It was bad welding by someone in the shipyard! My bags didn't get wet and it didn't take too long to get all the bags out. They closed the front compartment door.

Our ship was on the left side of the convoy and the big hospital ship was to our right. One afternoon at about two thirty, we had a ringside view of a man on the big hospital ship jumping overboard. They had men stationed on all sides of the deck with a life preserver ring close by. We saw the man who jumped trying to get to the ring. The Navy signalman on our ship went to work moving the shutters on the big light. One of the destroyers launched a speedboat to the rescue. Our convoy didn't stop or slow down. We saw what was happening on our right side. They got the man out of the water and went back to the destroyer. The speedboat was then hoisted up on to the deck of the destroyer with the men still in the boat. After that the destroyer came alongside the hospital ship and they shot a line to the hospital ship. They transferred the man to the hospital ship by breeches buoy, which wasn't fun. One moment the man was in the air and the next moment he would be back in the water. One of the Navy men told us that the man was from the mental ward of the hospital ship. He must have had mental trouble to jump off the ship when he was coming back to the USA. The next day another mental patient from the small hospital ship did the same thing, but they told us that he didn't try to come to the life ring. The Navy men searched the area but couldn't find him. They tried.

We loved to watch the schools of porpoises that stayed alongside the ship all the time. The sailors told us they were after the food scraps that were thrown overboard. They also said when you see porpoises in the water you won't find sharks around.

I found a few of the ship's daily newsletters titled "Heave Ho" that I saved. Here is some of the news from them:

- June 5 Monday We passed Gibraltar at 18:10 last evening. We went 14 to 17 knots an hour. At noon today, we should be approximately 1200 miles from Naples.
- June 6 Tuesday We are 550 miles from Gibraltar and approximately 1600 miles from Naples.
- June 9 Friday Distance last 24 hours – 350 miles. Average speed 14.7 knots. From 350 to 420 miles a day.
- June 10 Saturday Average speed 14.4 knots. We have traveled 355 miles in the last 24 hours.
- June 11 Sunday Average speed 16.7 knots. We have traveled 408 miles. Rain squalls.
- June 12 Monday No news – just some drawings. But today we saw some birds flying. It can't be long now. We should see land tomorrow.

We came into the harbor at Newport News, Virginia, mid-afternoon on Tuesday, June 13, 1944. The captain came on the speaker and told us we would stay in the harbor that night and dock the first thing the next morning. We were sure the hospital ships went into the docks first. The sailors were busy chipping off paint on and around the gun turrets and repainting them. The merchant seamen were busy taking care of the rest of the ship. We went to the dock about six o'clock Wednesday morning and left the ship with our bags at approximately eight thirty. A military band welcomed us. It was a very good feeling to be back in the States.

On the dock was a Red Cross booth with coffee and doughnuts for a twenty-five cent donation. I had to get in line, but it was good. We went to a train station close by and got on a train to Camp Patrick Henry, Virginia. After we arrived there, we were led to a barrack and then to a mess hall. At the mess hall, we were welcomed back to the States by a mess sergeant. He told us this was a special mess hall and we were his guests. We didn't have to go in a chow line. We would be served at the tables and he had orders to cook anything and as much as we wanted. We just had to tell the ones who were working the tables. We had never been treated like that. I don't remember what I ordered, but I remember the milk—*real* milk! They had bottles of milk on all the tables at all times. We went back to our barracks and got a bunk.

After a little while, someone said we should check out the PX. So, off we went. We asked directions and soon we were there. When we got there we found a line of men waiting to get in. We asked what the line was for and were told it was for ice cream. So we joined the line and we were soon inside the PX. As I got close to the counter, the young lady who was dipping the ice cream stopped and said that was it. The officer who was in charge hadn't shown up. The young lady said she wasn't dipping anymore and she would not let anyone help her. I was third or fourth from being served. Some had offered to help but she said no. We had nothing else to do so we stayed in line. About thirty minutes later the camp commander came in. He was a general. He talked to the young lady, but she didn't change her mind. The general told someone to go and get the PX officer and the general started serving the ice cream himself. The young woman was still standing there. We all knew that the woman and the officer were in trouble. The general was mad. About the time the officer arrived, I had moved up in line and was at the counter. The general told the officer he wanted the woman relieved from duty and off the base, never to work on the base again. Then, he had a few choice words for the officer, ending with the order for him to remember these men had just returned from the war. We felt bad for the woman, but she should not have refused help when it had been offered to her. The ice cream was very good. It was the first I had tasted since I had been overseas. We returned to the barracks and turned in for the night.

About six o'clock the next morning, a GI came and told us he would be our guide while we were at Patrick Henry and he would lead us to a mess hall at seven o'clock. After breakfast, we went back to the barracks and he told us to put all our clothes and blankets into one barracks bag because we would be turning them in for new ones. About mid-morning, he led us to a building and he told us to toss the bag and all inside. At the supply building we got new things. He informed us the next day we would be leaving Patrick Henry. That was good news. My orders were dated the 16th of June and I was told I would be leaving to go home the next day. On June 17th I left by train to go to Camp Shelby in Hattiesburg, Mississippi. I would have a 22 day delay en route to Miami Beach, Florida, and I was due there July 14th. I got my orders on June 20th at about noon but was told I had to get paid that afternoon. There were 16 of us from the Mobile area with this order:

<u>From Camp Patrick Henry, VA</u>
<u>Special Order Number 148 Dated 20 June '44</u>
<u>Army Service Forces</u>
<u>Fourth Service Command</u>
<u>SCU 1427</u>
<u>Camp Shelby, Mississippi</u>

The finance officer with a guard and two other GIs set up a pay table outside a building and we got started getting paid. This was about three o'clock in the afternoon. There was a private in front of me. The officer said the records showed he had not been paid in a long time and he counted out a lot of money on the table. The private said the records were wrong and he was due only one month's pay. The officer told him to pick up the money and leave, but the private would not do it. He said he would get drunk, lose it or someone would rob him and he would lose a lot of paydays for a long time. We were at a standoff. I was next in line to be paid, and I had to get to town by five o'clock to catch a bus to Mobile from Camp Shelby. I saw that neither the officer nor the private was going to change their position, so I asked the private if he was going home and if his mother was living. He said yes. I told him to pick up the money and go to the base post office and buy a money order for his mother. That seemed to fix the problem.

I got paid and got a cab to the bus station. I got on the bus and it was full. It was a small bus and every seat was taken. We were on our way to Mobile on a small, slow bus. About five miles from Hattiesburg, the bus stopped and a very old lady got on. She had to stand in the center part of the bus. No one made a move to give up his seat, so I did. She thanked me and I had to stand all the way to Mobile. We got to the bus station about nine o'clock that night and I got a cab to Roper Street where Myrtle was living. It was a wonderful feeling to be home. The next morning Myrtle and I went downtown to buy me a pair of brown dress shoes. I had gotten a shoe stamp while I was at Camp Shelby and I bought a pair of Florsheim shoes. I wore them and they sure felt better than the GI shoes.

"Home and on to Miami Beach"

On the morning of June 21, 1944, Myrtle and I went to Atmore by bus to live with her father and mother and visit with family and friends. Time passed by quickly and I enjoyed it very much. I would meet friends in town and they would give me ration stamps for gas. Mr. Dean, Myrtle's father, let me use his car a number of times.

Mr. Dean set up a fishing trip for me. Mr. Turner from Bay Minette, the farm agent for Baldwin County, arranged for a fishing guide to take us on a trip to Mifflin Lake in Baldwin County. Mr. Dean and I were at Mr. Turner's home about three o'clock that morning to leave on the fishing trip. Mr. Turner was in the kitchen cooking breakfast for us. After breakfast, we left Bay Minette to meet up with the guide. We found him at his boat waiting for us, and what a boat! He had a fishing rig. It was a very large boat for four persons and it had a large outboard motor. We arrived at the lake early and started fishing. No bites. The guide said he thought it was the heat; it was too hot for the fish to bite. After a few hours, he said we might as well go in and call it a day. That we did.

Before I left Atmore I went to the ration board office to get stamps. The office had been a ladies' dress store and was between the 1st National Bank building and Escambia Hardware building. We had to have ration stamps for almost everything we used. The lady at the office said I could only get a gas stamp for five gallons.

I said, "Lady, I have just come back from a year overseas and I think that I should get more than a stamp for five gallons."

She wasn't nice to me at all and said, "That's all you are getting."

That made me mad. It wasn't what she said but the way she said it.

"Lady, you need that gas stamp more than I do, so you keep it and give me the other stamps." That was what she did and I was glad to leave that building.

I had to leave the next day for Miami. I had to be in Pensacola by noon on July 13th. I arrived at the station and met up with a S/Sgt. I had met on the ship from Naples who lived in Mobile - Harold E. Soles. The train left Pensacola at one o'clock for Jacksonville. We changed trains there and got on one that ran from New York to Miami. That was a fast-running train. We arrived in Miami about ten o'clock in the morning on July 14th. We got a cab to take us to Miami Beach.

I had to report to AAF Redistribution Station #2, Miami Beach, Florida, on July 14, 1944. I had to ask where I was to go after I got there and was told to go to the big hotel with the big fountain in front. That was where everyone was to report and they would tell us what hotel we were assigned to. I was assigned to the Sovereign Hotel and it was the last hotel on the beach going north. It was next to the Firestone Estate. I went there and was told what room to go to. It was a really nice hotel. I was not told anything else, except when to go to the dining room for meals. I was tired after that train trip so I went to the dining hall and ate a meal and went back to my room, took a shower and went to sleep.

The next morning about eight o'clock, a GI clerk woke me up and asked me why I wasn't down in a meeting in hall number so and so. I told him no one had told me about a meeting. He told me I should have seen it on the board when I came into the hotel the day before.

"What's so important about this meeting?" I asked.

He told me to get dressed and get on down to it. That I did and when I entered the hall a colonel was speaking to a large group. I sat down at the back and he asked me why I was late to the meeting. I answered that I was asleep and no one had told me about the meeting. He asked me when I had arrived and I told him I had arrived the day before. He seemed to accept my being late and continued with his talk. He told us we were to be there two weeks. He pointed out that we had to live with civilians again and to not behave like we did overseas. We had to watch our talk and our actions. We had to attend meetings. We were going to be examined in both body and mind by a number of doctors. He welcomed us, told us to enjoy our stay at Miami Beach and to check the board in the lobby of our hotel.

We did stay busy, but I enjoyed the stay there. The doctors were good to us and they did a thorough examination of us. They were set up in different hotels on the beach. We got to do a lot of walking. One day I was scheduled for a dental checkup. It was one o'clock in the afternoon. I got in the chair and after the dentist spent about five minutes looking in my mouth, he told me he wanted all the dentists on the floor to see my mouth. I had all my teeth and no fillings and no decay. He asked me for my permission and I told him okay. All of them said it was something to see after a year overseas. The flight surgeon had told us we would be the first large group to use pure oxygen for such long periods of time and the medical profession didn't know how that would affect our lives in the future. They did know pure oxygen would affect the enamel on our teeth. So, I was happy to get a good report. They cleaned my teeth and I was sent on my way.

Some days we had to watch a lot of films and other days we were not busy all the time. I took a sightseeing tour on the Indian River boat and the guide pointed out the homes of the rich and famous.

After noon one day, a clerk from office headquarters came to the hotel and was walking the halls asking for Shiver. I asked him what he wanted me for. He told me his mission. He had a train ticket to Texas and some papers for me to sign. He said I was to sign them and he would be on his way back to the office. I told him I wanted to read them before I signed them. He gave all of them to me. It didn't take me long to see I didn't want to sign anything. I told him the Army Air Corps had kept their word, but they were two years late. I had tried to get into cadet training to be a pilot when I was at Atlantic City in 1942. Now, two years later, the orders had caught up with me. I found out if I signed these papers, I was signing up for four more years. I gave the papers and the train ticket back to the clerk and told him I didn't want them. He told me he didn't know what to do with them. I told him to send them back where they came from and put a note with them that I refused to sign up for four more years. He still wanted me to sign them but I told him, "No! No Way!" So he took them and left. I had no desire to stay four years more.

Our two weeks in Miami Beach were over. Approximately thirty men were being sent to an AAF Redistribution Station in Lincoln, Nebraska, for reassignment to another place.

"Next Stop - Lincoln, Nebraska"

It was time to leave Miami Beach. We left on July 28, 1944. Some of us were to go to Lincoln, Nebraska, for processing and to be assigned to various bases. Most of the bases were in the western states. In the group I was with, most were flying personnel. We met as a group and were carried to the train station. We were told to go to the last car of the train and climb aboard. It was an old type car, but it wasn't one of the boxcars converted to GI cars. It had soft cushion seats. The person in charge of us took roll call and discovered we were short one GI. He asked if anyone knew anything about him. Someone said he had told him he would be at the train before it left the station. The person in charge answered, "He needs to hurry up. This train is pulling out in ten minutes and it waits on no one."

Someone at the window said, "I see a red convertible coming with the top down, a blond driving, and a GI is with her."

Someone else said, "That's him!"

The car stopped, but the GI stayed in the car. Almost all the windows had GIs with their heads out yelling at him, "Come on! The train is moving!"

He got out of the car and ran and got on. He stepped inside and said, "You fellows wouldn't leave a man, would you?"

Coal burners pulled this train car and the smoke and ashes were bad. In the daytime some of the windows would be open and that let a lot of smoke and ashes in. Being in the last car on the train was really bad, because a person would receive a whiplash when the train traveled fast and went around curves.

There were about thirty of us in the car going to Lincoln. The GI who was almost left in Miami was a T/Sgt. and called us "his boys." He was some kind of guy - nice looking, about six feet tall, happy, always smiling and laughing. I have lost some of my notes, but I think the train trip to Lincoln was about four or five days and nights. I remember we went to Cincinnati, Ohio. We were shifted from one train to another and sometimes we were left sitting by ourselves for a long time.

One time, as we were going through Illinois or Iowa, we had a fifteen-minute stop at a station and there was a young lady with a large tray of small bottles of milk who came over to our car. Of course, our windows were open, but she would not give us a bottle unless we came to the platform and got it. Our T/Sgt., the one who called us "his boys", asked her if he came to the platform if she would give him enough for all of his boys. She said she would but he had better put his shirt and tie on, because there were MPs not far away. Our T/Sgt. put on his shirt and tie and went to get the milk. As we looked at her, she handed him one little bottle of milk. He told her she had just promised him milk for all of his boys. She said, "That's all you are getting."

We saw he was mad; he said, "You shouldn't have lied to me."

He threw the bottle on the cement and got back in the car. He took his shirt off and no one said anything to him. In a few minutes two MPs came up to the car. One came in the car and really told us off and said he wanted the one who had just thrown that bottle of milk on the walkway. No one said a word. The MP was a stupid person to think that a GI was going to squeal on another GI. The MP was walking up and down the car and was still asking for the guilty person to speak up. Then the MP really got mad and told us he and his fellow MP were going to have the whole bunch of us off the train and in the brig. That was when our T/Sgt. went into action. He got up from his seat and told the MP it was time for him to leave and join his friend. He said he was the one who threw the bottle and he would be the one who was going to take care of the two MPs.

"The best way to end this problem is for you to get off this car and you and your friend tell everyone that it's been taken care of."

None of us knew what was going to happen next, but the MP left the car. At that time, the train started to move and we were on our way to Lincoln. No one said a word about that again.

We arrived at the redistribution center in Lincoln on August 2, 1944, to spend a few days waiting on orders to be shipped out to another base. We had to take calisthenics each day except Saturday and Sunday. We hadn't done that since gunnery school days and it was hard to get accustomed to it again, especially with the corporal who was in charge of us. I would say he enjoyed being tough on those with higher rank than he was. That's what we told him.

They always tried to mix up a new group when one arrived, and they did a real good job at it. I was in a group that I hadn't been with before. In my group was an old master sergeant with almost thirty years of service. It was very hot that morning (about ten o'clock) and that little two-bit corporal wasn't having any mercy on us. He was giving the old master sergeant a hard time and I told the corporal to get off his back.

"He can get out if he can't take it," the corporal said.

The master sergeant thanked me and told me that wasn't anything new. He needed six months more to finish his thirty years of service and everywhere he had been lately, they had been extra hard on him.

"But I'm sticking it out. I'm going to show them that I can do it."

A number of others told the corporal to let up on him, but he wouldn't do it. The sad thing about the corporal was that he didn't realize he had made a big fool of himself by what he had done and said.

We had to have a big parade on the last Saturday I was in Lincoln and I was assigned to be on the front right corner spot.

During the next week, I was with a group that left Lincoln by train for Casper, Wyoming. I was glad to be assigned to a B-24 base and to be leaving Lincoln. We left Lincoln on August 10, 1944.

Chapter 13

STATESIDE DUTY

"Casper, Wyoming"

I arrived in Casper by train from Lincoln and was assigned to the 211th Combat Crew Training School – Section E, as a flight engineer instructor. When I completed my combat missions, I was relieved from flying for a period of ninety days. That letter from the 98th bomb group flight surgeon was dated May 18, 1944. It was for rest and rehabilitation for ninety days. At the end of that period, I was supposed to be paid for three months' flying pay. Flying pay was an extra one-half of your regular pay.

In the first days at Casper I was helping in the ground school in the flight engineer's building. There were some things I could teach the crew flight engineers on the ground, but most of the teaching had to be done in flight. One day I wasn't needed at the day school and I was resting on my cot. Someone from the squadron operations office came and told me the major who was the head man over all the training wanted me to meet him on the flight line as soon as I could get there. And I was told to check out a chute. I told the person I didn't know if my ninety days of flying relief were up. He replied the major wanted me and not to keep him waiting. I got a chute and went to the flight line and found the operations officer with a non-military man. I was introduced to the chief test pilot and trouble-shooting man from Consolidated Aircraft Company. I did not know what the mission was or where we were going. The major told me the plane was ready to go and it had already been pre-flight tested.

"Let's go - get on and get it in the air," he said.

I would soon find out our mission. The major had told the Consolidated man he was a better pilot and he was going to show him. The major told me what my job was. He gave me a book and a stopwatch and told me to time the book in the air. They were going to stall the plane time after time and I would keep a record of the book's airborne time off the table for each stall. It wasn't a good thing to be doing. We were up about 10,000 feet, and the rear section was really shaking when the plane was in stall for a long time. I told them the rear section was taking a beating and I thought it best for them to stop and call it a draw. The major told me to go to the rear and check on things. I said I would and for them to not get it into a stall while I was back there.

About the time I arrived in the rear section, I thought the plane was coming apart. I was at the right waist window and was checking the vertical stabilizer when the major pulled the plane up into another stall. My body went everywhere in the back and as quick as I could get on my feet, I went to the flight deck. Before I could say anything to the major he stalled the plane again. I mean it was in a bad stall. The B-24 had lost all motion except for sliding down—tail first. The major was in the left seat and the Consolidated factory man in the right one. Usually a pilot can get the front down and get the plane's air speed up and get control of it. The major was doing everything he knew to do but it didn't work. The factory man took control of the situation. He pulled the major's hands off the controls and said, "I've got it!"

I was looking at him, but I don't know what he did or how he got that plane out of that situation. But, he did and I was glad. Not a word was spoken during our return to the base or after we were on the ground. I didn't say anything to the major or the factory man about that trip, and that plane ride cost me two months' flying pay. To be paid flying pay, I had to fly a minimum of four hours. My August 1944 flight record had a flight of 2:40 on August 23 and 6:20 on August 29, 1944. Ninety days from May 18, 1944, should not have been a factor when I was ordered to fly on August 23rd. I did not fly in that 90-day period. But they did count it and it cost me flying pay for two months. That plane trip went on my flight record: August 23rd, 2 hours and 40 minutes. When I got my pay on September 1, 1944, the finance officer told me I was getting only August flying pay. I told him I was due three months' flying pay.

He said, "NO WAY!"

"I was made to make that flight," I said.

He told me I was not going to get it and I never did. A few of my friends received the full three months pay, but they didn't fly any time during August.

The only good thing I received from that flight was a good friend I made that day – the Consolidated factory man. He came back to Casper two or three months later to investigate some planes that went down and he and I got together and had a long talk. We had seven planes lost in a period of a week and he was sent to Casper to find the reason. He called a meeting with the engineer instructors to help him find the answer for the lost planes. No one knew what had happened. I shared with him my experience with one crew on a night flight. The flights were from 4:00 a.m. until noon and the night flights were from 4:00 p.m. until midnight. The planes were serviced and re-fueled twice every 24 hours except when they were due for the 25, 50, 75, and 100-hour inspections. On this flight, the plane was using an excessive amount of fuel; I talked it over with the pilot and the co-pilot and told them about the problem. The pilot told me, in no uncertain way, that the major in charge of training had told them that no plane's wheels could touch the runway before midnight. I was the only instructor with this crew. The pilot had been turned loose as being qualified to be a first pilot. That was the trouble with Casper's training program. They were turning pilots loose too soon. The engineer instructors have to be with the crews two to three weeks after the instructor pilots have turned them loose. Most of the pilot instructors had their wives or girlfriends in town and they wanted to check the pilots out so they could be free.

So I told the pilot and co-pilot, at best, we needed to get back to the Casper area. They agreed and we got back close to the base. That was about 10:00 p.m. I checked the fuel again; we needed to land and get some more to finish the flight time.

The pilot said, "No way. We can't land until midnight."

I asked him what was going to happen when the props stopped turning.

"I don't know," he said.

I told them *I* knew what was going to happen - we were going to fall and fall fast. I told both pilots I would take full responsibility for landing; they still said no. Then, I said one of them needed to contact the tower and tell them there is one engineer instructor who is leaving this plane in the next five minutes. The pilot said, "You wouldn't dare!"

I told him, "I have had it with you, and as soon as I can get the bomb bay doors open and this chute clipped on, I'm leaving."

He replied, "I'll call the tower and land."

We got to the base and landed. Before we finished the landing roll, I saw a jeep heading to the end of the runway. I thought I knew who was in it. The driver motioned for us to pull off the runway and we did. The driver of the jeep was a master sergeant and the other was who I thought it was - the major. I opened the bomb bay doors and the master sergeant got on the flight deck and started checking the gauge tubes. That was when I got mad. The major was close enough to me to hear what I was saying. I asked the master sergeant if he thought I didn't know how to check the gauges. About that time the major asked the master sergeant if the fuel was low enough to justify the early landing. The master sergeant said, "They should have come in an hour ago."

I said it took me at least an hour to convince the lieutenant we had to come down and get fuel. I asked the master sergeant if he had been in combat and he said he had not. I said I had, and I didn't appreciate someone thinking I couldn't read the gauges. I got credit for fifty missions and went on a number of others I didn't receive credit for. I asked the major if he wanted us to get some fuel and go back up and he said, "No, call it a night."

That made me happy. I told the Consolidated factory man the major was pushing the crews too hard and they were scared of him, and the pilot instructors needed to spend more time with the crews before they turned them out on their own. After the meeting was over, the Consolidated man told me he wanted to talk with me some more and we had about an hour together, just the two of us.

He asked me if we had much trouble with the super-charger ducts when I was overseas, especially the new Honeywell control system. I told him we did, but we didn't have but a few new planes in our group. He wanted to share with me his troubles about trying to find a solution to the problem. He said he couldn't see the trouble, but he knew it was there. After many days and many sleepless nights, he saw the problem. If that doorplate in the exhaust duct controlled by the Honeywell's new system happened to get close to the center position, then the exhaust force, which was stronger than the electrical controlled system, would send the plate closed. Then, a duct would be blown off. The problem was corrected by changing the linkage to the duct plate.

He asked me if I was going to stay in the Air Corps after the war. I told him, "No Way!"

He gave me his phone number and address and told me to contact him when I left the service. He said he had a job for me. I thanked him and told him I wanted to go back home and stay in Atmore, Alabama. That's what I did and I'm still here.

Soon after this the major at Casper told me he wanted me to go with him on a check-out flight to see if a 2nd lieutenant was ready to be assigned to a crew. We took off and it didn't take me but a few minutes to see that this young 2nd lieutenant was a very good pilot. He was *really* good, a natural-born pilot. He had a ready answer to any question the major asked him, and the major really put him to the test. I thought he was too tough on the young man, but I didn't say anything. This man was good, but not a smart aleck. The major told him to return to the base, and if he didn't have any trouble with the landing, he had passed the test.

There was, as usual, a strong crosswind blowing and the lieutenant had lined up to the correct side of the runway. Just at the plane's touchdown, a strong crosswind hit the plane and the wing dipped and the lieutenant kicked it onto the runway with the rudders. The major came down hard on the lieutenant and told him he should have used the ailerons to level the wings when the wind hit the plane.

"Isn't that right, sergeant?", he asked me. "Have you ever seen someone use the rudders and kick a plane in like that?"

I said, "Major, the lieutenant did what he had to do. The wing controls are too slow on the B-24 and he had plenty of runway on that side. Yes, I have seen that type of landing a number of times overseas. In my way of thinking, any landing you can walk away from and the plane is in good condition is a good landing."

The lieutenant gave me a nod and a smile came on his face; I knew he appreciated that compliment at that time when the major was giving him a hard time. The major asked for it and I had the opportunity to help the lieutenant. That was the last time the major asked me to fly with him and I don't think I ever saw the lieutenant again.

"Training Combat Crews"

There has to be a starting point in everything we do. In flying a B-24 bomber, someone has to be with a man when he sits at the controls for his first time. He has to learn to take off and land the plane. Casper was a first-phase training base. The men we were training were men who sometimes had a little two-engine plane flying time, but most didn't have any two-engine plane flying experience at all. I have seen some of these young men, sitting in the seat while the instructor was talking to them before the engines had been started. They would get so excited and nervous and start to sweat - the drops would be as large as small peas. After a week or ten days they were not sweating and were enjoying their training.

When I first started flying at Casper, I was flying with a number of different instructor pilots and was having no problem with any of them. Then I met a Captain Sumner. He and I worked well together and he asked me to join up with him as a team. We went to operations and they put us together as a team for which we were glad.

Sumner had been in the Pacific Theater and had to ditch two times in the ocean. The first time the crew of ten all got out of the B-24 after they went down in the water. They got the two life rafts and emergency supplies out before the plane went under. The sun was bad for them and the supplies didn't last long. Death took its toll on the crew and by the time they were found, there were only four left. He told me each time one of the men died, there was nothing to do except roll the body out of the raft. When a rain cloud came, they would use their shirts to catch water. They would catch fish and eat them raw. The four that survived were rescued on the 22nd or 23rd day - I have forgotten. On his second ditching the crew was rescued on the third day. I enjoyed working with Captain Sumner and we helped a number of young men to become good pilots.

Understandably, some young men would advance in training at a faster pace than others. They couldn't be too far apart in their advancements, because there was a schedule and a new group would be arriving. At first, on take-offs and landings, it would take about twenty or twenty-five minutes for each one and our nerves would really be tested. After a few days, the trainees could be making touch-and-go landings and could advance to handling emergency problems that might happen. The captain and I would talk it over and I appreciated working with him. He would ask for my opinion on the pilots' progress, especially on their ability to handle emergencies. They didn't know when they would be faced with one. The captain would tell me what and when he would do a certain thing. The pilots had to act fast and make the proper move without thinking it over. Hesitation could be the difference between life and death. They could have one or more engines lost on take-offs and landings. They had to know on what part of the runway they could abort a take-off or would have to keep going.

The bad weather that came in the fall and winter in Casper meant some days there would be no flying. We would get behind on our schedule when there was a snowstorm that passed through the area. Myrtle and I had an apartment in Casper, and she would put me out the back door of the apartment at one o'clock in the morning when I was on a morning flight. I would have to walk one and a half blocks to the main street and then, twelve more blocks to meet my friend, who had an old car. I was to be at the pickup place, which was at the center of Casper, at 2:30 a.m., and we would arrive at the air base at approximately 3:00 to 3:15 a.m. The engineer instructors would check in and wait for the word to come if the training flight was canceled, on, or delayed. If it was on, we would get our gear and go to the flight line. One particular morning, as we met in the building, we thought the flights would be cancelled. It was still snowing - not too bad, but all the anti-icing and de-icing stuff had been removed from all the planes. Just before daylight, we received the orders to go out to the flight line and prepare for take-off. I met Captain Sumner at the plane and the first thing he told me was, "The major is on the warpath this morning about the weather, and he told us we would get the planes in the air come hell or high water."

The flight line men were sweeping the snow off the wings and some of them were washing the prop blades with some chemicals. The crews were at the planes, but we had to wait on the men cleaning the planes. The captain and I were away from the others and he asked me, "Do you think that we can fly this morning?"

I answered, "No."

He told me, "We're number one for take-off this morning and the major is in the tower to give us orders. What are we going to do?"

I thought about the situation and said, "If you will go along with my plan, this is it and I know it will work, because I know the major. If another plane can get in the air this morning, then we can. You say we're number one. You will be in the co-pilot's seat. As we are checking the magnetos out, we will be on the runway. When we go to check the magnetos on number three engine, you can cut both "mag" switches at the same time and then turn them back on at the same time. At the time they are turned back on, there will be a very big noise and plenty of black smoke. The major will have a fit and order us to get off the runway and let another plane have our place."

The captain asked me if I thought that we could get away with it.

"We can, because no one will know about this but you and me. I'm not telling anyone, are you? There is something that you must do. Be sure you cover your hands and fingers so that the crew pilot doesn't see what you are doing with the switches on the number three magneto."

The captain asked, "Will you feel right if we do what you just told me to do?"

"Yes, it's survival of the fittest."

He told me okay. The men finished their cleaning job and the major began to bark orders out using a lot of profanity. We got the engines warmed up and he told us to get the show on the road and in the air. As we pulled onto the runway, I was standing between the pilots, leaning actually on the backs of their seats. The captain took a glance at me and smiled as he spoke to the lieutenant and said, "Let's check out the mags and then we'll do what the major wants us to do. We'll try to get the show on the road and in the air."

When the captain manipulated the number three engine switches, it actually made more noise and smoke than I had thought it would and the major did put on a show with his profanity and cussing. He told us to pull off the runway and let the next plane go and for us to try to get the engine cleared up. The number two plane pulled on and ran up their engines for their take-off roll. The plane's wheels were still on the runway at about three-quarters down the runway, and the major was screaming, "Abort take-off! Abort! Abort!"

It was too late. There was no way the pilot could stop in that short span. Everyone was hoping that the plane could get up before the runway was gone, and it did. As the plane was at the end of the runway, the wheels were about a foot off the ground.

The major was still screaming, "Return to base! Return to base!"

The plane had to go about two miles before the pilot could get up enough to turn and return to the base. The captain and I were relieved to see that plane safely back on the ground. We never did say anything about this to anyone and we didn't discuss it ourselves. After this, the captain and I would give each other a nod and a smile when we would meet. I don't know if the major learned a lesson from this episode or not, but I do know one thing. We need to accept the weather we get and remember to respect it and know what we can and cannot do in it.

It was still snowing some and it continued for several days. The Casper Air Force Base was approximately fifteen miles from town and we would have to go to the base and sign in, even if we knew the weather was too bad for flying. We would have to check in early each morning and stay until all flights were cancelled. Then we could leave. The only break we received was a few days we got off after a group had finished their training and the new group had not yet arrived. All instructors enjoyed that time off, but we knew it wouldn't last. The snow would fall and then we would have a little warming trend for a day or two and the ice would melt a little; then a blizzard with ice, snow, and wind would move in. Talk about cold. It would get *cold*!

I could never learn to walk on ice especially with the leather-soled GI shoes we had. I would try to walk through some snowdrifts almost as high as my shoulders, then I would step on some ice and down I would go. I would have to dig out and go again. Some snow would always get down my collar and that was cold, especially about 1:00 a.m. - the hour that I would leave the apartment. I would walk through the snow to the main street where I would catch my ride to the base. I was glad when I made it okay. The city would keep the main streets scraped, and at that time in the morning there wasn't much traffic on the streets.

In the afternoons when I would ride the bus to our apartment street, I would get off the city bus at the drug store. When I stepped off the bus, the people would gather up to see me cross the street. Sometimes I would make it without falling and, if the weather wasn't too bad, I would take another street to the apartment and walk the twelve blocks. I promised myself if I ever got back home I was going to stay there - and I have.

At times when my friends and I were going to the base in the mornings, the car would hit an icy spot on the road and would spin around a few times, but we wouldn't be going fast and no damage was done. Some mornings, when we were waiting at the engineers' building, we enjoyed tuning in to the weathermen calling in their reports at 4:00 a.m. They were located at the outposts on mountains in all the northwestern states. There were some cold places, other than Casper. Some would be as low as minus 40 to 45 degrees. They would give their name, location and their weather report. We enjoyed hearing them.

My friend's old car, about a 1936 Chevy four-door, was having clutch trouble. I checked it and told him the clutch had to be replaced. He went to a dealership in Casper and an independent shop, but he couldn't afford to have it done at either place. A couple of others and I were paying him a little money for our rides, but it wasn't much. We all were in need of the car getting repaired, so I told him I would check on the parts' cost and he and

I would put the clutch in. I checked at a parts place and told them about our needs and our shortage of funds. They quoted a good price for the parts. I told my friend he and the other two riders could pay for the parts. He could still drive the car, but the clutch was slipping badly. He would have to take it easy and not take off fast until it was replaced. He got the money for the parts and he and I went to the parts store and picked them up. It was a rebuilt unit and I signed a statement I would be responsible for the return of the old parts.

We got a break in the weather and started back training crews. I told my friend that on our first day off we had to get that clutch in and we did. There was a small shop, not far from the apartment where Myrtle and I lived, where I had planned on getting the loan of a jack in order to get the front end jacked up and blocked. I asked to borrow their jack and got turned down. It was a very cold day and I told the man who owned the shop I was sorry to have bothered him. I asked him to come outside and show me where his property line was on the left side of his shop and he did. I then told him we were going to change that clutch right there - just off his property.

The car owner had a box of tools and I had borrowed a line-up spline tool from a man at the car dealership. My friend asked me if I was sure we could do the job. I told him I had helped my father with clutch jobs before. I had my friend drive his car across a small ditch and we went to work. He had an old blanket to put on the ground. It was cold, but it wasn't snowing or raining. About four hours later, we had the clutch in and adjusted. We returned the line-up tool to the man at the dealership and the old clutch unit to the parts place. I got my friend to take me to the apartment, and he and I were happy to be finished and get in out of the wind and cold.

The apartment Myrtle and I had in Casper was downstairs in the rear of a large building that had four apartments in it - two up and two down. The roof was high-pitched, so the snow would slide off. However, large, long icicles would form from the roof, and Myrtle and I would have to break them off with the screen door before leaving the apartment. We had a small sitting area with a couch in it, a bedroom, a kitchen, and a bathroom. We used the back area to come and go to our apartment.

On the next block to our rear was the home of the police captain. I got to know him and we became good friends. When I had a day off and when he had some break in his work, he would ask me to go to town with him. I enjoyed those times with him, especially when he and I would sit on a park bench and observe the old men with some of their friends going to the Old Union Bar.

Casper was an oil and cattle convention town. At the center of the town was the Old Union Bar and a block away was a block full of new and used covered wagons and other supply business places. That's where ranchers would meet up with friends they hadn't seen in a long time. We were where we could see them coming and going and he would tell me about them and where they lived. This is an example of one of his short descriptions:

"Now here comes Mr. So-and-So. He owns the Double D Ranch forty miles from here. He doesn't have any idea how much he is worth. He comes to town two or three times a year and stays a week or two when he's here. He has a number of oil wells on his property. He's snowed in about six months a year. His ranch is up on Casper Mountain. He's a cattle and sheep man. He and his spread have a commissary and a little school, and you could say it's a little community."

That's just one example. That would be repeated time after time.

I was with two or three of my friends one time and we went in the Old Union Bar and met "Old Joe," the barman and heard his stories about the rough old days. We spent about an hour with him, hearing him tell story after story about what happened on a day or night when so-and-so was killed. He was a very old man then, but he could get excited while telling stories and showing us the bullet holes in the tables and walls.

He had to stop his stories and tend bar when some of the old men would come in with their friends. Old Joe would serve them, but there wouldn't be anyone paying. We asked about that and Joe explained, "Some of my old friends give me money up front, others pay later. Most of the time, we get together and settle up once a year, but we trust one another."

It was interesting to watch what a great time the old men were having and to hear Old Joe tell about the 1880's and 1890's. I'm sure he had many more stories he didn't tell us.

If we went in to any store in Casper and bought anything, when we paid for it we would be given our change back in silver dollars and they were heavy. If we owed a dollar and paid with a $20 bill, the clerk would give us nineteen silver dollars in change.

The mountains around Casper would start to get snow on the top around late August or the first part of September and the roads would have signs warning they would be closed after a certain date. the road to the air base, we could see all kinds of animals moving about. We would hear stories about how many different animals some hunters would kill. I would see some hunters coming into Casper with the animal they had killed that day with their permit tag tied on its head. They were supposed to go by the game officer's headquarters and have the permit tag removed and the kill registered. I heard stories about hunters waiting until after dark to come in so they could bypass the game officer and not turn in the tag and keep it and use it again. There was a large freezer locker business in Casper, and the news was out the game officers were checking the freezer lockers and a large number of hunters had been arrested.

In the Casper area there were five oil refineries, including a Standard Oil refinery that hadn't been operating since 1929. It was not within the Casper city limits when it was built, but, in 1929 Casper extended the city limits to bring the refinery into the city. That's when it stopped production and, I was told, the company had firefighters there all the time since operations had ceased.

"My Friend 'Kentucky'"

One afternoon about three o'clock, a friend and I were walking on the Casper base close to the base headquarters building. I saw a GI pushing a lawn mower and I told my friend I thought I recognized that GI. There was not another GI who wore his fatigue hat on his head like Kentucky did.

"When we get a little closer to him, I am going to call out to him and see if he is who I think he is. I was with him when I was in basic training in Atlantic City, New Jersey."

After a few more steps, I yelled out "Kentucky" and he came running to us. Before I could say anything to him, he grabbed my hand and said, "Shiver, how are you? I'm glad to see you."

I introduced him to my friend and asked him where he had been since basic training.

"Shiver, I've been having a good time enjoying life here in Casper and not worrying about anything. I'm just pulling KP and guard duty, cutting grass and making people laugh all the time."

"Kentucky, you haven't changed. You did that in Atlantic City and you gave that drill S/Sgt the works. He set out to change you, but you always had us laughing at him trying, and then, he had to give up on you. You would make him so mad and flustrated with you that he wouldn't know what to do. You would always have the last laugh."

We enjoyed the time with Kentucky, but we had to leave him and he got back to his grass cutting. I told my friend there wasn't another Kentucky in the world.

A few days later, a M/Sgt. hanger chief, who also knew Kentucky, told me this story about what happened one winter when a blizzard hit:

> There was snow and ice and it was really cold. I was driving the "officer of the day" around that night and Kentucky was not on his guard post. We couldn't find him anywhere. I told the officer he must be in one of the hangars.
> The officer asked, "But which hangar?"
> I told him I didn't know, but we would start out with the hangar closest to the place where he was supposed to be and go from there. We went in the first hangar and couldn't find Kentucky. We then went into the boiler room and there was Kentucky, in the corner, behind the boiler, sitting on the floor with his GI coat on, fast asleep. I woke him up and then, the officer took over. He dressed him down a couple of times and you could tell it didn't do any good. Then, the officer lowered his voice

and said in a nice tone, "Kentucky, what if someone had come while you weren't on your post and fast asleep in this hanger and got one of those planes? Wouldn't you feel bad?"

Kentucky got up, stood at attention, and remarked, "Sir, if anyone wants one of those planes on a night like this, he's welcome to get it." The officer put Kentucky back outside on his post and we left.

We never checked on him anymore that night but I wouldn't be surprised if Kentucky didn't go right back into that boiler room after we left.

The M/Sgt. told me he and the officer didn't say anything else about Kentucky after that. I told the M/Sgt. Kentucky always gets the last laugh and another thing about Kentucky - he never worries about anything. He is still a private and he wouldn't have it any other way.

While we were in Casper, a friend was always asking me questions about our way of eating down South. He was from the North. Myrtle and I invited him to have an evening meal with us and he accepted. I told Myrtle to have fried chicken and biscuits with the other usual side dishes and she did. The meal was cooked after he arrived and that smell of chicken frying was great. She put on a very good meal and we enjoyed it. Before he left that night, he thanked us saying he really enjoyed the chicken and hot biscuits.

"A Friend Who Bailed Out Over France"

I had a friend in Casper, Wyoming, who was a flight engineer instructor there at the same time I was. He was with a group that had been in England. He had to bail out over France on one of his missions and this is the story about his rescue and return back to England. He was tall and slim with light-colored hair. He was picked up by the Free French and hidden until night. They were close to Paris and told to stay there. Sometime that night, a beautiful woman would come get him. She came for him about midnight and told him her plan. She had a room in the best section of Paris.

Her room was on the second floor directly below the German Officers' Paris Headquarters. She told him he would be safe with her.

"I'm taking you to my room until morning. Tomorrow, we will get you on your way to England," she said.

They gave him a change of clothes. He said this was a great group the woman had working very close to the German High Command in Paris.

She and a man came and took him to her room. Early the next morning, she took him to a little printing shop owned by an old, small man. The man took his picture and then she took him down the street away from the shop. He was placed in front of a big store showroom with his back to the street and was told to stay there and not move. She said she would be back as soon as his papers were ready.

He said time passes slowly in a situation like that, but suddenly, things went from bad to really bad. Two German officers came by and stopped. They moved a little and the one next to my friend accidently touched his arm. The officer looked at him face-to-face. My friend said, without thinking, "Excuse me."

He told me, "That officer and I looked at each other for a few moments and then, the officers walked away. I almost stopped breathing for a while. That was a close call for me, but things went well for the return back to England."

"Helping Close the Casper Base"

When I was getting ready to leave Casper, I was told by a first lieutenant he had picked me to help him close one of the hangars. When I asked why he had chosen me, he told me I was older than most of the others and I had the rank to get the job done. He assigned four GIs to help me. We met in the hangar supply room to tag everything. We were to attach a tag to each item, showing the proper nomenclature and the correct Army number on it.

We had an Army catalogue to use, but that took time to hunt up all the information and tag everything. There was only one catalogue and when someone was slow in looking up a number, two or three of us would be waiting to use it. I asked the lieutenant if we could tape a number of the same things together and put the number on the tag.

He said, "No. There is an old saying – 'there is the right way and the Army way.'"

I told him we were getting nowhere with our job and we needed some relief. He took me away from the others and told me there wasn't and wouldn't be any inventory records made on anything in the supply room.

"I'm not telling you to do this," he said, "but, if I were you, I would fill my coat pockets full of those small sockets and wrenches, then walk out to a snow pile and unload them."

He told me the items wouldn't be found until spring and the Army wouldn't get any money for them anyway. The small items would be bid off in piles of odds and ends.

It didn't take long after that to clean the supply room. We tagged the large tools and a few small ones. We cleaned out a chest of drawers and I asked the lieutenant what to do with the chest. He told me to get a truck and take it to the dump where it would be burned. I told him I would like to have it. He said he would complete a paper request for me to have it shipped to my home, but I would have to pay the shipping charges. He helped me get it ready for the shipping truck to pick up and I went to the truck line's office in Casper to pay for the shipping.

When I returned and thanked the lieutenant, he said he had one more job for me to do for him. One of the barracks on the base had a lot of things in it which would need to be tagged and moved to a warehouse. Items included both jungle and arctic kits included in the B-24 planes when they arrived at Casper. When the planes left the factory, both kits were included since the manufacturer didn't know where the planes would eventually be sent. There were also de-icer boots from the leading edges of the planes' wings and stabilizers. All items had to be tagged and numbered.

We were able to find the numbers for everything except the large protector plates. The plates were made of 1/2" steel and five to six feet in length, which made them very heavy. We had to move everything to a big warehouse at the rear of the base. The lieutenant told me to unload the plates on the ramp of the warehouse and to ask the warehouse manager to tell me what to put on the tags.

I had four men with me to help in addition to the truck driver from the motor pool.

He backed the truck up to the unloading ramp and we unloaded it, but we had to wait a few minutes for the manager.

The warehouse manager was busy with another truck driver who had two South Bend metal lathes loaded on his truck. One of the lathes was about six feet long and both looked new; they had all the attachments with them. They had quick change gears on them as well. The same truck had a large number of tarpaulins on it. The truck driver counted out $1200 to the warehouse manager for the load, but I didn't see any papers exchanged between the two of them in the sale.

The manager came to me and I asked him to give us some numbers and names for the steel plates we had placed on the loading ramp. He got mad because they weren't already tagged. I told him the catalogue in the supply room didn't have the numbers and names for them. I explained we would tag the plates with the numbers he would give us and carry them into the warehouse. He told me he would give me the information for the tags, but we couldn't tag them on the loading ramp. He said they would have to be loaded back up and hauled back to the hangar. When I asked him why, he said, "Because I say so."

I told him he was being too hard on us, because the plates were very heavy. I said we were doing what we were told to do. I said, "Mister, you can do with these steel plates what you want to, because we are leaving them with you."

I told the men it was time to go and we left the warehouse. The man kept talking to us, but the truck driver and the other men were happy with what I had said to the manager. We returned to the hangar and I reported to the lieutenant about our trouble with the warehouse manager. He told me I had done the right thing.

I was glad to get the supply room and the barracks cleaned out. Now, I was ready to leave Casper.

"The Train to Ardmore, Oklahoma"

When I was leaving Casper, Wyoming, I was given the orders for the ones being transferred to Ardmore, Oklahoma. There were twenty-three persons on the orders for Ardmore, but only eleven were going on the train. Three of the eleven were WACS, and that left eight GIs for the trip that day in one of the old boxcars which had been converted to carry GIs. I was a T/Sgt. and the highest ranked GI left on the orders, so I was in charge. I did not ask for the responsibility, but I couldn't get out of it. I tried, but I was told I had it anyway. We were supposed to leave Casper at 1:00 p.m.

We were in the old boxcar at the end of the train, but the train hadn't moved. I had a S/Sgt. I had already asked to be my helper, so I told him to keep the men in the car while I went to see why we were delayed. As I arrived at the station, I found out the trouble. One of the WACS was drunk. And I mean drunk! She was a private first class, small, Indian, and a beautiful girl. When I walked up to the station, she ran to me, jumped up and hung onto my neck and called me her sergeant. She had refused to board the train with the other two WACs, one a corporal and the other a private first class. The corporal was in charge. As the others were explaining what had happened, she was still hanging onto me and asking me to help her, saying she was not getting on the train with the other WACs.

There was a large crowd around trying to help get her on the train and they had the scratches to show for it. There were two MPs, some policemen, the police chief, the conductor of the train, and some of the train station employees trying to get her on the train. She had them all wanting no more of her clawing and scratching and I didn't blame them. They asked for some help and I told them I would try. I got the little WAC off from the crowd and pleaded with her to get on the train. She told me she would go with me, but not with the other WACs. I went to the crowd and told them the news. I told them I would take care of her and would bring her to the WACs' Pullman car later that afternoon. That was all I could do - take it or not. The WAC corporal told me she and the little WAC got into an argument over her drinking problem and it had gone from bad to worse. The corporal thanked me and the little WAC and I went to our old boxcar and got on board. The train finally left at 2:00 p.m.

277

I told the men about the problem they had at the station with the WAC and that she would be with us until that evening and no one was to touch her. We would let her lie down on one of the benches and I thought she would sleep the drunk off. I was right - she did some sleeping. About 7:00 that evening I tried to get her awake but no luck. I went to the conductor and told him about her sleeping and that I needed to report it to the WACs. He told me what car they were in. I found them and gave them the news about her and assured them I would bring her to them as soon as I could. It was about eleven that night before I got her up. The little WAC told me she would go to her bunk, but she wasn't talking to the other two WACs. I told her I had made plans with the conductor to take her to her bunk. She asked me if she could come back in the morning and I said she could. She returned the next morning at about nine o'clock and spent the day with us. I didn't have any more trouble with her or the men.

We arrived at Ardmore about six o'clock that evening. There was a staff car for the WACs and a GI big truck waiting at the station to pick us up and carry us to the base. The little WAC refused to get in the car with the other WACs and insisted on riding with us on the truck. I told the WAC corporal I had gotten the girl all the way from Casper, so why not let her ride to the base headquarters with us. I had decided I would put her in the truck cab with the driver, but she insisted on riding on the truck with us. I told her the truck didn't have any seats on it and we would have to stand.

She said, "I will stand with you men."

She had to have help getting on. When the truck was about two blocks from the headquarters building, she started jumping up and down and shouting, "Big Red, Big Red! Come to the headquarters building!"

She told me she and Big Red had been through basic training together and she wanted me to meet her.

I said, "Okay."

She introduced me to her friend as "my sergeant" and the little WAC told her about her trip down to Ardmore. "Big Red" was a mess sergeant - three stripes - and in charge of the WAC kitchen and mess hall. She was not too big of a woman, but compared to her little WAC friend she was big. She had red hair and told me she appreciated what I had done for her friend.

I checked in and turned in the papers for the others. What a relief that was for me. I left the HQ building and went to the squadron day room and met Sergeant Treace there. My stay at Ardmore is in the Treace story, which follows, except for this: One evening, I met up with Red while I was at the PX and she wanted to talk with me. She wanted to know if I would escort her to the PX about two times a week. I asked her why she needed an escort. She told me every time she came, there was always someone whistling and saying some things to her and she was afraid to be out at night by herself. I told her I was trying to get to Pueblo, and I didn't know how long I would be in Ardmore. She told me she was looking for someone to help her.

"There will be no hanky-panky stuff with me," she told me.

I told her I was married and I showed her my wedding ring.

I had to ask, "Why don't you come to the PX before it gets dark?"

"I'm the mess sergeant and I'm always making salads, pies, and cakes for the next day. That has to be done after the evening meal. That takes time and then I have to clean up the kitchen and have it ready for breakfast. If you will help me, I will treat you with a salad and dessert after we return from the PX each time."

I told her I would help her. She would tell me the day, time, and place to meet and it worked out fine for both of us. It usually would take about thirty minutes to go to the PX and then we would be back at her mess hall. She would have my plate fixed and in the cooler. She had to keep the lights off, but some lights outside the building would give enough light for us. She was a good cook, and I think she fed me four times before I left Ardmore. The WACs sure ate better than the GIs!

"Staff Sgt. Harvey L. Treace"

I left Casper, Wyoming about 2:00 p.m. on March 8, 1945, and arrived at Ardmore, Oklahoma, in the evening on March 9th. I was assigned to a squadron as a flight engineer instructor on B-17 planes. I wasn't going to fly on B-17s; it was not what I wanted. I had a bad feeling about Casper sending me to Ardmore and not to a B-24 training base. As soon as I got to the squadron area, I went to the dayroom to see if I knew anyone who happened to be there. As soon as I walked in I recognized Staff Sgt. Harvey L. Treace at a pool table and he saw me.

I was a friend of Sergeant Treace when I was in the 344th squadron overseas. We became close friends, although I was never on a combat mission crew with him. He would confide in me about his life in Kentucky. He grew up in a rural mountainous area and he was married and had a little girl he had never seen, because she was born while he was overseas. But, that little girl was the pride of his life. We called Treace, "Trigger Treace", because he had a reputation with his tail turret shooting. He had been a tail gunner on Colonel Kane's crew on the August 1, 1943, mission to Ploesti oil fields. His wife and little girl were living with Treace's grandmother. He was always gambling and sending money orders to his wife. At that time in the Army, you couldn't get more than $200 on a money order, but there wasn't a limit on the number of money orders you could get. Later on, there was a limit on the amount you could send. Your limit was no more than the pay grade you were paid.

When I saw Treace by the pool table at Ardmore, he came to me and said, "Shiver, you have come to the worst base in the Air Corps."

He said he needed to talk to me in private. We got off by ourselves and he unloaded to me what had happened to him.

"Shiver, you knew I gambled all the time I was overseas and I won a lot of money. I sent about $20,000 to my wife and told her to save some for our daughter and to buy what she and my Grandma needed to live on. When I got home, I found out my wife had left our little daughter with my Grandma, had run off with some man and had not spent any money on anyone but herself. My little girl didn't even have shoes or clothes to wear. I had my allotment changed to benefit my Grandma and I haven't heard from my wife."

Treace told me he didn't know what he would do when he found her. He thanked me and said that he needed someone to tell his troubles to.

He told me what I needed to know about Ardmore Army Air Base. He was a gunner instructor and had tried to get moved to another place, but hadn't been moved yet.

"An instructor here is responsible for anything the student does wrong and they make the instructor sign a statement of charges and you have to pay for it," he told me.

He told me I should start to work on getting transferred. I thanked him and we shook hands; I went to the squadron office and tried to get the ball rolling to get transferred to Pueblo, but I got nowhere with my request. The squadron commanding officer told me it was impossible to get transferred out of Ardmore. He had tried for two years and was still there. I asked him to write a letter to the base commander for me, but he refused. I told him I would not fly on the B-17 and that was that.

"You need to put me somewhere so I can do a ground job." I told him.

He assigned me to AC-222 AF BU-Sqn (Air Crew Supply). So, I had a job on the ground. I checked out chutes, headsets, and oxygen masks to crews who were flying and, at times, I checked some back in. After a few days I went back to the squadron office and tried again to get transferred out. I asked permission to go to the commanding officer of the base in person to ask for a transfer. The squadron CO told me I didn't take "no" for the final word. He told me he would send the request for me. I thanked him and left the office feeling better. There is an old saying – "There is a right way to do something and there is the Army way".

I have a copy of the letter dated March 13, 1945, from the Office of the Director of Operations and Training at the Ardmore Army Air Field stating the standardization board had acted on my request and had recommended I should be sent to Pueblo. The order didn't get in print until March 24th and I received my orders to leave on the 25th. I was a happy person. I was being assigned to the 215th AAF BU – Pueblo AAB – Pueblo, Colorado – Maintenance F Sqn.

<u>Headquarters</u>
<u>Ardmore Army Air Field</u>
<u>Ardmore, Oklahoma</u>

(Special Orders)   24 March 1945

16. Under the provisions of AR600-68, as amended, and upon recommendation of the Squadron Commander, the Fol. EM, 222nd AAF BU, Sq E, is authorized to wear the Good Conduct Medal.

    T/Sgt. (748) John J. Shiver, Jr. 34335079

"Pueblo, Colorado"

I left Ardmore, Oklahoma at 2:28 a.m. on March 26, 1945, by train going to the AAF Base at Pueblo, Colorado. This train trip was the only time the Army gave me a ticket for a Pullman (sleeper) ride. I did get to sleep about five hours and it was appreciated. I arrived at Pueblo late afternoon that day and went out to the Air Base and checked in. I found out the next morning Pueblo was changing to a B-29 training base. They were training Chinese crews to fly the B-24s and they didn't need B-24 men. I was told that six B-24 flight engineers were going to attend a transition class to be B-29 flight engineers and I could join them. It was my choice.

On the B-29 plane the flight engineer had a seat in the flight cabin behind the co-pilot and had a large board of instruments to check and keep records on. The readings had to be recorded every thirty minutes. The flight engineer had a set of levers and switches for all the engines' controls and had to control the fuel consumption and fuel transfers when needed. The pilot had a set of control levers he could use in emergencies, but the engineer was usually the one who started the engines and did the running up as the pilot requested. This led us to refer to the B-29 pilots as airplane drivers. They didn't appreciate that, but a B-29 flight engineer was busy all the time.

I enjoyed the short B-29 school and we had a good instructor. The instructor came to me after our final exam and told me I was the only one who had passed. He said he was going to give the others another fast review course for about a week, and then give another final exam. He gave me a choice of taking the review course or leaving the others right then. I told him I would take the review course and stay with my friends. He said I had made a wise decision. A person will always learn something in a review course. We had a fast week of instruction and we all got passing grades. We were now ready to go back on flying status and flying pay would help. Flying pay was an extra one-half of base pay. They gave us a choice of keeping our rank or being made a flight officer. Most of the men would rather keep their non-commission rank. That was my choice.

I sat down to sign my papers and decided to read them before I signed. If I had signed, it meant I was signing up for four more years! I had enough points to get out of the Army at that time, and I was trying to, but my records were not up-to-date. The sergeant-major at the base headquarters said I had only 95 points, but I told him I had 105 points. He showed me that my records didn't show my #3 and #4 air medals. I told him they showed my earning a silver leaf on my air medal, along with two bronze leaves. I had eight air medals.

He kept saying, "Your #3 and #4 air medals are not on your records."

"My silver is on my records. How could I have a silver medal on my records, if I had not earned my #3 and #4 air medals? What does that silver represent?" I asked.

"Silver is for #5, but #3 and #4 are not on your records, so you are going to stay in the Army for five more months."

He was right. I got out in September 1945—five months later. I tried to get in touch with the 98th Bomb Group but couldn't. They were coming back to the States. I gave up. A sergeant–major is the "Top Dog" at any base. His word is final, but I told him he was wrong and he was stupid to believe I hadn't earned my #3 and #4, because my record showed I had earned a total of eight air medals.

I got in more trouble after I refused to sign the paper to go back on flying status. They told me I would be given a Master Sergeant's rank and I was to be a hangar chief. I didn't want that job, so I refused it. They had three or four of the hangars made large enough to get the B-29s into them. Since I wouldn't take a hangar chief's job, they told me I had to take the job of overseeing and taking charge of #1 and #2 engine inspections on a night shift.

The engines had to have the valves adjusted, spark plugs changed, all of the engine cowling covers cleaned, and a number of things done and checked depending on the number of hours on that engine. I had about sixteen men on the night shift—7:00 p.m. until 7:00 a.m. The plane would be towed into the hangar and we would get busy. Records would be put down on all work done and initials put down by the one who did that job or that check. The first thing that had to be done was to get all cowling covers off and put them on the carts to be taken to the building at the end of the flight line to be steam cleaned. The carts were towed by a tow motor, but a man had to go with each cart to be sure they got cleaned and back to the hangar in time to be put back on the plane.

At every inspection all spark plugs were changed. Each engine had thirty-six spark plugs to be changed. The rear bottom cylinder back plug was always the one that gave us the most trouble getting it out without bringing out the cylinder threads with the plug. That cylinder was the one that got the hottest. There was a rule that if a shift damaged a cylinder, they had to change that cylinder. If the shift ended, that shift had to work overtime to finish the job.

We would use a small fire extinguisher and freeze that plug and then, if we were careful we could get it out. We had to get everything ready for this operation and we had to time it just right with no brass around. Someone with a bucket and mop would be ready to clean up the mess made. Then someone would have to take the fire extinguisher to the place to get it recharged and have it back to the hangar before we needed it on the other engine. Everything was working out well until one night about ten o'clock when the man with the extinguisher didn't get back to the hangar on time. I sent one of the men to see what had happened to him. He returned and reported our man had left the supply depot with the filled extinguisher and headed back to the hangar.

One of the men told me the man had been into Pueblo that day and just got back to the base in time to change his clothes and report to his job. He was known around the base to be a heavy drinker and his favorite place in Pueblo was a bar on Union Street. This street was across the railroad tracks and was known for its brawls and fights. Some of this bar's customers were Mexicans who worked at Wickwire Spring Foundry and Iron

Works located close to Pueblo. This man was known around the base to be a graduate of MIT, but he had a big problem. His problem was alcohol. A number of times he would come back from Pueblo with his face showing he had been in a fight. We could have made the night without this man, but we needed the extinguisher. I sent a man to his barracks to see if he had gone there. He came back with the extinguisher and told me he found the man asleep on his bunk with the extinguisher by his side. He said he didn't try to wake him up. I told him he did the right thing. I said we could make the shift without him and I would tend to him later. That I did.   The next evening, before the shift started, we had a good talk - just the two of us. This GI was a buck sergeant and a good man for what we used him for. As long as he didn't pull any more deals like he did the night before, I wouldn't turn him in. I am sure he would have lost his stripes if I had turned him in. I told him I was going to hold that over him; if he had another episode, then I would let the axe fall. He thanked me and I didn't have any more trouble with him.

I had to use the men who were assigned to me. Most of them would do a good job, but I had a buck sergeant from Arkansas who gave me trouble all the time. He was a slacker in the jobs I assigned to him and was always complaining, saying I was giving him all the bad jobs. I told him that wasn't true, because I passed all jobs around. One night I had assigned the job of checking the valves on the #2 engine to him. The B-29s had an 18-cylinder engine, and that meant there were thirty-six valves to check the clearance on and adjust if needed. It wasn't such a bad job, because we used a "Go & No Go" gauge to check the valves.

After a short time I saw him sitting on the stand steps. I asked him why he wasn't checking those valves and he told me he had just finished them. I went and got the clipboard to see; it was checked and initialed. I was in a hurry and didn't read the initials. The shift ended and I went to the mess hall, and then to my barracks. I got a shower and hit the cot for some sleep. (I never could get used to that night shift. Nights were made for sleeping!)

At about ten o'clock, I was awakened and told the engineering officer wanted me right away. I dressed and went to his office. He was a major and I had met him before and knew him. He was at his desk and told me to have a seat. I sat down and he told me why he had sent for me.

He said, "Shiver, the B-29 that was in for inspection last night had to return to the base this morning—#2 engine out—valve trouble. I checked and your initials were on the valves' check line. I know someone else put them there. Tell me, who did you assign to that job? I know you didn't do it."

I was in a tough spot. That good-for-nothing buck sergeant with a wife and two kids living off base in Pueblo had put me in a bad spot. If I told the major who did it, he would give the buck sergeant exactly what he deserved and his family would suffer. I took the responsibility for it, because I didn't think the major would do anything to me. I got out of that bad situation and came out fine. I told the major I had checked the valves, since my initials were there. He told me he didn't believe me, but he knew me and figured I had a reason for what I was doing.

He smiled at me and said it would be taken care of. "Am I right, Shiver?"

"Yes, sir!" I replied.

The major told me he had another thing he wanted to talk with me about. I told him to go to it. He told me he was going to stay in the service after the war was over and he would like to have me as his assistant. "I have a little pull around here. I want you to go to OCS for three months and come back to Pueblo as a 2nd lieutenant and work with me. I will work on your promotions as fast as I can. I can keep you with me, and I think within a couple of years, you will be a captain."

I told him I appreciated his offer, but I wasn't staying in the service. "I have enough points to get out now, but my records are messed up and my old group is on a ship coming back to the States now. I'm getting out as soon as I can. I thank you, but I have to refuse." The major told me he wished me success.

I left the office and returned to the sack for some rest and sleep. I couldn't get that buck sergeant off my mind. I knew how I was going to handle him and I was going to try to make a man out of a bad nothing. When we arrived at the hangar that evening, I didn't assign that sergeant a job, but told him to wait until I got the others on their work and then I would get back with him.

I came back to him and told him to follow me. I went outside the hangar where no one could hear me and I let him know about my session with the major that morning. I let him know I did what I did for his wife and two children - not for him. I knew they would suffer, if I had told the major he had put my initials on the valves' check line.

"Now you straighten up and act like a man!" I told him. "You know you can't keep on doing what's wrong without getting into trouble. I'm giving you another chance. If I have any more trouble with you or hear about anything bad you've done, I'm going to the engineering officer and he'll come down hard on you. The first thing the major will do is bust you down to a private and put you in the brig where you will wear a big "P" painted on your fatigue clothes. Everyone will know you are a prisoner and are waiting to be court-martialed. I'm done with you! Do you understand? This is it!"

He thanked me and told me he was sorry about what he had done and appreciated my not telling the officer about him. I again told him I was giving him a chance to straighten up and be a man. After that talk, I didn't have any more trouble with him. There wasn't any more complaining from him. He was a different person.

When I was in Pueblo, I was assigned to a barracks with T/Sgts. and M/Sgts. in it. One of the men was M/Sgt. Weiss from headquarters and he worked in an office where a major was his boss. He was always telling us about him wanting to finish his thirty years in the Army Air Corps and return to his home on Chesapeake Bay near Baltimore, Maryland. His home was on the Bay Shore and he wanted to spend his later years fishing. He had been a crew chief on General "Hap" Arnold's plane, a long time ago when he said you only needed a big roll of wire and pliers to keep it flying. The boss over him, a major, was always filing insubordination charges against him. M/Sgt. Weiss knew General Longfellow in Colorado Springs. The general was the top man over the 2nd Air Force (the Training Command), and Sgt. Weiss would call him and the charges would be dropped. That major wouldn't stop filing the charges.

The sergeant came into the barracks one afternoon and he was really mad. The major had filed another charge against him and the sergeant had called General Longfellow again. He told us that day's call to the general was the last one.

"After twenty-nine years and nine months in the Army, I'm getting out. I have had it with that major," he said.

He told us the major wanted to see him leave the Army Air Corps as a private, not as a M/Sgt. He said he had been working on the old planes since the Army had them in the Signal Corps. Some of his friends tried to get him to change his mind and complete his three months. He told them he had already signed the papers to leave, and he was getting out before he did something bad to that officer. Then, he would really be in trouble. He told us he was doing what he had to do, and he did leave the Army.

There were two other M/Sgts. in the barracks. They were always pulling pranks on each other - especially if they had been drinking in town and had returned to the barracks feeling good. They would try to outdo each other, if they could think of a prank to do. One of them came back to the barracks alone one night about ten o'clock and turned on the lights. He woke everyone up. It was a Saturday night and I was there. He went from one end of the barracks to the other and got everyone awake. He told us he had tried to get his buddy to come back to the base with him, but he wouldn't do it.

"I know he is mad at me for leaving him and he is going to do something to me tonight when he gets back. I want someone to help me to swap his cot for mine now," he said.

Their cots were on opposite sides of the barracks directly across from one another at a foot-to-foot position. He took his blanket and rolled it up and placed it under the sheet to look like someone was in the cot. All barracks had at each end two five-gallon buckets on a shelf - one with sand and the other with water. Everyone was awake waiting to see what was going to happen. We didn't have to wait very long before the other sergeant returned. He was talking loudly as he came into the barracks and took the water bucket off the shelf. He came charging down the center of the barracks still talking to himself.

"I'll show him what he gets for leaving me in town by myself," he said.

His buddy's cot was in the middle part of the barracks and there were no lights except a small light at each entrance. Everyone sat up to see what he was going to do. He stopped in front of the cot which he thought was his buddy's and threw the bucket of water on the cot. His buddy was sitting on his own cot on the opposite side of the barracks.

His buddy shouted, "You just wet your own bed! I got you tonight! I thought you were going to do that to me."

He got up and helped his friend clean up the mess.

There was an extra cot with a dry mattress in the barracks and they got it for the sergeant's bed. The wet one was turned in to supply for a dry one. I was told these two sergeants had been doing pranks to each other for a long time. They had to have been good friends to laugh after a prank like that one.

"Grady Gaston's Story"

Grady Gaston was a T/Sgt. from Alabama. Some of the men told me that when Grady was flying combat duty in the war, he had to bail out over the jungle somewhere and had spent a long time surviving there by eating raw berries and snakes. They told me not to ask Grady about the ordeal. He didn't want to talk about it. Later, while I was still in the Air Corps, I read about Grady's survival in the newspaper. There was an article in "Ripley's Believe it or Not" about Grady's episode, but I had forgotten how long he was in the jungle.

At Pueblo, Grady was operating a radio station at the rear of the base to help get Chinese crews back to the base when they got lost. He would get another base operator from another state to help him. They would both get a location where the plane was to help the pilot. When they found the lost plane, they would give the pilot a reading to come in on. He came into the barracks from the radio shack and I went over to him, met him and asked him what part of Alabama he was from. He told me Frisco City. I told him I was from Atmore. I could tell he was really nervous.

I told him, "It's a small world after all—two of us from South Alabama who lived only thirty miles apart and never met. Now here we are meeting for the first time in Pueblo. Glad to meet you."

I left him; I would see him other times, but I never talked to him about his survival episode. After I got out of the service, I went to a baseball game in Monroeville when Atmore was playing a game there. Grady was on the team from Monroeville and was playing that afternoon. After the game I went down on the field and spoke to him. I didn't talk to him very long, because I could tell he was still very nervous and didn't want to talk anymore. We shook hands and parted.

My son, Jeff, recently sent me a book he had found about Grady's experiences with the plane's crash in the northern bush territory of Australia. Grady and two other crew members survived. Seven others were killed in the crash or didn't survive the ordeal in the jungle. The book, *The Crash of Little Eva,* was written by Barry Ralph. I recommend it to anyone who enjoys war history. The author did a very good job researching historical documents to tell it like it happened. Here are some of the facts about Grady's ordeal:

Grady was 22 years old and the radio operator on the crew. The crew's plane was a B-24D and named "Little Eva," 321st squadron of the 90th bomb group. They were on their first mission on the evening of December 1, 1942. The bomb load was eight 500-pound bombs. The pilot's name was Norman Crosson. They were on a mission to bomb Japanese destroyers. On the bombing run, the bomb racks didn't release the bombs, and they were going to another target when they found themselves coming into a storm. Night was coming and it was getting darker, so they headed back to their base. Their instruments went bad because they were in a violent storm and fuel was getting low. They were lost and didn't know if they were over the Coral Sea or land. They had to bail out, and that's where Grady's ordeal began.

Grady was found after 141 days in the Australian jungle. Seven men died in this tragedy. I know Grady's nerves were very bad because I saw that myself. After reading the book, *The Crash of Little Eva,* I can understand why Grady never wanted to talk about his experiences in the jungles of Australia.

"More about Grady Gaston"

This episode happened on a night when I was not working at my hangar job. It was about nine o'clock and Grady who worked in the radio shack on the backside of the Air Base at Pueblo, where they were training the Chinese crews who flew the B-24s, hadn't made it in from the shack yet. He was usually in the barracks by seven or eight o'clock at night. About nine-thirty Grady arrived and he was mad. Someone asked him what he had been up to that made him so late and so mad. He told us about a Chinese crew he had been trying to get back to the base. They were lost and he had gotten a shack radio operator at another base in another state to help him. They determined the plane's location for the crew and Grady gave them the information to get back to Pueblo, but he couldn't get them to the base. One time he got them within thirty miles of Pueblo and he told them they should be able to see the lights in the sky from Pueblo. They still hadn't gotten to Pueblo, but on the next location, they had gotten turned around and were going in the opposite direction. He told them he was going to locate them one more time and give them the information to come home on.

"That's it," he radioed them. "I have worked with you for the last four hours and got my friend to stay with me, but enough is enough. I was supposed to close the shack at six o'clock and now it's nine. I'm going in now. I hope you make it in okay."

The Chinese crews ate in the same mess hall as the GIs. That was fine with me, but I didn't like rice all the time. The mess sergeants cooked rice for every meal, and we would watch the Chinese go for it. They could put the rice down and go back for more. I'm sure that they enjoyed their meals at Pueblo more than I did; rice wasn't what I wanted to eat all the time.

I met a T/Sgt. while I was at Pueblo who had been an engineer on a B-24 that flew supplies over the "Hump" (Himalaya Mountains) in China. Their plane was attacked and shot down by some Japanese Zeroes. The crew had to bail out over the mountains. On the way down, the sergeant got hit a number of times by a Zero that took a shot at him on the way down in his chute. He told me he had passed out after he was hit several times on the way down. He landed close to a Chinese family's farm. They found him and took him into their home. They lived close to a little village and the village doctor nursed him back to where he was able to be carried out of the mountains. He woke up several days after they had fixed him up. There were three wounds on his upper body and two on his legs. They did a very good job. None of the bullets had hit a vital part of his body. I saw the scars on his body. He told me he enjoyed pulling off his shirt and showing his back to a GI who was talking about his wounds. The Chinese family was very good to him and he was and will always be grateful for their help and especially for not turning him in. The Zero must have shot up all of its big ammo at the plane. They had two wing guns that fired about .30 caliber ammo, and he was glad it hadn't been the big stuff.

"When I Was at Pueblo – Sad News"

President Franklin D. Roosevelt died on April 12, 1945, at Warm Springs, Georgia. I was at Pueblo, Colorado, then and I have no record of the exact date, but we stopped all flights and work for one day to show our respect and sympathy for our President and Commander.

"VE Day – Good News"

President Truman announced the war in Europe had come to an end and Nazi Germany had unconditionally surrendered on May 7, 1945. The time was 2:41 a.m. (French time). The papers were signed at a little red school house, which General Eisenhower used as headquarters. I don't remember if we stopped all work that day, but it was a great day for all of us.

"March Field, Riverside, California"

I left Pueblo by rail on July 12, 1945, with thirty other men going to a B-29 base in Riverside, California - (March Field) – 239th AAF BU on Special Orders Number 192 dated July 11, 1945. I was glad another T/Sgt. was put in charge on this trip. We arrived at Riverside on July 14, 1945, and went out to March Field Air Base by truck. After a day or two, I was assigned to a hangar working on B-29s. They asked me to accept a hangar chief's job and if I agreed I would become a M/Sgt., but I refused the offer. I wanted to get out of the service. Some of my work was on the B-29s in the hangar I was assigned to, but most of the time I was working on the planes parked on the flight line.

It was hot in July and August out in the open area with no cover over us or the planes. There were concrete ramps everywhere and the planes would get so hot we couldn't touch them, but after a few hours we got used to the heat. At the end of the workday, we didn't have to clean the ramps like we did the hangar floors. The concrete ramps would be cleaned for us. That was a plus! At the end of the day, we would put our wrenches in our toolboxes, carry them into the hangar supply room, and go back to our barracks.

While I was at March Field, I saw my first freeway. Someone told me it went to Los Angeles. I was walking through another squadron area late one afternoon with another GI. We were taking a shortcut to the PX when I noticed a T/Sgt. sitting on the steps of the barracks a short distance from us. I told the GI with me the GI sitting yonder looked like a man from my hometown - Atmore, Alabama. By that time, we were at the steps and I said, "It's Root Lowrey!"

Root got up and reached out his hand to me. As we shook hands he said, "John Shiver! Glad to see you."

I replied, "Glad to see you. Where have you been?"

Root was a T/Sgt. and a flight engineer on a B-24 in the Pacific Theater. He wanted to get out of the service, too. We were waiting for the headquarters office orders to send us to Atlanta to be discharged.

The shipping orders were posted on the base bulletin board each morning for the ones who would be shipped out soon. It was up to us to keep a watch for our names to come up. While I was checking the board one morning, I saw a notice that caught my eye. I read it and it was telling any GI who was married and had been overseas that the Army owed him some extra money. They had paid an officer $2.00 a day for his wife's meals and had paid an enlisted man's wife only $1.25 per day. I found Lowrey and we went to the finance office to check on it. They said we could get 75 cents for each day we were overseas, but since we were being shipped out in a few days we couldn't file for it there. It might take a few weeks. We were told to file a claim at our separation center. We tried to do that and they wouldn't help us. Lowrey and I tried after we were discharged, but no luck. There wasn't even a reply from the records center in St. Louis. That's the Army's way of not paying. When we owe them any money, they will get their money; but if they owe us, we can forget it. That's what I did. I just forgot about it.

The Atomic Bomb (A-bomb)

The first atomic bomb was dropped on the City of Hiroshima, Japan, on August 6, 1945. That evening I was lying on my bunk in the barracks when I heard the news on the radio about a B-29 dropping an "A-bomb" that had the destructive power of 20,000 tons of TNT on the Japanese city of Hiroshima. I couldn't believe one bomb could be that powerful. We had no knowledge of the atomic bomb at that time. Later, on August 9th, the second bomb was dropped on Nagasaki and we thought the war would soon be over. That was good news to us. Then on August 14th, President Truman announced hostilities had ceased with Japan. The Second World War was over and the proclamation of V-J Day would come at the formal signing of the surrender terms by Japan. VJ Day was September 2, 1945. All of this happened while I was at March Field in Riverside, California.

"The Hangar Card Episode"

A day or two after President Truman announced the war was over, we were told the base was going to celebrate the war's ending by closing down operations the next day and throwing a party for everyone. The base party was going to be held at the big gymnasium. It was going to be a big picnic with all kinds of sandwiches, salads, and drinks for free. The hangar chief told all the M/Sgts. and T/Sgts. assigned to that hangar to come to the hangar at seven o'clock the next morning. When we got there, he told us there was a B-29 out on the hangar parking ramp that had to leave early the next morning. It had to have the fuel control unit replaced on #3 engine and someone had to change it that day.

"How do we determine who is going to do it?" I asked.

There were about ten of us there in the hangar chief's office and he was the boss over all of us. He made a suggestion we draw cards and the low card would work that day. He also told us he wasn't drawing a card.

Everyone agreed and someone said, "Shiver, you draw first."

I asked, "Why me?" Then I said, "Okay."

I picked a card out of the deck and turned it over. It was the ace of spades. I said, "That's a good draw! You can't beat that! The best card in the deck!"

Someone spoke up and told the group Shiver was the one to work that day. "That's the low card in the deck when drawing cards here at this base."

I said, "You must be joking! You all know that's not the rule. You want a fall guy and you found one. I'll work today while you're all having fun! Take off!"

The chief told me where the new control unit was and said to me, "They ganged up on you and you couldn't do anything about it."

I told the chief he was right and I couldn't do anything but work. I had to get at it. The fuel control unit was on the topside of the 18-cylinder engine and it was very heavy. I knew I had a day's work ahead of me. The first thing I had to do was roll the work stands out to the plane, place them, lock the wheels and get my toolbox up to the top area. I went to work and I didn't stop until mid-day. I went into the hangar to the water cooler and rested about thirty minutes and then went back to my job. I didn't have anything to eat, but I was thinking about the eats I was going to get when I finished that job!

At about 3:30 that day I was ready to come down. I told the hangar chief he had to inspect the job and put the top cowling on. He told me he would do that for me. I put the old unit and my toolbox in the hangar. I washed up and took off for the gym. I got to the gym and I had a surprise - no food left! They were out of everything! The PX was closed for the day. I went to the barracks and filled up on water.

The next morning the chief told me he inspected my work and I had done a good job. The B-29 left March Field early that morning. I never heard anyone say anything more about the card drawing in the hangar office that morning.

"Checking My Toolbox into Supply"

After the war was over with Japan, they stopped some of the training operations at March Field. They had told us to turn in our tools to the hangar supply room. The tools were stored in the supply room, but they had to be checked and inventoried by a certain supply clerk. That turned into a bad day for us. The line was long and it wasn't moving at all. That was the Army way - "hurry up and wait." After a long wait one of the GIs came out and told us what the long delay was about. He had the correct number of sockets and wrenches, but not the right sizes. The supply clerk would not accept the extra sized ones and asked the GI to sign a statement of charges for the missing sizes, but he wouldn't give the odd-sized ones back to the GI. So, the GI had refused to sign the statement of charges. That explained the long delay. The GI won out when he wouldn't sign the charges and he was right in refusing. We always needed two of the same size sockets or wrenches when working on the planes. We knew what we had to do. We couldn't have two of the same size. Everyone started checking and swapping the sockets and wrenches. There were a lot of loud noises around that supply room area that morning. I checked my tools in and got away from that noise in a few minutes. I always watched my toolbox and if someone got one of my tools he knew to return it.

"Helping Forest Rangers Fight a Fire"

I was moved to a special barracks in March Field, waiting on my orders to leave Riverside by rail to go to Atlanta and get my discharge from the Army Air Corps. They gave me a tag with my name and rank on it and told me to tie it on my bunk. One afternoon at about two o'clock, I was asleep on my bunk and a clerk woke me up and told me to report to the gym at once. I knew it had to be something about my leaving March Field. I went immediately to the gym and was told someone would be there about three o'clock to talk to us. There were a few GIs there and more coming.

In a few minutes someone in back of me called my name. I turned and found an old friend from the 344th squadron I hadn't seen in over a year. It was B.J. Summerhays. We talked for a few minutes and he told me to come outside with him. He wanted to show me the car his father had waiting for him when he returned from overseas. It was a new 1942 Packard Straight 8, four-door sedan. That was some car.

We talked a few minutes and he told me he was also waiting to get out of the service. He said he wasn't living on the base at March Field, but was living at one of his parents' homes. I knew his father was a rich man, because Summerhays received a small newspaper every month with the name "Summerhays Society" on it. Summerhays was a friend of mine and a regular person to all. He told me his parents had a big house in Los Angeles and one in Beverly Hills. Both of them had a maid and a cook at all times. I asked him what kind of business his father was in. He said he owned a large advertising company and one of his accounts was the Goodyear Blimp that flew all over the United States. He asked me to stay with him after I got out of the service. I thanked him and told him I was going home to my wife in Atmore, Alabama. I didn't want to live anywhere else. He told me his father would give me a good job with his company, but I refused.

About that time the officer in charge told us why we were called to the gym. A Navy plane had crashed at the top of San Bernadino Mountain and had set the forest on fire. They needed help. He started calling out names. I was one of the first ones called and told to get in the back of a big Army truck. We had to stand up and the officer stopped calling names when the truck body was full. There was just one truck and he told the rest of the GIs to return to their barracks.

The truck driver was a typical Army truck driver, driving fast and faster and then using the brakes. We went through San Bernardino as fast as the truck would go and then went up San Bernardino Mountain. That was some wild ride – no guard rails on a road cut out of the side of the mountain. We went past Lake Arrowhead up to the top of the mountain – twelve thousand feet. We stopped at a large tent the California Forest Rangers had set up. They told us they were going to feed us in a few minutes and then they would take us up to our job site. They gave us a very good meal and then we left the tent area. They led us to the top area of the mountain and assigned us our work. I was put with a group of about ten or twelve GIs and we were to control an area of four or five acres with two or three rangers telling us what to do. The rangers had already contained the fire to the top of the area and the tall trees had burned down to the lower trunks of the trees. Some were still burning and we were to put out the fires using shovels and dirt. We didn't have jackets or any kind of coats and we were really dirty and cold.

About one o'clock we said the next tree stump that started to burn we would help so we could get warm. It wasn't long until a ranger came by and began talking to us. The other rangers had left about midnight. He informed us we were to put the fires out – not to start them. We pointed out to him we didn't have jackets like the rangers had and we did what we had to do. We were cold, but we put out the fire as he requested anyway. We got extra cold before daybreak. They told us to walk to the big tent about six o'clock where we would get breakfast. That we did and they fed us very well – better than the Army.

The Army truck was there to take us back to March Field. We left the tent area about eight o'clock and headed down the mountain road. We called it the "Rim of the World Road". We were frightened the day before when going up the mountain, but we were scared to death coming back down. The driver was a wild man and we feared we would never stop falling if he missed one of the curves. We were happy to get back to the base alive. The truck got us back to the gym, and I went as fast as I could go to my barracks to get a shower and hit my bunk. I didn't do anything but sleep until the next morning. It was a bad job helping those California forest rangers, although they fed us well. We worked that night in ash and dirt that was about six inches deep. I think it was about a week later before I got all that smoke out of my lungs. I found out I didn't want a ranger's job.

"Leaving March Field for Fort McPherson, Atlanta, Georgia"

My orders to leave March Field came on August 30, 1945. I was one happy person. Fifteen other GIs and I left Riverside, California, in a railroad coach put on the end of a passenger train in the late afternoon of September 3, 1945.

We were told it would be a fast train trip to Atlanta, but that was not true. We spent a long time waiting for trains we met. We would go on a side track and wait for a train to go by time and again. I remember small Mexican boys coming along selling soft drinks for 25 cents a bottle, when the regular price was only a nickel.

I didn't think we would ever get out of Texas. We arrived at the Houston station and we stayed a long time. When we finally left the station, the flagman on the train came to our car and asked if he could stay in the car with us. We were happy to have him. He told us about the engineer who was driving our train to New Orleans. The engineer was mad because the train was eight hours late getting to Houston, so the flagman told us we would be getting a fast train ride. He was right.

Since we were the last car on the train, we were beginning to worry about being in an accident. The flagman told us we would be coming to a little train station in about thirty minutes and the engineer would have to slow the train, so he could catch an order on his arm loop from the woman who operated the station. The order would tell him whether or not the track ahead was clear to New Orleans; if not, we would have to go on a side track. The flagman said he would have to catch the order from the station operator if the engineer didn't.

The engineer didn't slow down and the woman operator jumped back as the fast train went by, so neither the engineer nor the flagman caught the order from her. The flagman told us the engineer had no choice but to stop the train and back up to get the order.

He said, "I will have to hop off the train when our car gets back to the station and I will hear the engineer and the woman operator go at one another. Both are mad. I'll try to keep them from hurting one another."

He hopped off as the train was backing up and went to the station operator. Some of the GIs got out of our car to watch as the engineer and the woman went at each other. They were a long way off, but they could see the engineer waving his arms from the cab and the woman pointing up to the engineer.

Soon we were moving again and the flagman came back to our car. He gave us a report on the train stop and told us we had a clear track to New Orleans, which was good news. He said the station woman and the engineer had a really big fight with their mouths. The engineer said it was her fault and the woman said she wasn't going to stay near the track when the train was speeding by so fast. The flagman said it was a good thing the engineer stayed in the cab.

We finally reached New Orleans and made a thirty minute stop there. I was happy, because I knew the train would be in Mobile soon and one step closer to home for me. After we left Mobile, we had to pass through my hometown, Atmore, Alabama, on the way to Ft. McPherson in Atlanta where I would be discharged. We went through Atmore at 10:00 p.m. and I stayed awake to see it. It looked just like I remembered it and I wanted to get off the train right then. I said to myself, "There's no place like home."

I took comfort knowing I would be home in just a few days. And I was - finally home safe and sound, finally home to Atmore and Myrtle.

Chapter 14

AN AIRMAN'S REFLECTIONS

"My Experiences with Army Air Corps Doctors"

Looking back on my years in the Army Air Corps, my experiences with the Army doctors were not good. I think most of the doctors were mad with the world, because they had to be in the service. I tried to stay away from them when I could. But, I'm going to tell about the times I had to go on sick call.

At Goldsboro, North Carolina:

I injured my right foot and ankle when I jumped from the top of a high wall on the obstacle course. It was very painful and blue-colored. The doctor told me nothing would help it. I asked him if he could tape it up and give me an excuse slip to miss calisthenics until it got well. He said, "No. The exercise will do it good; you're not getting an excuse slip."

I left – mad at him and the Army.

At Benghazi:

One of the crews at Benghazi had a softball and bat with them when they came to the squadron. Some of the crew had gloves, but not enough for all the players. There wasn't anything to do one afternoon, so a game was being played. I was the shortstop on one of the teams. A hard-hit ball came to my right and I thought I could get it. I did, but I paid a price for catching it. I had a blistered, red hand immediately. I left the game and went to see the flight surgeon. He looked at my hand and told me there was nothing he could do for me. He said if he had an aspirin, that might ease the pain a little, but he had none. He said it would be okay in a few days. I told him I was sorry I had bothered him and would try not to do it again. That man wasn't feeling any pain. He had been drinking. I smelled it when he talked to me. It was several days before my hand got back to its normal size. I didn't play anymore without a glove.

At Casper, Wyoming:

When I was flying at Casper, I went to sick call early one morning. I was having some trouble with my heart. It would have several fast beats, and then it would miss one or two. That scared me. I told one of my friends about it. He told me it might be caused by Casper's high elevation, but to go have a check-up to be sure.

The doctor who examined me gave me a quick check and said my heartbeat was normal. If it acted up again, I was to come by and let him check it while it was having one of those spells. A few days later, one afternoon about four o'clock, I was in front of his office when my heart started to act up. I went in and told him my heart was having one of those spells right then; so here I was. I could tell he was mad about my coming into his office at four o'clock. I was right. He pointed to the clock and told me sick call would be at eight o'clock the next morning. I told him I was only doing what he had told me to do and I hoped I wouldn't have to see him again. I walked out and I didn't have to go on sick call again. My heart never gave me any more trouble.

"The Flight Engineer of the B-24"

As the flight engineer on the B-24, I had a full-time job. If I wasn't busy, I would be in a minute or two. There was something to do or check all the time. I would go to the plane to which I was assigned to meet the crew chief. He would tell me all about the condition of the plane and some things I would need to know. For example, he might tell me to be easy on the #4 engine as it was to be changed in a few days.

He and I would go over the things he had done overnight from the last mission. Then, I would begin the pre-flight checks. I never took someone's word that something had been checked – I checked it myself. I checked the fuel in the tanks to be sure they were full and checked that the cap seals were in place. I checked the bombs to see if the lock pins on the fuse blades were in place and made sure the boxes of ammo were on the plane.

I had a three-sided slide rule to use to figure the weight position in the plane. Each crew member and his equipment were counted at 200 pounds each. The fuel load, oil weight and bomb weights were added, so the center of the weight in the plane would be known. That information was given to the pilot and co-pilot when they arrived from the mission briefing session. They would know how to set the control tab wheel to assist on take-off with this information.

After the crew arrived, the assistant flight engineer could help finish some of the checks. The gunners in the rear section would sometimes hang some of their equipment on the control cables and that was a no-no. They would be told not to do it, but some would still do it and after take-off, I would go to the rear section and give them some plain talk about it.

The auxiliary power unit (called the put-put) had to be started for power while we were still on the ground. It would be stopped before take-off and, after we were in the air the generators were switched on. As flight engineer I had to make the manifest list and hand it to the crew chief before I closed the bomb bay doors. I had to open the top hatch door in the flight compartment and climb up and sit while the plane was taxiing to the runway. Then, the top hatch door was closed and I would take my position between the seats of the pilot and co-pilot.

I had to call out the air speed to the pilot on take-off. Sometimes the pilot would say to me "now" and I would say "no, not yet". I would tell the pilots and co-pilots the runway at our rear is not going to help us – it's what's up front that counts – let's use it.

After we would get into our place in the formation, I would synchronize the props and we would be on our way to the target. After a fighter attack, I would check the plane for any damage and all gunners would call in; then, we would continue on to the target. When we would get to the IP (Initial Point for a bombing run), I would open the bomb bay doors and call the bombardier to tell him they were open. The plane would be on the bomb run and sometimes the ack-ack attack would be bad. It would seem such a long time before the bombardier would say – "bombs away". That was what it was all about – dropping bombs on the enemy and getting another mission credit.

After the bomb drop we would head back and the plane would be attacked again by fighter planes. We hoped our escort fighter planes would come to our rescue. Sometimes they did and other times they did not. After an attack, as the flight engineer, I would have to check for any damage and try to make repairs. I would check the fuel levels all the time and if fuel transfers had to be made, I would do that to balance the plane. The fuel was in the wing tanks and the engines didn't use the same amount of gas. I would fill out the flight records and tell the pilot of any troubles we might have.

When we arrived back at the base, we had to get in our landing order. As engineer, I would call the air speed to the pilot as we made the landing. When the plane was parked, I had to get the flight records completed and get with the crew chief to tell him about the condition of the plane. Any time we got back to home base, it was a good day.

"The B-24 Liberator Bomber"

The B-24 Liberator Bomber was a four-engine plane built by Consoldated in 1939 in San Diego, California. Later they were built in other places by Douglas, Ford and North American. There were over 18,300 B-24s built for service during World War II. Some were built for the Navy with a single vertical stabilizer and some cargo type planes were built. The B-24 was newer, more efficient and much more versatile than the Boeing B-17 plane. It was a good bomber, but its most valuable work may have been in the war against the German U-boats in the middle of the Atlantic Ocean. The B-24 was the only plane that could get there and take care of the submarines. Winston Churchill used a modified B-24 as his personal plane.

I went to the 50th anniversary of the B-24 plane in 1989 at Fort Worth, Texas. It was also the annual reunion of the 98th Bomb Group. It was a week of different events. On Friday night, I went to the "B-24 War Symposium" at a large theater in the Fort Worth Civic Center. There were eight or nine men giving lectures and answering questions from the floor. There were a number of microphones and anyone could ask anything he wanted about the B-24. In the group of men were Air Force and Navy men, retired generals, admirals and one civilian – the man Consolidated had put in charge of the B-24 project, who later became the CEO of General Dynamics Company. The group of men told us we could be proud of our part in the war effort. They didn't say the B-24 won the war, but they said if we had not had the B-24, the war would have taken much longer to win.

The B-24 was a very good bomber and I should know – I always wanted to fly. I had 299½ hours credit on my combat record and about 2,000 hours total flying time on the B-24. It was a good plane – no, I would say it was a _very_ good plane.

B-24 Specifications

Type – Heavy Bomber
Powerplant – 4 – 1200 hp Pratt & Whitney R1830 Twin Wasp Radial Engines
Maximum Speed – 300 mph

Range – 2850 miles
Service Ceiling – 32,500 feet
Weapons – 10 - .50 Caliber Browning Machine Guns
Bomb Bays – 2
Weight – Empty – 34,000 lbs.; Maximum – 60,000 lbs.
Wing Type – Davis Wing
Wing Span – 110 feet
Length – 66 feet 4 inches
Height – 17 feet
Wing Area – 1,048 Sq. feet

"It was A Very Good Plane"

"An Airman's Wife"

During the fall of 1938, while still a student at Escambia County High School in Atmore, Alabama, I met Myrtle Dean, who attended Baldwin County High School. We met on a double date and dated off and on until 1941 when we began to go steady. We both wanted to marry, but we knew I would be going to war soon. I told Myrtle there was a chance I wouldn't return, but she said she would take that chance. We were married on the evening of May 27, 1942. J.W. Terry and his wife, Jewel, took us to Pensacola, Florida, where we were married by Harvey E. Page, Escambia County Judge.

We spent our first night together in my apartment on North Main Street in Atmore, which was owned by Wheeler Crook, who also owned the City Café. The next day, we moved to the Pipkin Apartments, which I had already rented for us. Our apartment was upstairs and I had already bought furniture for it.

At this time I was working for Long-Steele Motor Company. I worked in the office for Mr. Robert Long, earning $50 a week. It was immediately after the Depression when times were tough. Fifty dollars a week was a fair wage then. Myrtle did not work outside the home at this time; she kept house for us.

Prior to our marriage I had registered for the service. Shortly after our marriage, I received a notice to report with a group leaving Atmore on July 20th to go to Fort McClellan in Anniston, Alabama. So, after only two months of marriage, I found myself leaving Myrtle. I was inducted into the Army on July 21st and was sent back to Atmore until August 3rd, when I left for Fort McPherson in Atlanta, Georgia. Mr. Dean and Myrtle's brothers immediately came and helped her move our furniture to Lottie, Alabama, where it was stored until we could once again set up house.

After basic training and maintenance school, I was able to find a room for Myrtle to join me in Goldsboro, North Carolina, where I was stationed at the time. The room was owned by Mr. and Mrs. Crowe, owners of a store in town. I was not allowed to stay with Myrtle and I had very little spare time because of training school. Sometimes I would go to school at night, so she was alone much of the time. The Crowes would let her work in their store when they were busy. I knew she was lonely, but this trip allowed us to be together some. We celebrated our first Christmas together there. Myrtle saw snow for the first time when she lived in North Carolina.

She left to go home to Atmore the first week of January, when I was getting ready to go to St. Louis, Missouri. After she got home, she got a job at Brookley Field in Mobile as a typist. She worked in a warehouse office typing orders for parts. She lived with her cousin, Luvenia, in a boarding house owned by Mrs. Hughes, located at 206 Roper Street. Because she did not have a car, she had to take the bus and walk while in Mobile. Sometimes she would have to work at night and ride the bus to the bus stop; then, she would walk the rest of the way home. She did not enjoy doing that.

Myrtle was unable to follow me to all of my assignments, because I was on the move so much. Before I went overseas, I had an eight day delay en route to Herington, Kansas. This was my chance to go home and see Myrtle. I rode the bus all night to Denver, Colorado, on July 4th, and then caught a plane to Chicago, where I caught another flight to Atlanta. Then I took a bus to Atmore.

Since I had used too many days traveling home and would need to use the same number of days to return to Kansas, our time together was short. I knew when I arrived in Atmore I was on my way overseas to war, but I could not tell Myrtle. I asked my daddy if he would tell her after I left and he said he would. Myrtle and Daddy took me to the airport in Mobile when I left. I don't remember when Daddy told her, nor do I remember her reaction to the news. I just knew I could not tell her.

After I finished my combat missions overseas, I returned by ship convoy to Norfolk, Virginia. From there I went by train to Fort Patrick Henry for processing. I then left by train to go to Camp Shelby in Hattiesburg, Mississippi. While there I called Myrtle to let her know I was on my way home. I spent one night in Hattiesburg. I was paid the next day and immediately took a bus to Mobile, then took a cab to 206 Roper Street, where Myrtle and I were reunited.

The morning after I arrived at Myrtle's apartment, we went to Metzger's Department Store where I bought a pair of Florsheim shoes. I was able to do that because I had received a shoe stamp while I was at Camp Shelby. It was nice to wear lightweight shoes again.

We left Mobile and traveled by bus to Atmore. She and I visited my daddy and he carried us to Lottie to visit and stay with Myrtle's parents. A few months after our time together, Myrtle was able to join me when I was stationed at Casper, Wyoming. She traveled by train there. She remarked many times about the soldiers aboard the trains being so kind and considerate of her. They helped her with her baggage throughout the trip. For a young woman traveling alone, this meant a lot.

The base was fifteen miles from Casper, where I got her a room in one of the nicest hotels in town. There was a cafe on the ground floor where she ate her meals. I was able to see her almost every day. After four or five days, I found an apartment for us located twelve blocks from the center of town. During the day Myrtle would spend her time cleaning house, washing and ironing. The weather was rough in Casper. When the blizzards came through, her wash would freeze on the clothesline. Snow was often piled up as high as our shoulders. It was definitely a different climate than what Myrtle was used to.

While coming home on the ship convoy from overseas, I had met Zollie Norwood and he was also stationed at Casper. Zollie's wife, Minnie, and Myrtle became friends and spent time together. Zollie and Minnie would come over often and play cribbage with us. Myrtle sometimes would cook a meal for some of my friends. They loved her fried chicken.

While in Casper, Myrtle became pregnant and had a miscarriage. I checked her into the city hospital, so she would receive the best care. She stayed in the hospital for a week. Myrtle traveled home by train when my time there was over. She had spent about three months in Casper. She would often recall those days, especially the weather.

Myrtle found herself once again with the Deans in Lottie, waiting for me to get out of the service. I was discharged in Atlanta on September 9, 1945. I caught a bus from Atlanta to Montgomery and then another south to Atmore. I was home at last and we could begin our life together. We went back to the Pipkin Apartments to live, but in a different apartment this time. We took our belongings out of storage and began our new life.

Myrtle never wanted to watch war movies or read my book about my experiences in the war. She always said she had lived through the war once and had no desire to live it again. She always believed I would return home to her from the war and that I did.

Final Thoughts

I would like to thank the Air Force Historical Research Agency at Maxwell Air Force Base in Montgomery, Alabama, for providing information that helped fill in the material I misplaced. Without their help this book would have been difficult to write.

I would like to thank once again my niece, Gwen Dean Myers, who spent countless hours working with me to make this dream a reality. Also, a special thanks to Sandra Fischer who typed and edited the manuscript, and my children, Martha Walker and Jeff Shiver, who supported and helped me throughout this two year process.

The Lord allowed me to fulfill my desire to fly in a way I never dreamed I would. He made it possible for Myrtle and me to marry and for me to obtain flying experience in the Air Force. My opportunity to enter cadet training came too late in my military career. My desire to come home and start a family with Myrtle had become more important to me than my desire to continue flying. I was blessed to have been married for 69 ½ years. Myrtle passed away on November 16, 2011.

I was nearly 90 years old before I started writing my memoirs. I feel blessed that I was able to go through WWII without any injuries, and that I have been able to see my reflections in print.

TO GOD BE THE GLORY FOR ALL THE GREAT THINGS HE HAS DONE IN MY LIFE!

www.ingramcontent.com/pod-product-compliance
Lightning Source LLC
Chambersburg PA
CBHW070631160426
43194CB00009B/1432